It's All Abut People
Dead and Alive

JOHN ANDREWS

ISBN-13: 978-1542911283

Dedication

I dedicate this book to my very best friend, my wife, Carol. Her constant love, undying support and loyal companionship have been the delight of my life. I have been guided by her wisdom and inspired by her faith. She lived in, worked in and we raised our children in the same funeral home where I grew up. She supported and encouraged me in every line of work I engaged in. And she personally experienced many of the events described in this book. I love Carol and I'm so grateful for the gift of her life, love and friendship.

Introduction

My wife says that her parents never told her stories, instead, they read stories to her. It was just the opposite in my family. My parents shared stories, all sorts of stories. Some were funny. Others were sad. Some were so interesting that we heard them over and over again. I enjoyed those stories because I knew they were true and they involved people I knew and events my family experienced.

Through the years when I'm with my brother and sisters we share the stories of our life. We talk about our childhood. We laugh about events that others might find uncomfortable. We recall the many people, dead and alive, that have had an impact on our lives. And as we share those stories we feel a close bond that can only come from shared unique experiences.

My family lived in a funeral home. Dad operated the only ambulance business that served the communities in two counties and he was the elected county coroner. So, our daily life was full of adventure. Dad would receive a phone call from the sheriff, jump in the ambulance and leave town with red lights flashing and siren screaming. As soon as he was back we were the first to hear the gory details that others would read in the papers. And those details would later become the source of interesting stories to be shared with family and friends alike.

There were lots of opportunities for story telling in my family because it seemed as if we had a constant stream of visitors at our home. Denver Swedes, old family friends, relatives and business acquaintances would show up unannounced. My parents would stop whatever they were doing and the conversation would begin. Since "children were to be seen and not heard" in our family, I remember quietly sitting and listening to the chatter, which always included stories about real people and bone fide events.

I was born and raised in a small rural Colorado funeral home. While in high school and college, I assisted my parents driving an ambulance. I accompanied my dad on coroner investigations, I helped embalm bodies, direct funerals and set monuments. Dad had a flower shop. While in high school I attended floral design school. I helped by making funeral sprays, festive floral arrangements, corsages, boutonnieres and seasonal flower displays. After college, I worked my way up through the ranks of an urban police department, owned a funeral home, attended seminary and then spent years serving congregations as an Episcopal priest. I then served as a Christian chaplain in a large hospital and later in a drug and alcohol rehab center. All those experiences exposed me to people and events that changed and shaped my life. The stories of my life were set in varied circumstances and among all types of people.

I've written these stories for several reasons. First, as I've aged I've come to realize how easy one forgets the stories and events of their life. I want to record events in my life before they are lost to memory. Second, as I enter the last years of my life I want to take time reflecting on what and who I've experienced. Finally, I think my life has been unusual and I want to preserve those memories for future generations to ponder.

CONTENTS

The Episcopal Priesthood

Early Life in a Funeral Home

The First Five Years of my Life

"Children are like wet cement.
Whatever falls on them makes an impression"

Dr. Hairm Ginott

I was born in Presbyterian Hospital in Denver, Colorado. As soon as I was able to leave I was taken directly to a funeral home. Daddy was an undertaker and our family lived in the funeral home in Castle Rock, Colorado.

I was the third of four children. Kendal, my oldest sister was 10; and Cindy, my next older sister was 7. It's hard to imagine being more fortunate than to have two doting sisters. They loved taking care of their baby brother. They changed my diapers, fed me, babysat me when needed, and they would play house making me their little baby. Those two girls loved me and spoiled me.

To make matters even better, my grandparents lived next door. Nana and Papa ate their meals with us and Nana spent most of every day helping my mother with housework and cooking. My grandparents

My sister Cindy and I having fun

both immigrated to the United States from Sweden. My mother was an only child and since Swedish was often spoken in her home as she grew up she became fluent in that language.

My grandparents were very proud to be Americans, but they and my mother often communicated in Swedish. My father was around Swedes so much that he was able to understand much of what was said. The grownups in our family decided early on not to teach the children the Swedish language because they could then talk to each other openly without the children knowing what was being said. Even though I wasn't taught Swedish, I loved the sound of that language.

Nana and Papa had a very heavy accent. My sisters and I would have fun asking them to say things like: "thirty-three and a third". It would always come out "turdy tree and a turd" and we would all laugh.

Papa grew up on a farm in Friel, Sweden, and he never forgot his agrarian roots. He built a hen house and a pigeon coop with an attached pen behind the garage of the funeral home. We awoke every day to the crowing of a rooster. We ate fresh eggs every day and occasionally feasted on squab. When Mother included chicken on the menu, Dad would prepare a bucket of boiling water, pick out the unfortunate bird, wring its neck, dip the bird in the hot water and pluck its feathers. I felt sorry for the chicken but I was fascinated by the messy process.

When I was born my family were still members of Augustana Lutheran Church in Denver, Colorado. The members of Augustana were all Swedes and all the services were conducted in Swedish. Shortly after my birth my parents arranged for my baptism at Augustana. After my baptism, Dad and Mom met with the pastor and told him they could no longer drive to Denver every Sunday for services. They simply couldn't leave the business unattended. Since there was no Lutheran church in Castle Rock, Pastor Lorimer told them to join the Episcopal Church. They did and they became very active in that congregation.

Christ Episcopal Church was a tiny one-room building. It had a pump organ, seating for about 75 people, and a raised chancel. Heat in the building was provided by a coal-burning furnace. There was a metal grate that was located directly next to the organ. Since my mother played the organ she soon became the organist for that congregation. One Sunday I was sitting on the organ bench next to her. It was cold and I decided to warm my hands of the furnace grate. I bent over and placed my hands on the grate and both hands were severely burned, leaving the marks of that grate on both palms.

Living in a funeral home was unique to say the least. Dad's office was at one end of our living room. Both girls shared a bedroom. There was a small circular hallway outside the entry to their room, and doors from that hallway led to my parent's bedroom, the living room, a closet, the bathroom and the kitchen. There was a shelf in that hallway where the telephone sat. When that telephone rang all activity in the house came to an immediate stop. More about that later.

Andrews Funeral Home, 4th and Jerry Streets, Castle Rock, Colorado.

My bedroom was near the back door to the house just beyond the kitchen. A small wood stove sat in the hall between the kitchen, my bedroom and the back door. Dad would start a wood fire every morning when he first got up. I remember waking every day to the smell of burning wood. And I'd hear the familiar voice of Pete Smythe, the morning rural newscaster who would begin his broadcast by reminding everyone he was speaking over the barbed wire network.

Just beyond the living room was a funeral chapel that could accommodate about 75 people. The family of the deceased sat in a small room off of the chapel. The embalming room and casket display rooms were hidden behind doors next to the chapel.

We had a black cat that had four white paws. As soon as she was able, Boots began presenting our family with litters of kittens. One time when Boots was pregnant she disappeared. A short time after her disappearance Dad was showing a grieving family through the casket room so they could make a selection. Much to Dad's horror he heard kittens meowing and found Boots and her litter in the foot of Dad's nicest casket! As it turned out the family liked that casket and selected it for their use. Boots and her litter were found.

When Dad was making funeral arrangements with families and when a funeral or rosary was being conducted in the chapel, my sisters and I had to QUIETLY play in my sister's bedroom. There was to be no loud talking, no giggling, and no one was to leave that room until Dad or Mother told us we could.

Our life really centered around that business. Dad had the only ambulance company that provided emergency service to 13 communities in two counties. He was also the county coroner for one county and, since the other county did not have a funeral home, he had to respond and assist the coroner in that county. The telephone in our house was critically important. We never knew when the phone rang if it was literally life or death. Someone could be having a baby and in need of an ambulance, or someone may have died and a coroner was needed. Our phone was so important that Dad had an extremely loud bell mounted outside the house so no call was ever missed. Kendal, Cindy and I were not allowed to touch that phone.

Family fun before my brother arrived.

Our phone number was 122. The phone was attached to a box by a long cord. The box had a crank that had to be turned in order to get the attention of the operator at the local telephone company. We were fortunate to have a private line. All my friends' phones were on party lines.

Dad kept the ambulance parked in a detached garage next to the house. It was always exciting to watch Dad run to that garage, back the ambulance out and leave the yard with the red lights flashing and the siren screaming. The ambulance would later become a center of my life.

The day after my 4th birthday a disaster struck. Mother gave birth to another son. I'm sure my parents had tried to prepare me, but apparently I wasn't listening. Before they brought that little guy home, my grandfather removed my bed and replaced it with a bunk bed. Learning to share that space, my toys, and the affection of my family would be one of the hardest challenges I faced in my early years.

About six months after my brother arrived, my parents bought a new hearse. It didn't come off a car lot, instead it had to be picked up at the factory in Lima, Ohio. Dad hired an undertaker from Denver to oversee our funeral home. My grandparents took full time responsibility for my brother, Tim. The rest of the family boarded the train in Denver and began the lengthy trip to Ohio. I don't remember the details; but I do remember passing near Cedar Rapids, Iowa. Someone said: "*There's Cedar Rapids.*" I quickly made my way to the window, searched the landscape, and finally said: "*I don't see the rabbits.*"

The new hearse was ready upon our arrival and after Dad inspected it we all climbed in that black Maria and began the journey home. Mom and Dad sat in front and my sisters and I stayed in the back. The new hearse also functioned as an emergency ambulance. So there was a stretcher and seats for two attendants. We took turns sitting and lying down. Did I mention that my sisters were not thrilled about a trip across the country in a black hearse?

Our family in front of the new hearse.

On the way home we stopped in Madrid, Iowa. My Dad's sister, her husband and their 8 children lived on a farm near Madrid. We stayed with them for several days. The highlight of that visit occurred one evening when the attendants' chairs and the stretcher were removed from the hearse, then all 15 of us piled in the hearse and drove to town to

attend a movie. You can't imagine the response when Dad stopped in front of the theater and we all jumped out. My cousins and I still talk about that experience. That was a great trip.

After we returned home I was again faced with the tough task of being a "good" big brother. Oh, the trials of being a big brother!

Mrs. Engle

"Enthusiasm and joy are Siamese twins – It's hard to find one without the other."

Peter McWilliams and John Rogers

When I was growing up my family lived about three blocks from the elementary school. Every day I walked those three blocks and that meant that I would pass Mrs. Engle's house. Mrs. Engle was an eccentric woman who actually lived in her car that was parked on the street next to her home. She must have been close to 80 years old at the time I was in Castle Rock Elementary School. Mrs. Engle never did any yard work. Her yard was a landscaper's nightmare. The trees were either dead or completely overgrown and filled with all sorts of debris that had blown in and become attached to the branches. The connecting bushes were so thick the ground underneath was not visible. There were noxious weeds throughout the yard.

To make matters worse, Mrs. Engle never threw anything away. Her house was packed with boxes of clothes, soiled dishes, trash, collectibles, and anything else one might imagine. She subscribed to both the Denver *Post* and the Rocky Mountain *News* which she never threw away, so her house had stacks and stacks of newspapers. As a matter of fact, that's why she lived in her car. Her house was so full of "stuff" that there was no room for her in that dwelling. Today Mrs. Engle would be called a hoarder.

All the children in town loved Mrs. Engle. She was kind, she was fun to talk to, and she knew every child's name. There was a constant stream of children who stopped to chat before school in the morning and after school in the afternoon.

Mrs. Engle was a Christian lady. I remember that one of the items that was always present next to her on the seat of the car was a black floppy Bible. That was her constant companion and the center of her relationship with the children in town. She would have every child who stopped to talk with her memorize a Bible verse. My passage was **John 3: 16**: "For God so loved the world that He gave His only begotten Son, so that everyone who believes in Him should not perish but have everlasting life." Every time I would stop to chat with Mrs. Engle she would ask me to recite that passage. If I recited it correctly, she would praise me. If I didn't recite it correctly, she would open her Bible, show me the verse and then ask me to recite it again. Believe me, I can still recite that passage from memory today. You see, Mrs. Engle loved the Lord so much that she wanted to share that joy and peace with everyone.

She lived to the age of 104. She spent the last years of her life in the Silver State Nursing Home. In my role as the elected coroner of Douglas County, I was often called to that facility in response to the death of a patient. Whenever I entered the long hall leading to the nurse's station, I would encounter Mrs. Engle sitting in a chair next to her room. When she spotted me, her eyes would brighten, her lips would form a smile, and she'd say: "Johnny, would you recite John 3: 16?" And I couldn't proceed any further until I did so.

Mrs. Engle loved the Lord. No matter where you found her … in a car parked on the street … or on a chair in the hallway of a nursing home … she shared God's love. She has been an inspiration to me and I hope her memory will be an inspiration to anyone reading this.

I Don't Have Anything to Do!

"Boredom is simply the lack of imagination"

Julie O. Smith

When I was born in 1943 the United States was at war. Food, fuel and many other items were rationed or simply not available. There was no television, I-phones, I-pads or I-pods. Children didn't have computers. We couldn't tweet, text, send e-mails or post on Instagram; there was no Facebook. Children entertained themselves without all the distractions.

FIRST GRADE 1949-1950

This was my first grade class. Nine of us in this photo remained classmates all the way through high school.

This was our sixth grade class. Mrs. Conrad, our teacher is standing next to her son, Ralph Bean.

When I was a child we played with other children … outside. We spent hours and hours playing hide and seek, climbing on the hay stack at the local feed store, shooting baskets at a hoop hanging from someone's garage or house.

One of my favorite activities occurred every winter. The dirt street located on the south side of the elementary school ran for one block. That street had a steep slope that ran from east to west for the entire block. Castle Rock sat at an elevation of 6400 feet, so we got lots of snow every winter. As soon as it was cold enough for the snow to stick to the ground, the town marshal would erect a wood barricade at the east end of that street, at both sides of the cross street and at the base of the hill, and another barricade at the end of the next block. That would give the children access to a two-block sled hill. The marshal would also deliver a 55-gallon drum to the top of the hill, place a stack of fire wood nearby, and then the kids would keep it burning all day so we had a spot to warm up after our two-block ride.

All the children in town owned sleds. Most of them were red with two iron rails and a wooden bar at the front to steer the blades. Kids would gather early in the morning dressed in heavy wool coats, several pair of jeans, and with their shoes covered with rubber boots that had medal clasps to keep them closed. Usually the air was crisp. There were times it snowed all day. It was always cold. The fire in the 55-gallon drum was a wonderful site after several fast trips down that steep hill.

No one supervised the play and there were seldom any accidents or problems. The only one I remember occurred when Keith Olson lost control of his sled and ended up under Dr. Rangell's parked car. He wasn't seriously injured. He walked to Dr. Rangell's office, was patched up and back on the hill in no time.

If we weren't sledding on the grade school hill, we were ice skating at the flooded tennis court located one block from my house on the southwest corner of the Court House Square. A 10-foot-tall chain length fence surrounded the tennis court; that fence sat on an 8-inch concrete curb. As soon the temperature remained near freezing, members of the volunteer fire department would drape the fence with heavy canvas curtains. They would also string metal wire across the top of the tennis court from one side of the fence to the other and drape shorter canvas curtains on those wires to keep the sun from reaching the floor of the tennis court. Finally, the volunteers would flood the floor with water which would then freeze and form a beautiful skating surface. The town marshal would again appear with a 55-gallon drum and all the wood we needed to keep warm.

I remember learning to skate using a pair of mail-order Montgomery Ward skates. They were the black lace-up variety that reached well above my ankle. It took a lot of time and patience to learn to skate. My ankles were weak and I'd end up with my legs bowled out and the sides of my feel bent and facing each other. Or, I'd simply fall on my face. But I wasn't alone. My friends would help me and I'd help them. In time, we mastered that skill and enjoyed many days each winter skating.

In the summer, we had the creek to play in. East Plum Creek ran along the west side of town about three blocks from my home. My friends and I would climb the fence surrounding the horse corral behind the Johnson's house, pet the horses and then scale the fence on the other side, landing on the path to the creek. There usually wasn't a lot of water running in the creek. We would spend hours building dams, playing cowboys and Indians, or floating sticks of wood we'd pretend were ships. Long spindly willows grew in the creek bed. We would cut the willows with our pocket knives and use them as swords, or make them into spears. And we'd catch frogs and tadpoles, take them home, place them in wash tubs and watch them grow.

The water was always warm enough that we'd take off our shoes and socks and wade. Oh, the fun we'd have at the creek!

Charlie Kirk was the Douglas County Agriculture Extension Agent and he oversaw the 4-H program. All the children in the county participated in different 4-H clubs. If they lived on a farm they'd have projects that focused on raising cattle, horses, pigs, sheep or other animals. The girls might be in a club that focused on food preparation, making clothes, or planning meals.

I raised rabbits and had a garden. When the Douglas County Fair and Rodeo occurred each fall, I'd enter my rabbits and produce from my garden to be judged. We also had to provide meticulous records of our work. The competition was fierce and I never won a ribbon.

Every summer a 4-H camp was held at a church campground near Deckers on the Platte River in Douglas County. I remember an event that occurred one night in the boys' sleeping

9

area. All the beds were metal bunk beds. I was on the bottom bunk and Ralph Bean was in the bed above me. When it was "lights out" we were all to be quiet and go to sleep. Not Ralph, he kept talking and talking and talking. Finally, someone snuck near his bunk and stuck a sock in Ralph's mouth! That produced the quiet we needed.

Before I was even a teenager my parents presented me with a .22 caliber rifle for Christmas. Ralph Bean, Keith Olson and I did a lot of rabbit and squirrel hunting in the summer. It was common for kids in our community to have guns and to openly carry them. That would never happen today.

I was also required to help around the house. My sisters and I were taught to "wire the flowers" that were used in funeral sprays and arrangements. So, when Dad had a funeral scheduled or he had to prepare flowers for a wedding or some other special function we could help by placing a wire in the carnations, or wire and wrap boutonnieres.

The funeral folders that came from the printer each had to be folded. Cindy, Kendal and I probably folded a million of those folders over the years.

Folding chairs were constantly being moved to make room for large funerals, or removed for more intimate small groups. We had a large closet near the chapel where the chairs were stored. It seemed we were constantly moving chairs. When funerals were scheduled in small churches in the county our chairs often supplemented the existing seating. We would stack the folding chairs in the back of the pall bearer limousine and then we'd unload them after the funeral was over.

When I was growing up none of the children in our family ever said: "I have nothing to do."

The Haystack

"Always jump in the puddles! Always skip alongside the flowers. The only fights worth fighting are the pillow and food varieties."

Terri Guillemets

My brother and I considered ourselves lucky because of a fortunate circumstance over which we had absolutely no control. Our family lived across the street from the Castle Rock Feed and Fuel Company. The feed store was owned by Carroll Hier, and his business provided farmers and ranchers with a wide variety of food for livestock, planting seeds, and hay.

Carroll was a kind and gentle-spoken man. He and his wife, Flo, played bridge with my parents; his two sons, Bob and Ed, were just ahead and behind me in school, and the Hier family attended our church. I liked Carroll because he always spoke to me when he encountered me at church or on the street. And, probably most important, he never seemed to mind when the neighborhood children used his feed store or hay stack as a playground.

Buggs Lambert and Charlie Weekley worked for Carroll, stacking hay and delivering sacks of feed. Both of those men were as gentle and kind as their boss. In spite of the problems the neighborhood children caused, neither man ever spoke in a loud voice, they never got mad, and they never asked us to leave. You will understand how remarkable that was as I describe the fun we had in that store.

The entrance to the Castle Rock Feed and Fuel was located on 4th Street. Just inside the entrance was a large counter with an office off to one side. Customers would enter the store, place their orders and pay their bills. A dividing wall with a small door separated the front of the store from the large feed storage area, which took up the remaining 2/3 of the building. The storage area had a large bay door facing Jerry Street. That door was directly across from our funeral home. Pickups and flatbed trucks could back into the storage area on the concrete floor. Hundreds of sacks of feed for horses, pigs, cattle and chickens lined the walls or were stacked in piles throughout the storage area. Most of those burlap sacks weighed 100 pounds.

When we went to the feed store, we entered the storage area through the open bay door. One of the games we played was tag. The object of the game was for the person who was "it" to touch another player. When physical contact was made, the person touched became "it", and the game would start all over again. The challenging part of the game was the requirement that anyone playing had to stay on top of the feed sacks or on the beds of any truck parked in the building. If someone stepped on the concrete floor they automatically became "it". Those playing had to be fast. They had to jump from one pile to another, and they had to plan ahead to avoid being caught on an isolated pile of feed sacks from which they couldn't jump.

The tag games went on for hours. The only time the work crew or customers bothered us was when they loaded an order, leaving a gap in the piles of feed sacks. When a game of tag started word usually spread on the street and the number of kids playing would gradually increase until there were six or seven laughing, screaming children jumping from pile to pile.

Tag was great fun, but it was also hazardous to one's health. One afternoon, while I was playing tag with Ralph Bean, Bob Lewis, Freddie Hurst and Keith Olson, I tried to leap from a stack of Purina Cow Pellets onto Carroll Hire's delivery truck. The distance was great and I ended up on the concrete floor with a broken arm. My friends helped me across the street. When I entered the funeral home office, my Dad took one look at my arm and pronounced it "broke". He drove me to Dr. Heaton's office and Arch took x-rays. He was able to set my arm without my having to go to the hospital in Denver.

As much as we enjoyed playing in the feed store, we enjoyed playing on the hay stack even more. The hay stack was located across the street from the funeral home at the rear of the feed store. The hay stack was always changing in shape and size. When a new order of hay arrived, the stack might be 12 bales high, 25 bales long and 20 bales wide. With some imagination and a lot of sweat, we would move the bales on the top to create a large hole in the stack. That hole would become a great fort or a magnificent castle or the interior of a ship. If we had lots of time and energy, we'd stack the bales to create an elaborate series of tunnels. Those tunnels were great for war games, with part of the kids playing American soldiers and the remaining kids playing German or Japanese enemies (it was during the 1940s and early 50s).

We could spend an entire afternoon in the haystack. When we were through playing we were full of hay. Our shoes and socks were filled with bits of hay, hay dust was clinging to our shirts and pants, and our hair was filthy. Our mothers wouldn't let us in the house until we were dusted off. After we took a bath we'd find scratches all over our body from contact with the sharp, brittle pieces of hay.

Every Halloween the hay stack became a source of material for pranksters. Late on Halloween night we would sit in our living room with the lights out and watch pranksters fill their pickups with hay bales. They'd drive to the main street in town and create "road blocks". On one particular Halloween before we moved into the living room to watch the hay stack, the funeral home office door bell rang. Dad opened the door and found a solid wall of hay. There was no way he could move the hay, but we could all hear the pranksters laughing on the other side.

One weekend afternoon our doorbell rang. Dad opened the door to find several frantic children. They'd been playing in the hay stack with matches and the dry hay caught fire. Dad yelled for mother to call the volunteer fire department, then he grabbed a garden hose and tried to fight the fire. When the fire trucks arrived, Dad continued to use his garden hose. He sure looked silly aiming his tiny stream of water as the firemen used their 4-inch hoses.

I have one sad memory associated with the haystack. It happened late on a Saturday afternoon. I'd been playing with others, but everyone went home, leaving me on the top of the hay stack alone. I must have been tired as I was quietly lying on my back looking at the clouds. Suddenly I heard loud, angry voices in the alley just beneath me. I crawled to the edge of the stack and observed a number of high school kids standing in a circle. Craig, a neighbor boy, was in the center of the circle and another boy was calling him filthy names and challenging him to fight. Suddenly the boy slugged Craig in the face, knocking him to the ground. The boy then jumped on Craig and began beating his head while others in the crowd kicked him.

I was probably 9 or 10 years old and I'd never seen anything that cruel before. The sight frightened and sickened me. I climbed down on the far side of the stack and ran home. I opened the back door and yelled for Dad. When he appeared, I told him what was happening and he ran to the alley. The fight was over, but Craig was lying on the ground, bleeding. Dad examined him and then helped him home. I've never forgotten the sight or the horrible feelings that it generated in me.

Years later, after I was grown, I was elected coroner of Douglas County. Carroll Hier had long since sold his feed store and he was the elected Douglas County Clerk and Recorder. We spent a lot of time together at election events, public hearings and political gatherings. Every Sunday our families worshipped together at Christ Episcopal Church. I always enjoyed being with Carroll and I respected him as much as an adult as I had loved him as a child.

A Funeral Home Ambulance

"Life happens at the level of events, not words"

Alfred Adler

Today it seems odd to even imagine a funeral home providing an ambulance service. But as odd as it sounds that is exactly what happened all across the United States from about 1899 until the late 1960s. The Wood Company manufactured the very first ambulances. Their motorized vans were battery-powered and traveled at an amazing 16 miles per hour. President McKinley was carried in a Wood ambulance after he was shot in 1901. Undertakers were quick to purchase vehicles like the Wood Company van because they could also be equipped to carry caskets. It was then logical that undertakers would assume responsibility for the transportation of the ill and injured. Their staff was on-call twenty-four hours a day and their primary business vehicle would carry people quickly, comfortably and horizontally. By 1930, nine out of ten funeral homes had ambulance services. In fact, the lyrics to a popular song went:

"The old gray hearse goes rolling by

And you don't know whether to laugh or cry."[1]

When Dad bought the Livingston Funeral Home in Castle Rock in 1938, the business included an emergency ambulance service that served two counties. None of the thirteen communities in Douglas and Elbert Counties had either a hospital or an ambulance business. The only people trained to provide emergency first aid were the full and part-time funeral home employees. All fire departments were volunteer and none of them had ambulances and none of their volunteers were trained first-aiders. The closest hospitals were located in Denver and Colorado Springs. And the only medical doctor was Dr. Alexander who practiced in Castle Rock.

Early Equipment

When Dad purchased the funeral home the sale included a black hearse that doubled as an ambulance. That kind of vehicle was called a "combination hearse/ambulance". When the vehicle was being used as a hearse the floor in the back contained ten or twelve sets of built-in rubber rollers. When a casket was placed on the rollers one would simply push the casket and

---

[1] Van Back, T.W., The 1,100-Year History of the Ambulance. *The American Funeral Director,* May, 1992, pp.44.

it would coast into place on the rollers. When the casket came to rest against a metal pin another metal pin would be inserted in a small hole at the rear of the casket to keep it from moving. When the vehicle was being used as an ambulance the rollers were removed and the holes they left were sealed with chrome plates. A stretcher was then added to the back on the driver's side. The litter was held in place by a metal bar that was attached to the wall. Another ingenious stretcher was added to the back on the passenger side. That stretcher contained four individual pods that could be locked in a way that either provided seating for two people, or the pods would lie flat to be used as a bed. The ceiling above the driver contained a storage compartment for first aid supplies. The ambulance attendant could gain access to that compartment through a small door that was located directly above the sliding glass partition that separated the driver's compartment from the back of the ambulance. The ambulance had a siren that the driver operated by depressing a metal switch located on the floor to the left of the brake pedal. There were two flashing red lights located directly behind the front grill.

Dad also had a black nine-passenger Chrysler limousine that could be used as an emergency ambulance. To prepare the limousine to be used as an ambulance one would remove the rear seat. The lid of the trunk would be opened and a stretcher could be inserted. The stretcher would be located with half in the trunk and the other half in the rear-seating compartment. The attendant would sit in the folding seat located directly behind the front passenger seat. The limousine contained a siren and red lights located behind the car grill.

The first aid supplies carried in the ambulance were very basic. A bedpan, an emesis basin, compress bandages, adhesive tape, a medal tubular arm and leg splint, restraining straps, tissues, and extra blankets. A portable oxygen cylinder was mounted on the floor next to the attendants' seat.

Volume and Charges

In the late 50s and early 60s Andrews Ambulance Service averaged about 150 calls a year. The main source of the calls came from the Douglas County Sheriff's Office, the Elbert County Sheriff's Office, the Colorado State Patrol and from the medical doctors who practiced in Castle Rock. Dad advertised in the Record Journal (later the Douglas County News) and the telephone book. His ads featured the funeral home but also listed the ambulance service. Since it was common knowledge that the funeral home was the only ambulance service available, we received calls from private parties

Tim, me and Russ standing by the three ambulances on the north side of the funeral home.

For many years, Dad charged $25 a call. He increased that to $35 a call in the early 1960s. The charge to the customer was the same regardless of the miles driven, the use of supplies or the number of passengers carried. Imagine paying that small amount to have an ambulance with driver and attendant respond to an emergency, provide first aid and then transport the victim with red lights and siren from anywhere in Douglas or Elbert County to a Denver or Colorado Springs hospital. Some of those ambulance trips could take one or two hours running emergency depending on the location of the call.

Part Time Help

Dad had to depend on part time help to assist with the ambulance calls. He used men who lived near the funeral home who either needed the extra cash or who enjoyed the excitement. Some of the men I remember working for Dad were:

Ernie Martin – owner of a small oil distribution company

Charlie Workman – a local contractor

Frank Bowman – a master electrician

Johnny Westbrook – a Colorado State Patrolman

Freddie Smith – a Douglas County truck driver

The Rev. Hank Hiddinga – a Baptist minister

Dave Block – a Trailways bus driver

Art Andrews – a miner

"Wimpy" Orbison – owner of the local pool hall

Dad also used men who worked full time for him. Some of those men included:

  Johnny Kracaw – a funeral director

  Ed Stevens – a carpenter and handy man

  Harlan Lowell – a carpenter and handy man

  "Red" Everett - a musician

And finally, Dad would use family members. My grandmother, Hulda Velin, was used as a mid-wife when Dad was called to transport women in labor. Nana helped deliver several of Mary Bernal's children. Both of Dad's sons-in-law, Russ Walker and John Abbott, were used as drivers and attendants whenever they happened to be at the house and Dad needed help.

My brother and I began riding the ambulance when we reached the age of 12. At first, we were only allowed to ride in the front seat on non-emergency calls. I recall many trips to transfer people from the hospital to their home after they were released; or to take invalids from their home to the nursing home. Mabel West would call Dad to transport patients from her nursing home in Palmer Lake to the hospital in Colorado Springs. Later she moved her nursing home to Castle Rock where she continued to rely on us to transport her clients.

I was always eager to go on those trips. I felt rather "grown up" riding in that ambulance. As soon as I was strong enough to lift stretchers I was allowed to sit in the back with the patient. Dad would keep the sliding glass window open between his driving compartment and the rear where I'd sit. If the patient needed anything Dad would tell me what to do. I think that was the first place I began to develop a sense of "pastoral care" and sensitivity to the needs of other people.

I was 14 years old when I went on the first emergency ambulance call. I recount that traumatic experience in the story titled: "First Fatal**.**" After that experience, Dad began using me on a regular basis. When I reached the age of 16 I was allowed to drive the ambulance and I became more and more responsible for oversight of the adults who worked as attendants.

Our family's life centered on emergency response. We could not take vacations like other families. We couldn't go anywhere together unless arrangements were made for someone to answer the phone or respond to our doorbell; and unless a full crew of emergency responders was available to handle the calls for service. Our home and our family life centered on emergency calls.

The Phone and Doorbell

Once that bell rings you're on your own. It's just you and the other guy."

Joe Louis

Most businesses depend on the telephone and doorbell, and since we lived in my father's business, our life revolved around the sound of those bells. When they rang, they could literally mean life or death. The person calling could be reporting an accident or someone ill. The caller could be the sheriff or the state patrol needing the county coroner. And just as easily the caller could be a young expectant mother who waited too long and suddenly she was in need of an ambulance.

When you called our phone, you reached the ambulance serving Douglas and Elbert Counties, the funeral home, and an assortment of other businesses. Dad had apartments for rent; monuments, flowers and furniture for sale as well as funeral insurance and pre-need burial polices. Oh yes, we also used that same phone for our private family calls.

At the time my parents bought the funeral home from Sam Livingston in 1938, the telephone number was 122. That remained our phone number until Ma Bell introduced Douglas County to the dial telephone system. That innovation brought about a change in our number. It went from 122 to Madison 8-3191 and later to 688-3191.

From the 1930s into the early 1950s the telephone office was located in Castle Rock near the Masonic Building on 3rd street just east of Wilcox. That office was staffed with an operator 24 hours a day. All phone calls went through that office. When a person picked up their telephone the operator would answer saying: "Number please." The person calling would then either give the number or the name of the person they were calling and the operator would make the connection using the switch board where she was sitting.

Since Castle Rock was a very small community everyone knew the operators and they, in turn, knew everyone in the community. In fact, they knew people in the community by the sound of their voices! That intimate knowledge had it's advantages and disadvantages. If someone in the family was ill, the operator might inquire about their health before connecting the person to the number being called. On the other hand, the operator just might also "listen in" on a conversation if it might be interesting. My mother was aware of that possibility so there were times she would call her mother by phone and they would converse in Swedish.

The primitive telephone system actually provided Castle Rock with its very first "answering service" for those involved in emergency services. Whenever the doctor, the sheriff, or my Dad weren't available at their home or office number they would tell the on duty operator the phone number where they could be reached. Then all emergency calls would be sent to that number. That wonderful convenience enabled my parents to play bridge at their friend's home, knowing that the telephone operator would transfer all emergency calls to that friend's phone.

In addition to the personal attention the operators gave their customers they provided two additional services everyone appreciated. They activated the fire siren every day at noon. The siren was located on top of the fire house in the center of town. It was so loud it could be heard anywhere in town. The noon siren was so accurate that people set their watches by it. At the sound of the noon siren businesses would close for the lunch hour.

The second valued service was using the fire siren to summon volunteer firemen to fire calls. All calls for the fire department went through the switch board. When a call was received the operator would activate the fire siren and immediately volunteer firemen would respond to the fire house. Cars and pickups with cheap sirens and red lights held in place with magnets would appear on the streets as those men responded to the call. The first volunteer to arrive at the fire department would call the operator, obtain information about the emergency, write the information on a chalk board, jump in the fire truck and speed to the scene.

Obviously, the operators were accustomed to handling emergency calls. They knew who to notify and where to find them. If there was an emergency and the emergency number happened to be busy, the operator would break in on the conversation and put the emergency call through. I remember many a time when our personal conversations were interrupted by an operator saying: "Please hang up. I have a call from the state patrol or the Elbert County Sheriff."

When the phone rang we never knew what to expect. We would assume a calm, professional tone and say: "Andrews Funeral Home." If the caller was reporting an accident and wanted an ambulance, we would refer to a sheet of paper with questions my mother had prepared. Reading from the paper we would ask: "Where is the accident? How many are hurt? Are any killed? Do we need any special equipment at the scene? Where are the remains?" We would record the information on a Law and Sons Casket Company note pad. Before we hung up we would always ask if there was anything else we needed to know.

Since the telephone was so important, it was vital that we be able to hear it ring. So, my Dad had the telephone company install an outside bell on the second story gable of our house. That bell was so loud that when it rang we could hear it one block away. When I was young I would get excited whenever that bell rang. It always had the possibility of being an exciting adventure. When I got older I came to hate that sound. It had become a call to action that took precedence over absolutely everything else at that moment. I came to respond somewhat like Pavlov's dogs. But instead of salivating, I'd prepare to encounter people struggling with painful injuries or death. I imagine that's why I react so negatively to telephones today. I want as little to do with them as possible.

The telephone wasn't the only link to the business. Many people came to our door. Through the years we were greeted by all sorts of crazy situations when we answered the door bell. One winter afternoon a couple rang the bell and when Dad answered they informed him they had two children in the back of their pickup with broken legs. The family had been tobogganing. The two children were sitting in the front of the toboggan when it hit a tree. They weren't near a telephone so they simply picked up the toboggan with the children still seated, placed it in the back of their truck and drove to the funeral home seeking help.

On another occasion, Dad and Mother were awakened by the doorbell. When Dad opened the door, he was greeted by a man who said his wife had died. Dad asked where she was and the man turned and pointed to the front seat of his car. She had died of natural causes at home and not wanting to put Dad out, the husband placed his wife in the car and drove her to town.

People came to our door for many reasons. They came to pick up plants and flower arrangements they'd ordered. They stopped by to pay the rent. They dropped in to order a monument or pay their funeral bill or look at the furniture Dad kept in his show room on the second floor of the adjacent apartment building.

The doorbell rang more frequently when we had a body in state. It was common practice for people to stop at the funeral home to view the body of the deceased prior to the funeral. The body would lie in a casket in the chapel. We would greet visitors, have them sign the guest book, and then take them to the chapel where they would pay their respects by looking at the deceased for a few minutes. If the deceased was a Roman Catholic a kneeler or prie dieu sat in front of the casket. Visiting Roman Catholic friends would kneel and say a prayer or recite the Rosary.

When there was a body in state one of us would have to remain in their Sunday-best clothes until at least 9 pm. If the deceased person was popular or well-known we could have a steady stream of people all evening. This constant need to answer the office door was why my dad wore a suit almost all day, every day. He even gardened in a suit, prepared to answer the door bell if someone came.

There was always a formal Rosary service for all Roman Catholics on the night before the funeral Mass. The Roman Catholic priest would conduct the Rosary which could be as well attended as the funeral Mass. I would assist Dad at the Rosary services by greeting people at the door and inviting them to sign the guest book. We weren't Roman Catholics but I was able to recite the Rosary before I entered high school.

I remember a most unusual experience which occurred in the late 70's when I owned the funeral home. I happened to be mowing the lawn one afternoon when a man parked in front of the funeral home, got out and approached me. The very first words out of his mouth were: "Do you have a red casket?" I thought he was joking but he looked and sounded serious, so I said: "Yes." "Let me see it." He said. Then he went on to tell me that his wife had died of cancer that morning. When she was in her 20's she had been a dancer at the New York City Music Hall. She had beautiful flowing red hair and her stage name was "The Long Stem Rose." That man had been to three funeral homes looking for a red casket. Ours was the only mortuary carrying what he wanted.

Since we never knew when someone would come to our door or call on the phone we had to be sure someone was in our home 24 hours a day. That meant we had to have part time help available to answer our phone and doorbell. Our most dependable help consisted of widows who lived nearby. Ruby Meyers lived in the same apartment Johnny Kracaw had rented for years. When she moved in she was told that one of the existing phone lines into her apartment was connected to the funeral home. Obviously, Dad had that installed when Johnny worked at the funeral home. Ruby was willing to answer our phone when asked.

Ruth Lewis was another widow who would answer our phone and doorbell when we were out of the house. Her husband, Ray, had been the Castle Rock Town Marshall and he was shot to death at the B & B Café in 1946. Ruth was left with four children to raise. She supplemented her income by washing clothes, helping us and she later started an answering service in her home.

When Carol and I owned the funeral home, we began using Inez Lillian. Years before, Inez had been one of the telephone company operators so she was well trained.

My grandparents lived in the apartment house across the street from the funeral home. On rare occasions Dad would ask Nana to watch the phone and doorbell. This didn't happen frequently because my grandmother didn't handle that responsibility well. To begin with, she spoke with such a heavy Swedish accent that she was even hard to understand when talking to her in person. Second, she never really understood the importance of good directions. If she was told that there was a plane down in Elbert County that was good enough directions for her. Finally, when we got our new telephone sets with multiple buttons for two phone lines, the hold feature and an intercom, Nana was unable to figure the system out. When the phone rang, she'd pick up the receiver and say "Hello". If the person on the other end didn't answer immediately Nana would begin punching the buttons on the bottom of the phone saying: "Hello … Hello … Hello". You can imagine what the person on the other end thought when they heard "Hello" and then the line went dead.

Nana had done her very best using the old telephone system. It had no buttons to push. There was a friendly operator on the other end who could re-connect her if there was a problem. She would even provide translation service if the caller struggled with Nana's broken English.

Aah for the good old days.

The Limousine

"You ride in a limousine the first time, it's a big thrill but after that it's just a stupid car."

Bruce Springsteen

One of the few advantages to growing up in a small-town funeral home was immediate access to a limousine. Name a teenager who wouldn't give up his ticket to a front row seat at an Elvis Presley concert if he could drive a long, black, sleek limousine. What many of my contemporaries only dreamt of, I had for the asking.

Every respectable small town funeral home had at least one limousine for either the pall bearers or the family of the deceased to ride from the funeral to the cemetery. Our funeral home was no exception. In fact, Dad had a limousine as early as 1938, the year he purchased the funeral home. It was black. It had four doors, front and back seats, and a pair of "jump seats" that folded against the rear of the front seats when not in use. That limousine could comfortably seat eight people.

Double fatal accident near Larkspur. CD Andrews is between a Colorado State Patrolman and Sheriff John Hammond. Phil Nolch is on the right.

There were many uses for that vehicle. To begin with, it was the sole means of transportation for our family. Mother drove it to Denver to shop. She used it as the family taxi to deliver her children to their piano lessons, Sunday School classes and 4-H club meetings. The limo was large enough for our entire family to comfortably enjoy a movie at the "47 Drive-In Theater". It was the ideal car to accommodate our large family on trips to Iowa to visit Aunt Hazel, Uncle George and their kids. And it was the only automobile my sisters, brother and I could use to learn to drive. In spite of the many family uses, the limo belonged to the business. Its primary use was to transport pallbearers and grieving family members. Its secondary purpose was to be an ambulance. Within minutes the interior could be converted from passenger car to emergency ambulance. All one had to do was remove the back seat, open the trunk lid and slide the stretcher in. The jump seat was then pulled into place providing a seat for the attendant to sit next to the patient. As clever at this conversion was you can imagine the stares it produced as it arrived at the scene of a traffic accident with the siren blaring and the red lights flashing.

Dad was using the limo as a coroner car in the above photo. The black limo will carry the two fatalities from this accident scene.

Many of the small churches where funerals were held did not have organs. My parents owned a small pump organ that could be used for funerals. Families would request my mother sing and play that organ. So, on the day of the funeral Dad and his help would fold the "jump seats" down and load the pump organ in the back of the limo.

When my siblings and I reached driving age it was Mother who assumed the role of driving instructor. I recall how excited I was when she took me on Lake Gulch Road for my first driving lesson. As soon as we passed Omer Memmon's farm house she stopped the car and traded seats with me. With my heart in my throat I drove from there to the Sidensticker ranch and back. That was the first of many excursions my mother and I took.

When my 16th birthday finally rolled around my Dad drove me across the street to the court house in the limo so I could take my driving examination. What a memorable day! After parking the car Dad handed me the keys and walked home. I took the written examination and then the state license examiner accompanied me to the limo. You may wonder what he thought when he saw the vehicle I was going to use; but, in truth he wasn't surprised. Remember this was a small town. Everyone knew us and everyone knew we drove the funeral home limousine. Without a word the examiner entered the passenger side and I nervously slid behind the wheel. I was told where to drive and what to do and each move I made was given close examination. I was told to parallel park that monster, a task the examiner admired. I used my arm to signal turns rather than rely on the automatic signals. I even slowed for the rail road tracks, a maneuver few teens ever observed.

By the time, we were driving back to the court house I was sure I'd passed. That is until we reached Wilcox Street. I stopped at the stop sign and looked both ways. In my excitement, I failed to see the white Ford sedan traveling southbound on Wilcox. As I stepped on the accelerator I heard a horn and realized I'd just pulled out in front of Undersheriff Beans Stark! He hit the brakes and screeched to a stop. I continued across the street and didn't say a word. I do remember the mental image that came to mind … it was a Colorado driver's license that had sprouted wings and was flying away from me. We arrived at the court house in silence. As I turned off the engine the examiner told me I passed. Then he cautioned me to look both ways in the future. Finally, he complemented me on my ability to parallel park a limousine. When I left the office with my license I could still hear him telling his next customer about my parking skills.

That big black four-door Chrysler limousine was my only means of transportation in high school and I loved it. When my friend Dave Stearns wanted to go hunting for hawks we would take the limo. He could sit in the back seat with two shot guns on the floor in front of him. When we spotted a hawk on a fence post or phone pole Dave would kneel on the floor and fire the gun out the window. Dave had a beautiful collection of stuffed hawks he'd shot from the back of the limo.

A limo is a wonderful vehicle for a high school date. My friends were forever asking me to double date with them. It was fun to pull up at a date's house and escort her to the black limo. And we always got a lot of comments when we arrived at a restaurant in that fancy car.

In 1960 my Dad had saved enough money to buy a new limousine. He special ordered it from Rickenbaugh Cadillac in Denver and he paid $10,000 cash for the car when it arrived. Dad ordered every piece of power equipment possible. There were buttons and gadgets all over the dash. As he was driving it home the temporary license fell out of the rear window and he was stopped by a Colorado State Patrolman. When the patrolman stepped to the driver's window Dad was pushing every button he could find to get the window to open. In frustration, he gave up and got out of the car to talk to the officer.

For some reason I'll never know, he and Mother decided it should be painted pink. Dad was so pleased with the color that he took the hearse and our second limo to the body shop and had them painted the same color. Jake Kroll, the most popular pallbearer in Douglas County also had a 1960 Cadillac he often offered as a pallbearer car. As soon as Dad painted his equipment pink, Jake did the same. Those pink funeral cars were the talk of the town.

The family limousine was used at all our family weddings. My brother, two sisters and I had the limo sitting outside the church and it took us to our receptions following the wedding ceremony. It was not only a classy touch, it also was a mark of who we were … members of the mortician's family.

Remain Calm and Confident

"What one had to do usually can be done."

Eleanor Roosevelt

When I first started riding the ambulance my dad impressed upon me the importance of my demeanor. He taught me to ALWAYS display an attitude of calm confidence regardless of how I felt. He taught me to mask fear and uncertainty with a calm and confident exterior. That was excellent advice. I found that presenting that demeanor not only boosted my sense of well-being, it had a calming impact on others. One memorable ambulance trip illustrates that.

Late one night when I was about 15 years old, Dad and I were called to the parking lot in front of the old court house in Castle Rock. A young husband was driving his wife to Denver to have their first baby. The young woman's contractions became so close and painful that they decided they needed help. The husband spotted a state patrol car pull into the parking lot and he stopped next to that patrolman and asked for help. The State Patrol called us and we responded. Let me tell you I was scared and at a loss as to what to do because at that point I had never helped deliver a baby. Not only that, but none of the first aid classes I'd taken had ever covered that emergency. Despite my fear and ignorance, I assumed my calm and confident demeanor. Dad and I helped the lady onto the stretcher, placed her in the back of the ambulance and instructed the husband to follow us to Colorado General Hospital in Denver. As dad drove out of town the woman's water broke. With a "calm and confident" tone of voice I asked dad what to do. "Make sure the lady's panties are off and determine if the baby's head is crowning." He said. "OK" I said. Then I asked him what he meant … "a crowning head". He explained in a voice loud enough to be heard over the scream of the siren. With a real lump in my throat – but a "calm and confident" look on my face – I told the lady what I was going to do, and I did it. There was no evidence of a crowning head. I thanked God in silence. During the rest of the trip I kept assuring the woman and silently praying for the Lord to slow the process down. To my great relief that prayer was answered. We arrived at the hospital with the same number of people physically present as we started with: Dad, a pregnant woman and me. On the way home Dad told me how proud he was of me. He said I kept the situation calm and cool in spite of the tremendous tension.

Another very difficult call involved Marshall Burgess, a mechanic who worked for his brother, Pete Burgess, at the Burgess Motor Company in Castle Rock. Marshall was known as a heavy drinker and he suffered from severe epileptic seizures. I vividly remember transporting him on two different occasions. The first time we cared for Marshall he was attending the Douglas County Fair. We were on stand-by near the main arena when someone yelled that the ambulance was needed on the north side of the grandstand. We drove the short distance and found Marshall on the ground suffering from a grand mal seizure. His body was absolutely ridged, his face contorted and he was violently shaking. I'd never seen anything like that and I was afraid he was about to die. I loosened his clothes and placed a tongue depressor in his mouth so he wouldn't bite his tongue. We lifted him onto the ambulance cot and placed restraining straps around him so he wouldn't fall off. I don't remember who was driving the ambulance that day; but whoever it was wasted no time on the emergency trip to Swedish Hospital in Englewood. The siren screamed during the entire trip, and I tried to verbally comfort Marshall even though he made no visible response to my effort. In fact, the intensity of his seizure did not appear to abate. When we transferred him to the emergency room staff there, I realized I was soaking wet from the nervous sweat I had produced during that trip.

The second time we transported Marshall he was having a grand mal seizure in front of his brother's business. That trip was a repeat of the first experience. Marshall survived both seizures and he probably had no memory of the events. I too survived them but my memory of the frightening illness is clear to this day. Both times I was afraid Marshall was dying and there was absolutely nothing we could do except get him to the hospital. I'm sure I exhibited a calm confident exterior but I was a mess on the inside.

My brother received the same training as I did and it paid dividends for him just as it did for me. One example involved an ambulance trip Tim took with one of our regular part-time attendants, the Rev. Hank Hiddinga. Tim and Hank transported an elderly woman from her home near the South Platt River to the hospital in Denver one summer afternoon. During the trip down the winding Jarre Canyon road the woman got sick to her stomach and she threw up. Hank was seated next to her in the rear of the ambulance, and he was prepared. At least he thought he was prepared. He held the emesis basin and a towel as the lady vomited. Then Tim heard Hank say: "*Oh my God!*" Tim looked in the rear-view mirror in time to see Hank place the emesis basin under his chin and heave. The woman said she was still sick and needed the basin back. She threw up again. Then Hank threw up again. There Tim was, traveling with red lights and siren, watching in the rear-view mirror as both the patient and his attendant were alternately vomiting. With a calm and confident voice Tim said: "Clean up that mess when you're through."

There was one occasion I was not calm and confident. Dad and I were called to an accident on the South Platt River near Deckers. It was very late and snowing hard. When we arrived at the scene the state patrolman told us the victim was drunk and belligerent. We examined him and placed him on our stretcher. He was semi-conscious, delirious and constantly moving, so we used restraint straps to secure him to the cot. As we began the trip to Denver the snowstorm increased and Dad couldn't drive very fast. The man began yelling and it began to look like he would work himself out of the restraints. The more I talked to the man in a "calm and confident" manner, the more he would yell and fight. Several times Dad stopped and we tightened the straps. It just seemed to make the man more combative and loud. I was deeply relieved when we finally arrived at the hospital several hours later. The call made me aware that there were going to be times I'd need more than a "calm and confident" demeanor.

I did see that demeanor work for dad one night. We were called to a head-on collision on I-25 a quarter mile north of the southbound exit to Larkspur. A drunk man had driven north from the Spur Tavern in Larkspur and turned north in the southbound lanes of the interstate. Within a minute the drunk struck a southbound vehicle head-on. When we arrived at the scene we found the drivers of both vehicles trapped under the steering wheels of their cars. Douglas County didn't have any rescue vehicles or specialized equipment to handle a situation like that, so it was up to us to extricate the victims. While I examined each victim, Dad asked the drivers of two 18-wheel transport trucks to disconnect their trailers and position their tractors in front and behind one of the cars. They then attached chains to their tractors and the wrecked vehicle. Slowly they pulled the car from two directions until we could remove the first victim. They performed the same maneuver on the second car and in no time, we were on our way to the hospital with both drivers. That experience left me feeling proud of my dad. I believe we saved two lives as a result of his efforts.

About 4 am one day Dad and I responded to another accident on I-25 at the Larkspur exit. It involved a cattle truck that had rolled over. The driver had fallen asleep and he was severely injured. The highway was full of dead and dying cattle. The odor of blood, cow manure and diesel fuel filled the air. One of the state patrolmen at the scene was walking from cow to cow shooting those that were still alive and injured. Another patrolman helped us lift the driver into the ambulance. We quickly left the scene and headed for Colorado General Hospital. During the trip I was so busy tending to the driver's injuries that I barely noticed that my body felt strange. I'd scratch my stomach and then my arm and then my leg. The tension kept me focused on my patient rather than on myself. That changed after we transferred the injured man to the care of the emergency room staff. Dad and I changed the stretcher bedding, put the cot back in the ambulance and started back home. I was still scratching myself, but now I was really aware of the intensity of the itching. I was miserable and I told Dad to turn on the interior light. I pulled my shirt up and discovered that my stomach was covered with round red spots. It was the hives. I was so miserable I suggested we run "red lights and siren" back home. When we got home, Dad gave me an antihistamine tablet and then filled the bathtub with warm water and Epson salt. I crawled into that tub and soaked until the hives began to disappear. To this day, I don't know what caused the hives; but I'm sure it had something to do with the unique environment at the scene of that accident.

My brother-in-law, John Abbott, and I will never forget an ambulance call we both worked as attendants many years ago. John, my dad and I responded to a single car accident on I-25 near the Greenland exit. The driver, a woman in her mid-50's, was alone. She had suffered a severe head injury and remained semi-conscious. John and I attended her in the back of the ambulance and Dad drove. We did the best we could to clean and dress the lady's wounds. About 20 minutes into the trip to Colorado General Hospital the woman began saying: "I'm sick. I'm sick." We tried to assure her but she didn't seem to hear us. Her only response was: "I'm sick. I'm sick." Suddenly she vomited a huge amount of dark coagulated blood. We weren't prepared for that and as we scrambled to get the emesis basin and towels, she vomited again. Blood was everywhere. It was all over her, on the cot, on the floor and on us. It was a major mess. Unfortunately, the woman had such severe internal injuries that she died shortly after we reached the hospital. When we got home it took us a long time to get ourselves and the back of the ambulance cleaned. After that experience all John and I have to say to each other is "I'm sick! "and that event comes to mind.

I take a lot of pride in the fact I never had an accident the entire time I drove an emergency ambulance. That doesn't mean I didn't experience some close calls. The most memorable occurred soon after I started driving the ambulance. I was 16 years old and Dad let me drive to an accident up Jarre Canyon. Dad was sitting next to me as I approached Johnson's Corner on U. S. 85. My red light and siren were operating. I turned on my left turn signal and slowed to make the turn off 85 onto highway 67. It appeared the oncoming traffic was slowing to a stop so I executed the turn. To my shock the oncoming car did not stop. I cleared his lane of traffic with about one inch to spare. Dad said: "Awful close." In a calm and confident voice, I replied: "Yes." Nothing more was said but I've never forgotten the experience. From that time on I never again assumed I would be given the right-of-way.

The ability to display a calm and confident demeanor has helped me throughout my entire life. When I was a police officer we were taught to project command presence at all times. That was exactly what my Dad taught me using the term calm and confident. I've used that demeanor as a funeral director, county coroner, priest and even as a parent. Thanks Dad for the good advice.

George Nixon

"The best way to meet a woman is in an emergency situation – if you're in a shipwreck, or you find yourself behind enemy lines, or in a flood."

Mark Helprin

George and his wife, Bertha, lived at 5th and Elbert, less than a block from our home. They were our neighbors. George raised pigs and he would regularly drive his old black pickup truck through our driveway to pick up our garbage which he used as feed for his pigs. (In the days before garbage disposals people would separate their food waste from other trash. That food waste was referred to as garbage.) He was a kind, thin man who wore bib overalls. I don't ever remember him speaking directly to me, but then I was just a young boy.

George served as sheriff of Douglas County for 14 years, starting about 1914. Before and after that he was a blacksmith. He was 81 years old and had been retired for at least 10 years. He spent a lot of his time drinking at the Village Inn – Bar and Grill.

Bertha was a small woman with white hair. She looked frail, but I imagine that her looks really didn't reveal the courage she must have had to love and care for a pioneer lawman.

One Sunday a very sad event linked the Nixons to my family. My parents had invited company for dinner. Mother had cleaned and prepared our home. Company, including my sister Cindy and her husband Russ, had gathered. My mother and grandmother were about to serve the meal, and my father and our company were moving from the living room to the dining room. My brother, Tim, and I had been playing outside and we were more than ready to eat.

Suddenly, Bertha Nixon, who was in her 70s, burst into the back door of our home. She ran into the living room screaming that George had shot himself, then she turned and ran for the back door. My mother tried to stop her, but she wasn't fast enough. Bertha pushed the back door open, jumped off the porch which was four steps high, and hit the ground running.

Dad hollered for mother to help Bertha. As mother ran for the back door, dad grabbed the keys to the ambulance and told his son-in-law, Russ, to follow him.

Bertha and mom ran through our back yard, north in the alley and then across the street to the Nixon's front door. Mom never did catch up to Bertha. Mom opened the front door and found Bertha standing in the front room pointing to the back porch. Mom rushed into the back porch where she found George sitting in a chair with a shot gun lying at his feet. The top of his head was lying open, his head and neck were covered with blood, as were his shirt and overalls. Blood and brains were splattered on the wall and ceiling.

Mother told Bertha to bring bath towels. She checked George's pulse and assessed the wound while Bertha was getting the towels. Surprisingly George was still alive, but it was obvious he wouldn't live long. Mother placed a large towel in the open wound and then wrapped another towel about the top of George's head to hold it in place. Then mother took Bertha into the living room and sat with her on the couch.

Within minutes, Dad and Russ arrived. They placed George on the stretcher and took him to the ambulance. Bertha got into the front seat with dad. Mom got into the back with Russ and George. They left the scene with siren screaming.

The trip to Denver took no time at all, but George died enroute.

I don't remember what happened to our company. I imagine they either went home or Nana and Cindy entertained them. I know that my brother and I thought the event was exciting. It wasn't often the ambulance was needed at a neighbor's home and I had never seen my mother respond as she did that afternoon.

As I reflect on that terrible day I feel some family pride. When trouble arose, our neighbors knew they could depend on my parents for help. This was only one of many times Dad responded to neighborhood emergencies. That was who and what he did.

But it wasn't something Mom often did. Yet she did not hesitate to help when Bertha burst into our home. She responded with compassion and skill. With no idea what to expect she went to the aid of a neighbor in distress. I can't imagine what Mom thought and felt when she found George. It must have been a shock. But as repulsive as it was, she did the best she could for George and then offered comfort and emotional support for Bertha.

There aren't many people who have to face that kind of situation and even less who would respond as nobly as my parents did.

First Fatal

"When we are children we seldom think of the future. This innocence leaves us free to enjoy ourselves as few adults can. The day we fret about the future is the day we leave our childhood behind."

Patrick Rothfuss

I was 14 years old. From the time I was 12 I had accompanied my father on non-emergency ambulance calls. I had never responded to an emergency. On August 12, 1957, at approximately 8:30PM, the phone rang. Dad answered it in the hall that connected my parent's bedroom, the bathroom, the kitchen, the girl's room and the dining room. The call was from the Colorado State Patrol dispatcher reporting a serious automobile accident on the highway south of Castle Rock. Dad was told that one person was dead and several people were injured. As soon as Dad obtained the information he needed he began calling men to help. He was able to reach two men, Johnny Kracaw and Wimpy Orbison. He needed one other person, and everyone he called was either not home or they couldn't help.

I had heard the original call and I stood in the hall listening as Dad attempted to locate men to help. I began offering my assistance, but Dad ignored me. After each call, I'd again offer to help. Within a very few minutes it was obvious he wasn't going to find anyone else, so he told me I could go. I couldn't have been more excited.

Dad and I got into the ambulance and pulled onto the street as Johnny and Wimpy ran to the garage to get the second ambulance. Dad turned on the red lights and siren, and my heart felt like it was going to jump right out of my chest. I had been dreaming of this day for a long time.

It was a warm evening. The highway was wet and slick from rain that had been falling. It took us no time at all to arrive at the scene which was only 2 miles south of town.

A Fort Carson soldier was driving south with his wife and a friend sitting with him in the front seat of the car. All three had been drinking and the driver was drunk. Just before the accident a southbound semi-truck and trailer had pulled onto the right shoulder of the highway. The soldier's car struck the left rear of the parked trailer. The soldier's wife was sitting in the middle of the front seat. She was propelled into the rear-view mirror and she died immediately from an open skull fracture. The other passenger landed under her on the front seat. The driver was not seriously injured. When we arrived at the scene the driver was wandering up and down on the shoulder of the highway.

Several state patrolmen were at the scene and one of them directed us to park directly behind the accident. Johnny Kracaw parked the second ambulance behind the one we had arrived in. Dad and I ran to the car and found the two victims in the front seat. It was obvious the woman was dead. Dad directed me to help him remove her so we could begin caring for the injured man. I got into the back seat and helped lift the woman. I remember looking at her face. I had never seen anything like that in all my life. In fact, I was so naïve that I had never imagined anything that horrible. We were able to get the woman out of the car and lay her on the ground near the front passenger door.

I was so upset by what I had seen that I stepped to the shoulder of the highway and threw up. Then I returned to help take care of the injured man. The man had stopped breathing. A quick examination revealed some sort of obstruction in his throat. A medical doctor had stopped at the scene to assist. He got into the car, examined the man, and announced that he would have to perform an emergency tracheotomy. He had no instruments. Someone gave him a pocket knife and he made an incision in the man's throat.

I couldn't believe what I was seeing. There was blood everywhere, and the car reeked of alcohol and gasoline. With my stomach churning, I again stepped to the shoulder and threw up.

My father could see the condition I was in. He told Johnny that he and Wimpy would take the man to the hospital in the ambulance, and I was to go back to the funeral home with Johnny in the coroner's car.

As soon as the ambulance left the scene, Johnny told me to give him a hand. We placed the woman in a black rubber crash bag, put her on a stretcher and placed her in the coroner car. Then Johnny returned to the soldier's vehicle to finish his investigation and collect pieces of the woman's head and brains. I watched but didn't help.

We rode back to the funeral home in silence. I felt physically sick and I couldn't have been more disappointed in myself. When we arrived, I helped Johnny carry the stretcher into the morgue and left without helping remove the body from the crash bag. I remember feeling greatly relieved that I didn't have to look at that woman again, but guilty for not helping Johnny.

I went to bed and cried myself to sleep. I felt like a coward who had failed both my Dad and myself. Dad and Mom never talked to me about that experience. And for months after that I would make myself scarce whenever we received an ambulance call. It took several months for me to get enough courage to even ask to go on an ambulance call again.

Early Morning Business Proposals

"The early bird catches the worm"

An English proverb first recorded in 1605

Dad was an early riser. I knew this because of his annoying habit that directly affected my life. My brother and I shared a bedroom which was located near the kitchen. Every morning from as early as I can remember, Dad would wake up at 5:30AM, go to the kitchen and turn on the radio. The twangy voice of Pete Smythe would invade the silence rudely interrupting our sleep with another episode of the "Barbed Wire Network".

Pete Smythe was KOA's morning DJ who created a radio program that he said was broadcast from Tin Cup, Colorado. He told his faithful fans that his broadcast location was so isolated that he had to use his neighbor's barbed wire fences to transmit the program. Whenever the station experienced technical difficulties, Pete would blame the problem on his neighbor, saying he had left his gate open. Dad liked Pete's humor so the kitchen radio was always tuned to 850 on the radio dial.

Tim and I could hear Pete's voice clearly because our bedroom door faced the hall leading to the kitchen. That wide hall contained a washer and dryer and a wood burning stove. That was the room Dad used to cut hair … our hair … and Nana's hair. He would place old Denver *Post* and Rocky Mountain *News* papers on the floor, put a kitchen chair in the middle and invite us to "have a seat." Then, he would save 50 cents each time he cut our hair, and more than that when he cut Nana's hair.

That hall had two more doors. One door opened onto a concrete porch with steps that led down to a flag stone patio. The other door was actually an open doorway that led into the kitchen. The doorway had a decorative wire partition that sat on top of a dish cupboard. The wire extended from the top of the cupboard to the ceiling. Mother kept her philodendron plants sitting on top of the cupboard and their vining leaves were intertwined in the decorative wire. An old white Philco radio sat next to the plants and that was where the Barbed Wire Network emanated from.

In the winter the furnace didn't produce enough heat to keep the kitchen, the washroom and our bedroom warm. So, after Dad turned on the radio he would start a fire in the wood stove. Then he would collect the milk and butter from the milk box which was located in the

33

wall next to the back door. The milk was delivered in the middle of the night by the Meadow Gold milkman. The milk was bottled in a glass container. The bottom of the milk bottle contained whole milk and the top of the bottle contained cream. The cream was poured out to be used on cereal or whipped as topping on pie or some other wonderful dessert. At least once a week Dad would use the cream to make pancakes from scratch.

Dad loved the early morning hours, Pete Smythe, and breakfast. If he wasn't eating pancakes, he was eating bacon, eggs and toast. And breakfast was always accompanied by steaming black coffee that was perked in a percolator that sat on the wood stove in the washroom.

I didn't like to get up early. I liked to sleep. I didn't like Pete Smythe. I preferred silence. But since I was the next to the youngest person in the house my preferences didn't carry much weight. Consequently, the last hour I spent in bed was filled with the voice of a corny DJ, the strong smell of coffee and burning wood. Those childhood memories are not something I treasure.

The one thing I did treasure was working on my Dad's ambulance. After all, I was the only kid I knew who was able to ride and drive an emergency vehicle. And since I enjoyed working on the ambulance so much I was constantly thinking of ways to improve or promote that business.

Maintenance of that vehicle was of utmost importance to me. I was forever scrubbing and polishing the floor, taking inventory of the first aid supplies, and testing the red lights and siren. One day, while washing the ambulance, I noticed that the tires were worn. Knowing that vehicle often exceeded 100 mph, I resolved to convince Dad to purchase four new tires. I knew that wouldn't be an easy sell because tires for a huge Cadillac ambulance were expensive. They cost in excess of $100 each. That was a lot of money in those days.

All of this happened when I was a high school sophomore. I happened to be enrolled in Miss Berdine's business class. Part of that class focused on creating business proposals. We were taught that effective business proposals contained details like cost analysis, return on investments, and the possible consequences of non-action. Using that approach, I prepared a "proposal to purchase tires for the ambulance." The actual proposal was only one page in length but it was filled with as much detail as I was able to muster.

Knowing that the best time to approach Dad was early in the morning, I was ready when awakened by the smell of coffee and the unique sound of the Barbed Wire Network. I jumped out of bed, dressed in the only suit I owned, and joined Dad for breakfast. He was surprised if not impressed. He asked if I wanted some pancakes. "Sure", I said. I knew he didn't appreciate small talk, so I sat in silence while he prepared the pancakes. When breakfast was on the table I simply handed him my business proposal. He read it in silence. Then he said he would think about it. Within several weeks, the ambulance had a complete set of new tires…with white walls no less.

The only other time I presented Dad with a business proposal was the year Continental Divide Raceways opened their new track south of Castle Rock. The raceway contained an oval track for stock car racing, a drag strip for drag races and a winding 2 ½ mile track for sport cars. Located half way between Denver and Colorado Springs, the owners were confident they could attract enough people to support their investment. Their advertisements carried a schedule of races that were to fill many weekends of the summer.

I really got excited as plans for CDR were announced. This would present us with the first opportunity to provide scheduled ambulance coverage throughout the summer season. WOW, I thought. I immediately began to prepare another early breakfast business proposal.

I spent hours determining the cost of paying a crew, finding and training enough people to provide "backup" coverage, equipping a second vehicle, and estimating the revenue from the additional ambulance trips the race track would generate. This time my proposal filled two pages. I was impressed.

Dressed in my suit, I again approached Dad at breakfast. This time he knew I was there to discuss business. As soon as the food was on the table, Dad said, "Now what?" I responded, "Dad, I'm not here to ask you to spend money, I'm here to show you how to make money." With his interest peaked, I handed him my proposal. He read it, but he didn't like it. He considered the ambulance business a losing operation. He provided the ambulance because no one else in the county had the equipment and he provided it as a public service

At the end of a long discussion, Dad again said he would think about it. He did. Within a month, we had sent a proposal to CDR and they invited us to provide ambulance coverage for the summer. We did and there were so few trips generated that we lost money.

The following year a Denver ambulance company bid and won the contract. Dad was pleased. And, in a small way, so was I. Instead of rising early to organize ambulance crews I got to lie in bed, listen to Pete Smythe and smell the coffee.

Kroll's Grocery

"Most of all – enjoy the journey"

Ken Poirot

I have known few people in my life as beloved as Jake Kroll. He was so well known that he was asked to be pall bearer at more funerals than absolutely anyone else in Douglas County. He served as pall bearer so often that he began buying Cadillac sedans that matched my father's hearse. Then, every time Jake was asked to carry a casket, he also drove the other pall bearers.

Jake Kroll was born on his family's homestead in Happy Canyon. He had three brothers and one sister. Jake and his sister, Betty, were lifelong residents of Douglas County. Betty married into the Lowell family but was widowed after three years of marriage. She and Jake lived within blocks of each other in Castle Rock. Betty was the post master of the Castle Rock Post Office for 41 years. Between Jake and Betty there was no one living in Douglas County they didn't know.

Jake owned and operated Kroll's Grocery, one of three grocery stores in Castle Rock. All three stores were within a block of each other. King's Fine Food Store was located on 4th street just west of the Castle Hotel and Café. Roger's Meat Market was located in the 500 block of Wilcox next to the Masonic Hall. Kroll's Grocery was just five doors north of Roger's. Jake Kroll, Ross King and Roy Rogers did all they could to support each other. If one store ran out of fresh milk a stock boy ran to one of the other stores and "borrowed" a crate of milk. "Borrowed" items were replaced when the next warehouse delivery was received.

Paul King, Ross King's son, once told me that every Friday evening, Jake would call Ross to find out what he would be running as "specials" on Saturday. That way Jake would be sure his "specials" wouldn't compete with "specials" at King's Fine Food Store.

While all three stores were small, Jake's was the largest. Kroll's had two cash registers while the other stores had only one apiece. Roger's had a large meat market, a small supply of groceries, and meat lockers that were rented for a nominal charge. King's had a small meat display case, and a small amount of groceries. Kroll's had a large meat display case and a full-time butcher, a nice selection of fresh produce, and the largest selection of groceries.

I was privileged to work for Jake during the last two years I was in high school. My good friend and classmate, Keith Olson, also worked at Kroll's. We both thoroughly enjoyed the work. Our duties included stocking shelves and delivering groceries.

Jake was an Associated Grocer, which meant that the majority of his groceries came from the Denver AG warehouse. Every Thursday, after school was out, the AG delivery truck, an 18-wheeler, arrived at Kroll's back door. Keith and I would help unload the truck. The driver would drop boxes of canned goods, paper goods and dry food onto a long metal conveyor belt and they would slide into the storage room. Keith and I would stack the boxes until the storage room was full of supplies from floor to ceiling.

As soon as the delivery truck left, Jake would hand us a stack of inventories. Each box was listed on that inventory. And Jake would have hand written the price he wanted on each item within each box. We would then cut each box open, determine the price of its contents, and begin marking each item with a metal price stamper. After marking the items, we them placed them on the shelf for sale.

Jake often bought his eggs from local farmers. The eggs would arrive in a large cardboard carton containing several hundred eggs. Keith and I would then take the eggs from the large carton and place them in cartons for display and sale. That task wasn't easy for two clumsy high school boys. It wasn't unusual for us to break three or four eggs. And since we were never trained to identify an A egg from an AAA egg, let alone a small from an extra-large egg – all eggs sold at Kroll's were marked AA Large.

In the summer farmers often arrived at the back door of Kroll's with fresh produce from their gardens. Jake would examine the produce and, if he liked what he saw, he'd buy it. Fresh home grown tomatoes were my favorites. Keith and I kept a picnic size salt shaker hidden in the walk-in cooler so that we could salt the home-grown tomatoes we'd eat on the sly.

By today's standards, Jake offered his customers some unusual free services. A customer could telephone their grocery order to the store. A clerk would place the order in a box, and those groceries were then delivered to the customer's home. On a normal day, we might have 20 home deliveries. Prior to a holiday, we could have 50 deliveries. Home deliveries usually left the store around 4:30PM so that the customers had their food in time to prepare the evening meal.

I loved making deliveries. The fact I was being paid to drive was almost too good to be true. But even better, I got to drive Jake's red pickup truck. At that age and time, I couldn't imagine better work.

We had a routine when we delivered groceries. We would go to the customer's back door and enter without knocking. We'd place the food on the customer's kitchen table and return to the truck for the next delivery. About half the time we would encounter the customer, and since Castle Rock was so small and everyone knew everyone else, we'd end up in a conversation. There were times the conversations lasted too long and we'd receive a phone call from Jake. On rare occasions, we were given a tip. It was fun.

Another service Jake offered was the option to charge groceries. A lot of people took advantage of that option including my parents. It was always a big event when Dad paid our grocery bill. He would usually pay that bill right after he received payment for a funeral. Dad would place the stack of itemized grocery slips on his office desk, then, with the aid of a mechanical calculator, check the addition on each slip. He would make corrections, bundle all the slips together and walk over to Kroll's. He'd discuss the bill with Jake, and then write a check. Jake would place the check in the cash register and then hand Dad a box of Roy Tan cigars (the fat kind) in appreciation. Imagine doing business that way today

Jake had a hard time finding and keeping good butchers. Most butchers were alcoholics. Often Jake would hire a butcher who would work dependably until the first payday. Then we wouldn't see the man until he'd drunk up all his pay.

Orville Sensible was an exception. He butchered for Jake for many months. He was an older single man who was polite and quiet. I liked Orville. He took time to show me how to cut up a whole chicken and he'd ask me to help him saw pork chops. One Friday afternoon, he invited me to go to the dog track in Colorado Springs. He and Duncan Lowell were going right after the store closed and they had room if I wanted to join them. I was very surprised when my parents gave me permission to go, and honored those old bachelors would take me. It was the only dog race I ever attended, and I lost every cent I bet.

Terry Keefer was another butcher who worked for Jake. Terry was in his late 30's, married and the father of five children. He enjoyed telling dirty stories and he loved to flirt with the young female customers. He drove a 1953 Oldsmobile coup and was forever challenging Keith to a drag race.

The coup once got Keith and me in trouble. It all started one Saturday when Terry arrived at work early. When Keith and I arrived, we found Terry's Oldsmobile parked at the rear of the store, backed in next to a tall pole that appeared to be carrying power lines. Terry's rear bumper was resting against a stabilizing guide wire that ran from the top of the pole to the ground. Keith and I pushed the guide wire around the end of Terry's bumper. We laughed thinking that the wire would be so strong that Terry would be unable to move his car.

That day was so busy that we forgot about our prank. At quitting time, Terry offered to give Keith and me a ride home. We accepted and all of us got into the front seat of the Olds. As he often did, Terry turned on his engine, stepped hard on the accelerator and popped his clutch thinking that his tires would spin as he left the parking lot. Instead the car lurched forward about one foot and his engine died. At the same time, we heard a loud crack and the lines above the car began to sag. Suddenly we realized that Terry's car had broken the power pole and, though we couldn't see it, we both mentally visualized it coming down on top of Terry's car. In unison, we screamed "HIT THE FLOOR" and we all sank down.

The pole did break and fall. It missed the car by inches. However, the car was draped with live wires. Keith told Terry not to touch any metal then he began yelling for help out his open window. People ran to our aid from behind the drug store. After examining the situation, they declared it safe because the pole wasn't carrying power lines. It was carrying telephone lines. We later found that ½ of Castle Rock was without phone service for hours. We never confessed to Terry, instead we offered to help him keep an eye on his car in the future.

That wasn't our only prank. One of the most successful pranks involved the stock boy at Christensen's Pharmacy. Harold knew that a hole the size of a nickel existed in the floor in front of the meat display case. If one were in the store basement and positioned to look up that hole they could see clear to the ceiling. On slow days, Harold was known to sneak into the basement in hopes of using that hole to look up women's dresses. Everyone in our store knew what he did and we were disgusted. So, a plan was put into place.

I ran to the drug store and told that boy that one of our classmates, an attractive girl, was talking to Terry at the meat display case. He almost knocked me over as he bolted into our back door. Down the basement steps he ran, positioned a box to stand on, and placed his eye up to the hole. Terry was above holding a large funnel. Keith was next to him with a pitcher of water. The resulting flow not only soaked the voyer, it washed his contact lens out.

Word of the prank spread quickly throughout the store and everyone was laughing when his mother happened to appear. She, of course, wanted to know what was so funny. After hearing the story, she made her way to the basement and found her son on his hands and knees searching for his lost lens. It wasn't a pretty sight watching him led out of the store by his mother.

Bobby Lewis was another stock boy who received our attention. He worked for Ross King and he was the person who usually came to Kroll's for extra milk or produce when his store ran out. Bobby would always talk with Jake and then go to the cooler for the necessary item. As often as we could, we would sneak to the door while he was in the cooler and lock it. Bobby would have to "cool" his heels until Ross missed him. Finally, Ross would call Jake and ask if Bobby was locked in the cooler again.

A group of businessmen in Castle Rock formed a group called the Downtown Businessmen's Association to develop ideas that would promote business. Naturally, the stock boys in all the grocery stores and the drug store decided to form a group. We called it the Uptown Business Boy's Association and began exploring ways to have fun. The greatest fun we created was a one-time ash pit burn off. The goal of the event was to see which of the stock boys could build the biggest fire in their store's ash pit. On the chosen day, all of us filled each of the ash pits in the alley behind the stores with as much cardboard, paper and wood as we could find. Then the fires were started. To our surprise none of them burned very well because there was too much material and not enough oxygen. What our efforts produced was smoke … lots of smoke … more smoke than we ever thought possible. The smoke startled citizens throughout town and the fire siren was set off bringing volunteer firemen to our "ash pit burn off." Those unwelcome firemen remained until all the smoke cleared from the area.

I only worked for Jake Kroll for two years. Those were perhaps the most fun working years of my life. Can you imagine what might have happened if Keith and I had worked for Jake through all four years of high school?

Burglary at the Kiowa Superette

"When I have listened to my mistakes, I have grown."

Hugh Prather

Sometime in the middle of the night my father woke me from a sound sleep to accompany him on an ambulance call. I dressed quickly, ran to the garage and opened the door. I had the ambulance backed out and the garage door closed by the time Dad arrived. I drove out of the driveway as Dad was telling me the Elbert County Sheriff called us to respond to Kiowa.

The Elbert County Sheriff's Office did not have a dispatcher. As I drove Dad said that it was Sheriff Yarnell's wife who called. She told Dad that the sheriff and the under-sheriff had discovered a burglary-in-progress at the Kiowa Superette. One of them went to the front door and the other watched the back door. When they announced their presence someone in the grocery store fired a gun. The sheriff fired back. After the exchange of gun fire, the sheriff radioed his wife and told her to have an ambulance respond to the scene. Since the burglars had not yet been arrested and the situation was still unfolding, Mrs. Yarnell instructed Dad to park the ambulance at the top of the hill on State Highway 83 just west of town and to stay there with our red lights flashing.

When we arrived, I kept the engine running and our emergency lights on. The main street of Kiowa was visible, but we didn't have a police radio so we had to simply wait until someone told us to move to the scene.

Finally, a sheriff's deputy drove to our location and told us one of the burglars had given himself up and the other one had shot himself in the head. He was still alive, lying on the floor of the Superette.

I drove to the front of the store. The sheriff met us and helped us get the stretcher out. We all entered the dark business as no one had yet located the light switches. We followed the beam of the sheriff's flashlight. The wounded burglar, dressed in black clothes, was lying on the floor with a pool of blood around his head. He was still breathing. We placed him on our stretcher and carried him to the ambulance. Sheriff Yarnell told us to take him to Colorado General Hospital.

Dad got in the back with the victim and I drove. I realized how serious the head wound was and so I was soon hitting speeds of nearly 100 MPH. The sliding glass window was open between Dad and me and he was keeping me informed about the man's condition. Shortly after turning onto Highway 86 at Franktown, Dad told me he thought the man had died. I said I would drive faster. Instead Dad wanted me to stop and return to Castle Rock with the body. I wouldn't hear of that and a brief argument ensued. I was determined we were not going to stop until we had arrived at Colorado General Hospital. I won the argument because I was driving.

Dad continued to press his side. He said he was sure the man was dead and he felt we would run into all sorts of complications if we continued to Denver. He was sure we would have to fill out reports for the Denver Police and the Denver Coroner's Office. That didn't matter to me. All I was interested in was getting our patient to a hospital where a medical doctor would assess his condition.

When we arrived at Colorado General Hospital the on-duty physician examined the man and confirmed Dad's pronouncement. The man was dead. Dad was right, not only about the burglar's death, but also about the many complications we were about to encounter.

Colorado General Hospital refused to let us take the man inside. The Denver Police arrived and escorted us to the Denver Coroner's Office located at Denver General Hospital. We spent hours filling out forms and writing statements. The longer the ordeal lasted the more I realized what a mistake I had made. I should have listened to my father. After all, he was the Douglas County Coroner and he was very experienced at pronouncing a person dead.

It turned out the man had a lengthy police record including many burglaries. I believe he had not only spent time in the State Penitentiary, but he was wanted on burglary charges at the time of his death.

This experience helped me realize the importance of listening to others, particularly my father. I had a real passion to provide the very best service to the people entrusted to our care. I believe Dad felt the same way, but he had the experience and wisdom to recognize when a change in circumstances was best met with a change in our response. I apologized for my stubborn unwillingness to listen. Dad never said another word about that experience.

Agony After Saving a Life

*"You never know how much you really believe anything until
its truth or falsehood becomes a matter of life and death to you."*

C. S. Lewis

The summer after my brother Tim had completed his freshman year in high school and I had just completed my first year at the University of Colorado, we were both working for Dad. On a warm weekend afternoon, we were sent to a traffic accident several miles east of Franktown on U.S. Highway 86. I drove the ambulance and Tim was my attendant.

The accident involved one vehicle. The east-bound driver had veered to the right, traveled along the shoulder of the road, and struck a large cottonwood tree. The car, visible from the road, had sustained major damage. A crowd of people were gathered around the victim who was lying on his back near the left rear of the vehicle.

Upon arrival at the scene, Tim and I went to the back door of the ambulance, opened the door and began removing the stretcher. Colorado State Patrolman Dutch Sandburg ran over to us. In a loud voice he said he thought the victim was dead.

Tim and Dutch took the stretcher and I ran to the victim's side. He had suffered an open skull fracture and his face was covered with blood. I placed my hand on his neck and felt movement in the vicinity of his carotid artery … he was alive. I hollered for Tim and Dutch to hurry. They placed the stretcher beside the man and Tim threw the pillow on the ground so the victim would lie on a flat surface. We carefully lifted him onto the stretcher and carried him to the ambulance.

As I helped Tim place and lock the stretcher, Dutch asked me where I was going to take the victim. I told him I would go north on Highway 83 to Colorado Blvd., and take Colorado Blvd. to Colorado General Hospital. Since we had no radio communications in the ambulance, Dutch said he'd have his dispatcher alert the hospital and obtain emergency clearance from the Denver Police Department.

With the siren wide open, I turned the ambulance unto Highway 83 in Franktown. With a moderate amount of traffic on the two-lane road, I was able to reach speeds of 80 and 90 MPH.

Several miles south of Parker, Tim hollowed that the man had stopped breathing. I told Tim to begin giving the victim mouth-to-mouth resuscitation. By glancing into the rear view mirror I could see Tim position himself and begin to administer mouth-to-mouth.

The closer we got to Denver the heavier the traffic became. The siren was almost in constant use, and I really had to concentrate on my driving. Occasionally I would look in the rear-view mirror to see how Tim was doing. I knew he had a difficult task and I would verbally encourage him.

When we arrived at the emergency entrance of the hospital, I was surprised to see a number of doctors, nurses, and attendants waiting for us. As I was backing the ambulance to the ramp, some of those waiting opened the back door of the ambulance and began removing the stretcher. By the time I got to the back of the ambulance, the stretcher was out and raised. Tim was still administering mouth-to-mouth. He and the victim were surrounded by medical staff. I watched as the entire group passed through the door to the emergency room.

Within minutes Tim appeared. The victim had been intubated and moved into a sterile environment. Tim was covered with blood from his eyebrows to his waist. A nurse took him to a sink and helped him remove his smock. She gave him a wash cloth so he could clean his face; then she had him rinse his mouth with some sort of peroxide.

After Tim cleaned up and we had completed all the necessary paper work, we got our stretcher and began to walk out. As we passed one of the doctors, I asked how our patient was doing. He said the man was still alive, but his chance of survival was slim at best. He said that it the man lived his brain damage was so severe that he would be a vegetable for the rest of his life. With that we got into the ambulance and began our drive back home.

For the first 10 minutes neither of us spoke. It took time for us to process all that had happened. We had risked our lives and used our skills to bring our patient alive to the hospital. Then we realized that all we had done may have left our patient and his family with the prospect of years of existence as a vegetable. We both had tears in our eyes as we talked about the experience.

By the time we arrived home, we had come to the conclusion we had done all we could … what we did was appropriate and proper … and we would never change our response. Our job was to do all we possibly could to save lives. We were not to make judgment about the future outcome of a patient.

We discussed the event and our response and conclusions with Dad and he gave us his full support. The next day the patient died, having never regained consciousness.

They Come in Three's

"In adversity, remember to keep an even mind"

Horace

Bob Anderson owned Barn, a rowdy bar and dance hall three miles south of Castle Rock. The Barn was known for its country and western music and the wild behavior of its patrons. People would drive from Denver and Colorado Springs to drink beer, listen to country music and dance. And on most weekends, they could also watch at least one bloody fist fight. Most of those fights didn't result in serious injuries but they often ended with one or both parties in jail. I remember one month we took more combatants to the hospital than the sheriff put in jail.

The first fight was the least serious. It involved two drunks who simply had a difference of opinion. Strong words led to threats which ended in a challenge to settle matters in the parking lot. One drunk was either stronger than the other or he'd had less to drink. And, for whichever reason, he over-powered his opponent. Once in control he beat the man unconscious and left him lying on the ground between two pick-up trucks.

Bob Anderson was a tall, thin cowboy who didn't seem to fear anyone. He often carried a lead-filled leather sap and a device called "the claw" in his hip pockets. He'd use the sap to subdue unruly patrons. The claw had a wrist cuff on one end and a handle that twisted the cuff as tight as the owner desired. Bob would use the cuff to grab his prey and hold him until help arrived. If his prey continued to fight, Bob would twist the cuff as hard as he could and the pain would bring his opponent to his knees.

On the night in question Bob's bartender told him of the fight and Bob headed outside. He arrived too late. The fist-a-cuffs were over and all Bob could find was the unconscious drunk. He asked an arriving patron to call our ambulance and he stayed at the man's side until Dad and I arrived.

The man reeked of stale beer and he was still unconscious when we arrived. Other than some minor cuts and a few bruises we couldn't find any other signs of injury. We stabilized his head and neck, placed him on the stretcher and loaded him in the ambulance. Dad drove and I attended the patient. About 10 miles from the Barn the man awoke. He had no idea where he was or what had happened. He kept fading in and out of consciousness until we arrived at Swedish Hospital in Englewood. He was treated and later released, a bruised, and confused cowboy.

The next weekend we were again called to the Barn. This time the situation was more serious. The country western band included a fiddle player who had convinced his girlfriend to tag along. As the evening progressed one of the patrons began talking to the fiddler's girl. The conversation led to a dance. The dance was so pleasant that it led to another and another and another. The budding romance became more than the fiddler could manage. He verbally shared his displeasure with his girlfriend and her dance partner. He told them to cease and desist. But the couple was having too much fun. In fact, they had decided to leave The Barn and find an intimate location to deepen their acquaintance. The real trouble began when they shared those plans with the fiddle player. He went berserk. He grabbed a large beer bottle, broke off the bottom and went screaming after his competition.

The ensuing battle was ugly. The fiddle player swung the broken bottle at his opponent and cut a deep gash in the man's neck. Blood began to flow from the wound.

The music stopped. Bartenders and patrons rushed to the wounded man's aid while members of the band disarmed the fiddle player. When order was restored the fiddler was told to "get out" and he hit the door running…without his girlfriend.

The sheriff's office wasn't large enough to have a dispatcher. When the sheriff was on the road his wife received his phone calls at home and then dispatched people as best as she could. That night Shirley Hammond called us. She said Bob Anderson was requesting an ambulance because someone had been cut. It sounded serious and sheriff Hammond was in route.

Again, Dad drove and we arrived within minutes. We unloaded the stretcher and took it inside. The place was quiet and it didn't seem to have as many patrons as usual. The fight had been so bloody that few wanted to stay. Others left believing they'd be tapped as witnesses when the sheriff arrived.

The injured man was lying on the floor with a man and woman kneeling at his side. There was blood all over the man's clothes and on the floor around him. One of the women had placed a Kotex over the wound and she was applying direct pressure. I was told that the wound was about six inches long at the base of the man's neck on the lover left side. Before the Kotex was applied the wound was pumping blood at the same rate the man's heart was beating. The Kotex applied with pressure had significantly reduced the bleeding. It was obvious that the victim was bleeding to death and we had no time to spare.

We lifted the man to the stretcher and I assumed responsibility for the patient. I placed a thick compress bandage on the Kotex and continued to apply direct pressure. Dad and several by-standers grabbed the handles of the stretcher and we all literally ran to the ambulance. Once the stretcher was firmly fastened, I sat on the floor at the head end of the stretcher. That position enabled me to apply pressure and observe the blood flow.

I was scared. It was almost certain that the man's artery was cut and he had lost a lot of blood. While pressure on the wound reduced the bleeding, it also reduced the blood supply to the brain. I was afraid the man would either die from blood loss or survive with brain damage. Dad shared my concern. When we got onto I-25 he pegged the needle of the speedometer at 120 mph, and that's the speed we maintained until we got to our exit at Hampden Ave.

The patient spoke only once. He looked at me and said he was going to kill the man who cut him.

Ambulances had to back down a ramp into the basement garage at Swedish Hospital. Ambulance patients were then wheeled the entire length of the hospital to an elevator, taken to the 3rd floor, and again wheeled back the entire length of the hospital

Once our ambulance was in that garage, Dad and I removed the stretcher and we ran with it to the elevator. The man had lost consciousness. Blood was dropping from the stretcher as we ran. The elevator ride seemed to last forever. When the elevator door opened, the doctor and his nurse were waiting. We filled them in as all of us ran to the ER. Once there, Dad and I had done all we could and the outcome was now the responsibility of that doctor and nurse.

Several days later we learned that our patient not only survived, he hadn't suffered any brain damage. I never heard if he got his revenge. If he did it didn't occur in Douglas County because we would have been called to that homicide.

The third incident at the Barn occurred the following Saturday night (actually very early Sunday morning). Dad again awoke me and told me to hurry and dress because we there had been another fight at the Barn.

Two serious fights in two weeks was too much for the sheriff. John Hammond and one of his deputies had spent the entire evening at the dance. But instead of preventing violence, their presence had provoked another fight. Near the 2 AM closing, John Hammond arrested one of the patrons for public drunkenness and disturbance. The man resisted and was injured in the ensuing struggle. Our ambulance was called to the scene as a result.

We found the man lying on the ground at the entrance to The Barn. He was surrounded by a small crowd and clearly under the sheriff's custody. John told us how the injury occurred and told us to be careful. I asked the man where he was injured. He wasn't interested in talking to me. He kept telling John Hammond how much hatred and anger was boiling inside him. Then he began yelling profanities at John. Suddenly the sheriff grabbed the man's shirt and belt and physically lifted his body onto our stretcher. The move was made so fast it surprised all of us.

As John held onto the man he told us to "strap" the bastard to the stretcher. John and I used one restraining strap to secure the man's chest and arms while Dad and a deputy secured the man's waist. Dad and I then rolled the stretcher to the back of the ambulance, opened the door and lifted the stretcher in. John Hammond was lifting the foot of the stretcher. As John leaned over to lift the patient kicked him squarely in the face with his pointed cowboy boot.

John was furious. Once the stretcher was locked in place, John pulled out his black leather lead-filled sap and began to crawl into the back of the ambulance screaming that he'd teach that "son-of-a-bitch" a lesson. The man kicked at John again. This time he missed and ripped a hole in the material that lined the ceiling of the ambulance. Dad and John's deputy grabbed John and pulled him out. While they were trying to calm him down, Bob Anderson and I used another strap to tie the victim's legs to the stretcher. (How would you have liked being "our" patient??)

John told his deputy to ride with us in the ambulance while he followed in his car. He was determined that man was going to spend the night in the Douglas County jail if he wasn't admitted to the hospital.

We took the man to Denver General Hospital. After initial treatment, he was admitted and taken to the detention unit with a hold from the Douglas County Sheriff.

John Hammond suffered only minor facial bruises. His major injury was to his pride. He addressed that injury by refusing to allow Bob Anderson to open his business the following weekend. The loss of revenue was so effective that it was months before we received another call to The Barn.

Ralph Maul

"Now, most dentist's chairs go up and down, don't they? The one I was in went back and forwards. I thought 'This is unusual.' And the dentist said to me 'Mr. Vine, get out of the filing cabinet.'"

Tim Vine

Years ago, there was a TV program called "Hee Haw" that featured Grand Old Opera singers and comedians. One of the regular skits on that program was a spoof on local TV newscasts. The "newsman" was a middle-aged character who wore bib overalls and spoke in a staccato style voice. He often mispronounced words and never seemed to have his facts straight, yet he spoke with authority. That "newsman" reminded me of Ralph Maul, the coroner of Elbert County when I was growing up.

Since Elbert County had neither an ambulance nor a funeral home they looked to us for those services. We responded to all deaths in the western half of the county and our ambulance responded to all calls for emergency transport. We encountered Ralph Maul often.

I never saw Ralph dressed in anything but bib overalls. He always had a "coroner's badge" pinned on the left bib strap. He looked funny. Ralph's wife was an invalid, but that didn't stop Ralph from taking her to view death scenes. On more than one occasion I watched Ralph go to his car, pick his wife up in his arms and carry her into a death scene so that she could view the details.

Two incidents involving Ralph come to mind. The first one was a natural death on a ranch south and east of the town of Elizabeth. A recluse had been living rent free on the rancher's property in an old brick chicken coop. The building was isolated and it contained neither running water or electricity. The occupant, an old man, would walk to town to pick up his pension check and purchase food for himself and his four dogs. When the merchants missed him, they called the sheriff and asked him to make a welfare check. When the sheriff located the chicken coop he found the door open and the dogs running loose. The animals were vicious. They wouldn't allow the sheriff to get out of his car. He honked his horn but got no response. Fearing the worst, the sheriff shot the dogs. When he approached the building he found the man lying on the dirt floor inside. He was dead.

Dad was called and I responded to the scene with him. A deputy sheriff met us and directed us to the chicken coop. The first person we spotted upon our arrival was Ralph Maul.

He was stepping over a dead dog with his wife in his arms. They were on their way to "view the body". It was surreal.

The second incident I recall involved the death of a rancher. The man died in his sleep. His wife realized he was dead and called the Elbert County sheriff who in turn called Ralph and us. Again, Dad and I responded, arriving before dawn. Ralph was already in the house. As we walked in Ralph was walking out, carrying his wife. He told Dad to take the body. After placing his wife in their car, Ralph returned with a blank death certificate he had signed. He told Dad to complete the death certificate and send him a copy. Dad asked Ralph if he knew the cause of death. "Yep", Ralph said, "it's that there thing that kills em in the heart." "A coronary occlusion?" Dad said. "Yap", Ralph responded and off he went.

If the producers of "Hee Haw" had ever met Ralph, I know that their skit would have been about county coroner's rather than local newscasters.

Johnny Kracaw

"It takes a long time to grow an old friend."

John Leonard

Our life revolved around the funeral home. We lived there. We shared the phone and the family car with the business. Funerals were conducted in our home, part of the house contained caskets for sale, and my father's office was located in our home. Since our lives were so close to the business it's natural that the people who worked for Dad were also an important part of our life.

Johnny Kracaw worked for my father during most of the time I was growing up. He was physically distinctive, standing at 5 feet 2 inches and weighing close to 100 lbs. He was a tough wiry little man who constantly had a burning cigarette in his hand.

Johnny was born July 29, 1894, in Franktown, Colorado. He married Helen Isenhart in Telluride in 1917. He and Helen had two sons, Robert and Kenneth. Johnny and Helen were divorced when the boys were very small. I never met Helen or Johnny's sons.

Johnny was a recovering alcoholic. Years of drinking led to his divorce. The York Street AA Club, located on York Street in Denver, was the place Johnny found sobriety. He was given every other weekend off and that enabled him to attend AA meetings twice a month. Once every year he celebrated the date of his sobriety by attending a "birthday" party at the York Street Club. Johnny considered my brother, Tim, and me adopted sons. So, every year Johnny took one or both of us to his birthday party. I remember feeling honored that he would take us. When he would stand, say: "My name is Johnny, and I'm an alcoholic whose been sober for X-number of years.", I felt a deep sense of pride to be with him. I probably attended half a dozen "birthday parties" with Johnny.

Johnny lived with his mother, Mary Ellen Tallman Kracaw (Mamie), in a downstairs apartment in the Odd Fellows apartment building located directly across the street on the south side of the funeral home. Dad owned that apartment building and Johnny's rent was part of his salary. "Mamie" Kracaw, like her son, was a small woman. She had white hair, was rather formal but kind and friendly.

Johnny had been a funeral director and embalmer for many years. At one time he either owned or worked for a funeral home in Telluride, Colorado. The business didn't provide him with enough income to live on so he worked part time cooking in restaurants and as a line walker for the Ute Power Company. Several times a week he would walk over the mountain pass from Telluride to Ouray checking the power lines for any potential problem. That must have been very hard work and Johnny told me it really kept him in good physical condition.

I've always been a good listener and I've always loved stories. I remember some of the stories Johnny told me. For example, he was involved in the horrible influenza epidemic that killed many people in 1918. He told me that he worked day and night embalming those who died. It was frightening work because there was a great danger that anyone who came in contact with the bodies would contact the disease and die. Johnny lived through the experience without ever getting it.

Johnny was a tough little man who spoke his mind. One story reveals this side of his personality. He told me that during World War II he responded to a traffic accident on U. S. Hwy. 85 – 87 south of Louviers near the Match Box Bar. He was a deputy coroner and had been called to investigate the death of a Japanese man who was killed when his car was struck head-on by a semi-trailer truck. Johnny told me that since America was fighting Japan there was a lot of prejudice against the "Japs". He said the driver of the semi felt terrible about the death of the man his truck struck. Johnny said he told them man not to feel bad because the accident eliminated a Jap. Then he told the man he thought he should be awarded a medal for what he'd done.[2]

In his later years, Johnny often forgot that he'd told me that story. So, I heard it over and over again. He though the story was funny. I didn't, but I never told Johnny that. Instead I'd politely listen and then change the subject.

A second story Johnny told demonstrated the callous side of his personality. It involved the death of a man who was struck and decapitated by a Santa Fe freight train. Johnny and my Dad were called to the scene which was near the Onsa Switch Station. When they arrived, a large crowd had gathered. Everyone knew that the man had been decapitated and they wanted to see what the body looked like. Johnny said that he and Dad quickly covered the body. They located the head under a freight car and covered it with a blanket. Then they took their time investigating the circumstances hoping that the people would leave. Not only did they fail to leave, but the crowd grew in size. Finally, Johnny lost his patience. Without saying a word to my Dad, he crawled under the train, uncovered the head and picked it up by the hair. "There you blood thirsty son-of-a-bitches; this is what you wanted to see!" He said people gasped and turned away. Within minutes the crowd left. Johnny had stooped to the level of the "look-e-loos" and people would remember his actions for years.[3]

As I've written in another chapter of this book, Johnny was one of the people present when I rode the ambulance to the first fatal I'd ever experienced. He and I worked many other ambulance and coroner calls together. As I recall some of those experiences it is easy to see how the shared trauma left us feeling bonded.

---

[2] March 19, 1942, 7PM, death of Frank Teraco Ishida, recorded in the Douglas County Coroner's book.
[3] June 11, 1941, Douglas County Coroner book, page 149

The funeral home ambulances were Cadillac's. They were huge vehicles. Being so small, Johnny would use a pillow to gain the height he needed to see above the dashboard when he drove. I can still see Johnny hustling across the street from his apartment to respond to an ambulance call with a pillow tucked under his arm.

One afternoon we responded to a traffic accident on I-25 about a mile south of the Larkspur exit. It had been raining and that section of the highway was always slick when wet. It was a single car roll-over accident. We took the driver to the Penrose Hospital in Colorado Springs. It was still raining as we drove back toward Castle Rock. We were northbound about one mile from the scene of the accident we'd just handled when a car passed us at a high rate of speed. Johnny laughed and said he imagined we'd be picking up that driver in a few minutes. Sure enough as we came around a curve in the road, the car that had passed us was skidding on its roof in the center of the northbound lanes of traffic. I turned on our red lights, slowed the ambulance and we stopped next to the car. I ran to the driver's door and peered in. The young man who had been driving was held in his seat upside down by his seat belt, uninjured but terribly frightened.

On another occasion, Johnny and I responded to a traffic accident at the rail road overpass just north of Castle Rock on I-25. Dolly Small lost control of her car and it hit the concrete overpass. Dolly's name wasn't descriptive of her size. Like Johnny, she was short. Unlike Johnny, she was extremely obese. In fact, she was so obese that, lying down, she appeared as tall as she did standing up! When we arrived at the scene, I went to her side and began to examine her. Johnny joined me. The first thing out of this mouth was: "Oh no, it's you Dolly!" She looked at him and said: "Oh no, it's you Johnny!" I knew what each was thinking. Johnny was thinking about lifting that heavy woman onto a stretcher. Dolly was thinking that Johnny could never lift her onto that stretcher. Johnny knelt at her side and said: "Dolly, do you think you can get on the stretcher by yourself … or better yet, into the ambulance?" Dolly laughed and said: "*Sure.*" I stopped the exchange by calling the state patrolman over to help us. We did pick Dolly up and we got her safely to the hospital.

During the summer of 1964, Johnny and I handled an ambulance call I can vividly remember. It was a hot afternoon and I was driving Dad's John Deere tractor on the land he was developing at the south end of the Castle Rock business district. My mother drove onto the property with her headlights on and honking the car horn. That was a signal to me that I was needed on the ambulance. As I got into the car she quickly drove onto Wilcox and breathlessly told me that there had been a shooting in front of the Douglas County Court house. She said that both of our ambulances were headed to the scene and that she would drop me off at the scene which was only blocks away.

As I jumped from the car I could see the first ambulance pulling to a stop in the parking lot directly east of the court house entrance. There was a crowd of people standing near a woman who was lying on the sidewalk near the two large wooden doors at the entrance to the building. I ran to the woman and found Dr. Arch Heaton kneeling at her side. He told me that she had been shot several times and we needed to get her to the emergency room at Swedish Hospital in Englewood as fast as we could. Johnny had driven the ambulance to the scene. He and I got the stretcher and took it to the lady's side. She was bleeding but she was still alive. As we were placing her in the ambulance I told Johnny to get in with her and I would drive.

I remember that as I was traveling down the exit ramp from Castle Rock onto I-25 the speedometer was at 80 MPH. Within moments I pegged the speedometer at 120 MPH and maintained that speed until we exited the highway at Hampden Ave. That was the fastest trip I ever made on I-25. Johnny and I didn't talk during the trip, but occasionally I would glance in the rear-view mirror and I could see him working with the patient.

The hospital had been notified of our pending arrival and we were met at the ambulance entrance by a group of doctors and nurses. Our patient had stopped breathing at that point. It took us less than a minute to get her into the emergency room. Johnny had been giving her external heart message, and a doctor took over that responsibility. Another doctor yelled that he was going to "crack her chest" so they could do internal heart message. With that, the lady's blouse and bra were cut off and an incision was made in her chest. The doctor put his gloved hand into the hole and began to message the lady's heart. The room continued to fill with medical people and equipment. Johnny and I removed our stretcher and left.

The woman died despite the heroic efforts extended on her behalf. She had numerous gunshot wounds to her chest and there was no way she could have survived.

We later found out the details that led to her death. She had gone to the court house to obtain a restraining order against her husband. Ardell Arfston, the Douglas County Undersheriff, was aware of the lady's domestic troubles, and he knew she was in the court house obtaining the order when he spotted the lady's husband standing outside the court house. Ardell was in a car and he stopped near the husband. He called the man over to his car and began to explain what a restraining order was when the man's wife walked out of the east door of the court house. Suddenly the man pulled an automatic revolver from under his shirt and ran toward his wife shooting. Ardell jumped from his car and began shooting at the man. Another deputy sheriff who was sitting in the basement sheriff's office heard the gunshots and ran up the steps to the east door. As soon as the shooting stopped he opened the door and found Ardell physically restraining the husband. The man's wife was lying on the sidewalk dying.

Dr. Heaton was shopping at Kroll's Grocery when the gunshots began. He ran to the wounded woman's side as soon as the shooting stopped.

My Dad and Ed Stevens responded to the scene with the second ambulance. After Johnny and I had left the scene, Dad and Ed, along with several deputy sheriffs, took the woman's husband to Colorado General Hospital in Denver. The man had suffered two gunshot wounds, one to his hand and another to his groin. One of Ardell's bullets had struck the man's hand and the man had accidently shot himself as he was pulling the automatic weapon out from under his shirt.

Dad said that when they arrived at Colorado General Hospital the man showed no remorse for what he had done. In fact, a nurse expecting a patient with a hand injury had walked up to our patient and asked if he had gotten his hand caught in a lawn mower. Our patient replied: "No. I was shot with a fucking 45!"

That man was later convicted of second degree murder and sentenced to the Colorado State Prison in Canon City.

I shared a number of adrenalin producing calls like that with Johnny. He was always cool and composed. Nothing could rattle him because he had seen it all.

I also spent a lot of time with Johnny in the embalming room   He did the majority of the embalming and I assisted him on many occasions. Some of them were rather memorable.

One afternoon I went with Johnny to pick up a body at a Denver hospital and bring it back to Castle Rock to be embalmed. It was a very busy time and Johnny really did need my help. When we arrived at the funeral home Johnny parked the hearse at the north doors. Those doors each had about 24 panes of glass in them and the doors often stuck shut. After we unloaded the body and placed it on the embalming table, I went back to shut and lock the doors. One of the doors stuck and without thinking, I pushed hard on one of the glass panes. It broke and cut an artery in my right wrist. Blood began to pump from the wound. I hollered for Johnny. He brought a terry cloth towel and tightly wrapped my wrist. In a disgusted tone, he said: "The only place you'll find sympathy is in the dictionary. Now go find your mother!"

On another occasion, Johnny was teaching me to embalm. We were wearing gowns and rubber gloves. My hands were wet. Johnny handed me a glass bottle of cavity fluid. Cavity fluid is the strongest embalming fluid used. It is almost pure formaldehyde. Johnny wanted me to practice opening the bottle. He showed me how to hold the bottle with the neck between my thumb and first finger. I was to strike the bottom of the bottle to loosen the lid, then I was to unscrew the cap. When I struck the bottom the bottle shot out of my hand and splintered as it hit the floor. The room was immediately filled with eye watering fumes. Johnny and I removed our gloves and gowns, opened all the windows, turned on the fan full blast, and got out of the room. It was hours before we were able to return. I don't remember Johnny asking me to open a cavity fluid bottle again.

Dad, Johnny and I were working together embalming an adult male who had an amputated leg. His wooden leg had been removed and was standing in the corner of the embalming room. As we were working, Johnny began telling us that he'd heard that the best place for an amputee to hide money was in their wooden leg. We all laughed. Then the room got real quiet as all three of us turned toward the leg. Dad began removing the flannel cloth that lined the spot where the stump went and he found cash underneath. The interior of that wooden leg was lined with $750 dollars in bills. When Dad told the man's family they were amazed and thankful. They had no idea he had that money. It was enough to pay for his funeral. We had to laugh because without Johnny's comments that man would have "taken it with him!"

 My Dad could be rather absent minded at times. One afternoon he and Johnny were embalming together. Dad finished his part of the work and he left Johnny to complete the job. As Dad walked out of the room, out of habit, he locked the embalming room door with Johnny still inside. Johnny didn't realize he'd been locked in until he finished about 30 minutes later.

Several hours later, while our whole family was watching television in the family room, we heard a constant banging noise. Actually, we had been hearing it off and on for several hours, but we thought it was coming from a neighbor's house. Finally, we became annoyed and we began to look for the source of the noise. It was Johnny, banging on the wall of the embalming room! In spite of Dad's apology, Johnny was as mad as a banty rooster. It took days for him to stop talking about the danger of working for Doug Andrews.

As Johnny got older and older he would often sit at his desk in Dad's office and sleep sitting up. That disgusted my mother who was always checking on him to make sure he didn't fall asleep and drop his cigarette.

Finally, Johnny reached the point he had to retire. Within a short time, he had to move to the Silver State Nursing Home where he could receive constant care for the emphysema that had taken over his lungs.

After I married Carol I didn't see Johnny for years. Then, one Sunday while driving home to Boulder after visiting my parents, who were then living in Canon City, I received a God-given impulse to stop at the nursing home and visit Johnny. Carol was open to the idea, so I made the stop. Carol remained in the car while I went into the nursing home. The receptionist told me I'd find Johnny in a bed in a nearby room. When I stepped into the room I found Johnny sitting on top of the bed in shorts. He had an oxygen cannula in his nose. He immediately recognized me. He said: "Hi John. You talk, I'll listen." It was an obvious struggle for him to breath. I talked to him for about 30 minutes. As I left he said: "Thanks!" He died several hours later.

I do believe that the impulse to visit Johnny came from God. I'm so glad I stopped and shared those few minutes with him. He was a man who I came to know and then to love. He was a lonely man who led a hard life.

Bill Jrlbacher

"If you press me to say why I loved him, I can say no more than because he was he, and I was I."

Michel de Montaigne

If you were to try to imagine what a grave digger was like, Bill would probably fit that image. He was single, illiterate, physically unattractive and very strong. He knew and used every swear word in our vocabulary.

Bill was a grave digger and he worked for my father for almost 30 years. My brother and I saw and interacted with Bill constantly as we grew up. Bill had a good heart and we loved him.

Bill lived with his brother, Adolph. They shared a small shack about one mile east of Castle Rock on Sellers Creek. The shack was on Omer Memmon's property and it had neither running water nor electricity. Bill walked to work five days a week.

Bill's mother called him "the strong one" and she called Adolph "the smart one". Adolph was "the smart one" because he successfully completed the 3rd grade. Bill was "the strong one" because he could physically overpower and out-work anyone his age or size.

Adolph didn't work. Instead he "kept" house. He was dependent on Bill to buy the food they ate. I can only remember seeing or talking with Adolph twice in my life. He rarely came to town and I don't ever remember him coming to our home.

Bill's primary responsibility was hand digging graves. He probably dug 50 or 60 graves a year. When Bill didn't have a grave to dig, Dad would have him water and mow the lawns, wash the cars, feed and care for the chickens, or help our two carpenters, Ed Stevens and Harlan Lowell.

Dad paid Bill twice a day. He received $1 at noon and either $1 or $2 at the end of the day. At noon, Bill would take his dollar and go to Roger's Meat Market on Wilcox Street. He'd give Mr. Rogers the dollar and Mr. Rogers would prepare him a large sandwich and a glass of milk. Bill would sit on a stool behind the meat counter, using the large wooden chopping block as his table. At the end of the work day Bill would collect his pay from Dad, return to Roger's Meat Market and use the cash to buy some groceries.

Bill didn't own a car and he didn't have a driver's license, so he walked to and from work every day. No matter how bad the weather, Bill would faithfully show up for work. In the winter, he would walk to town, then he would shovel snow from the walks at the funeral home and at each of the four apartment buildings Dad owned. When the weather was especially bad Dad would drive Bill to the pasture gate located about one mile from the shack. Bill would walk home from there.

Since Bill and Adolph's shack had no running water, Bill couldn't bath at home. He stunk. His clothes were filthy, his hair was unkempt, and he never blew his nose. He commonly had snot hanging from the end of his nose. He'd snuffle, it would momentarily disappear only to reappear. We were forever giving Bill a tissue but that didn't make a lot of difference.

Bill would get so dirty and smell so bad that Dad would insist that he bathe. Dad would take a large medal wash tub to the flower room in the garage, heat water and fill that tub then Bill would undress and bathe. Everyone in our family knew when Bill was going to take a bath. It was a big deal! Bill was very modest. The flower room was "off limits". I remember my brother and I once went to the door of the flower room while Bill was bathing. I knocked on the door, then in a high-pitched voice I said: "Is anyone in there?" Bill hollered that he was and no one better enter that room! He kept cussing as Tim and I laughed and laughed.

Mother would wash Bills clothes on the day he bathed. Those times were few and far between; but, everyone rejoiced when Bill bathed and got into his clean duds.

My Dad would have Bill help move heavy furniture when one of the apartments was rented "furnished". Dad would always caution Bill to "be careful", "don't damage the furniture". Bill would say: "OK". Then he would pick up his end of the item, and without fail, slam it against a wall or another piece of furniture. "Oops", he would say over and over again. I honestly believe that he thought that "being careful" meant saying "Oops" when you hit something.

Bill's vocabulary was limited but his knowledge of profanity was deep, wide and blue. To say that every other word was a swear word was not exaggerating. He knew every filthy word in the English language and he was very creative in the way he constructed his sentences and phrases. When my brother and I were real young we quickly learned not to ask Mother what was meant by some word or phrase we heard Bill say. If we were really curious we would ask one of the men who worked for Dad. Often, they would fake ignorance.

Over the years my Dad fired Bill at least five times. That would occur when Bill would come to work drunk, or when he and my Dad would get into a serious argument. Bill always went home after he was fired. He would come back to work the next day. Dad would remind him that he had been fired. Bill would respond: "Hell, Doug, if I listened to you I wouldn't have a job." Both of them would laugh and Bill would resume his work.

Once when Dad fired Bill, he got a temporary job with a local farmer. The farmer had Bill climb into a silo to shovel feed onto a conveyor belt. The conveyor belt was run by a gasoline motor that was located within the silo. The motor wasn't properly vented and Bill was overcome by the carbon monoxide fumes. He was unconscious when the farmer found him. The man put Bill in his truck and drove him to Colorado General Hospital in Denver. Several hours after that accident, Dad happened to have an ambulance call and he delivered his patient to the emergency room at Colorado General. As Dad was unloading his patient, Bill who was lying in one of the examining cubicles, heard Dad's voice. Bill began yelling at the top of his lungs: "Doug, help me! Doug, get me out of here! Help me, Doug, help me!" Dad recognized Bill's voice. He went to his side and tried to calm him down. Bill wasn't interested in being calmed, he wanted to go home. So, Dad loaded him on the stretcher and brought him back to our house. Dad prepared a bed in the flower room in the garage and Bill stayed there for several days until he recovered. After his recovery, Bill returned to work for Dad.

Bill was a good grave digger. He dug his graves by hand. When Dad knew which cemetery was to be used he would have Bill load his tools in the black limousine and off they'd go. If the grave was at Cedar Hill Cemetery in Castle Rock, Dad would take the cemetery records, locate the correct spot and make an outline of the grave. If the grave was at any other cemetery Dad would call the cemetery custodian who would meet Dad and Bill and show them where the grave was to be located.

My mother would prepare Bill a sack lunch and Bill would take a canvas bag full of water. As soon as he began digging Dad would return home. By 4PM Dad would return and find Bill done and patiently waiting. One of Bill's proudest accomplishments was the fact that he once hand dug two graves in one day and was waiting for Dad when he arrived.

Some cemeteries were harder to dig in than others. The Franktown cemetery was full of large rocks. There were times that dynamite had to be used to open the grave. When that was necessary an experienced blaster was hired and Bill would stand by to clean up the rock and shape the grave.

Winter was a difficult time to dig graves. Sometimes a fire had to be built over the ground where the grave was to be dug. The heat would thaw the frozen ground. Bill would also build a fire to warm himself during the day.

When Dad would return to pick Bill up he would be pulling a large wooden trailer behind the limousine. That trailer contained a large cemetery tent, artificial grass mats, a metal lowering device and a wooden "rough" box. None of the cemeteries had grass. They were full of unsightly weeds, dirt and rocks. Bill would have thrown the dirt from the grave to one side. Dad and Bill would drop the wooden "rough" box into the grave. The rough box was the container the casket was shipped in from the casket factory. That box became the "vault" for the casket. It was used because morticians had no other way to dispose of them, and they could recoup the cost of the shipping container by selling it as a grave liner.

After placing the box in the grave, Dad and Bill would place large 2 X 12 X10 foot boards along the sides of the grave, and 2 X 12 X 4 foot boards at the end of the grave. Then they would drape the artificial grass greens over the boards and the sides of the grave as well as the mound of dirt that had come out of the ground. They would then place the lowering device on the boards and erect the tent. Finally, they would place a dozen wooden folding chairs on the artificial grass facing the open grave. All this work made the grave site look attractive and pleasant.

Upon return to the funeral home Dad our pay Bill $10 for digging the grave. Bill and Adolph ate well when Dad had a funeral.

Every Christmas Eve Bill would be invited into our home at about 3PM. My mother would have included Bill in her Christmas shopping. She would buy him sox, underwear, bib overalls, warm gloves and a wool hat. She would wrap each one of those items separately and placed all of them in a large bag. She would include a few items for Adolph. Dad would prepare Bill and himself a large stiff cocktail and they would sit at the kitchen table to enjoy it. The rest of our family would drink egg nog and all of us would talk and laugh. Bill would leave for home with an extra $10 that afternoon. I always enjoyed that time. I felt good that my parents would treat Bill with kindness and attention.

After Bill "retired", he and his brother were admitted to the Silver State Nursing Home where they lived out the rest of their lives. They are both buried at Cedar Hill Cemetery.

I loved Bill and I'm grateful for his life and the opportunity I had to share some of it.

High School and Early College

"I have never let schooling interfere with my education."

Mark Twain

Douglas County High School, the only high school in the county, was small. About 200 students were enrolled in the four-year school. My class of 54 contained 14 boys and 40 girls. Nine of my classmates and I had attended all 8 grades of Castle Rock Elementary School together. The rest of the class came from all over the county.

DCHS had an active sports program including football, basketball and track. I wasn't interested in sports so I didn't participate in any of those activities. Instead, I worked after school.

I worked at West's Nursing Home during the first two years of high school. The nursing home, which sat on the east side of the Denver and Rio Grande Rail Road tracks near the center of town, was owned and operated by Ray and Mabel West. You wouldn't call the nursing home "a rest home" because unless the patients took out their hearing aids they couldn't avoid the loud noise from the trains, pulled by steam engines, which passed within 100 yards of the nursing home.

Mable was a tough boss. She expected nothing but perfection from her employees. She had me making beds, emptying bed pans, helping Ray prepare the meals, delivering meal trays and then washing dishes after the evening meal was finished. I didn't mind Mable's attitude because the joy of interacting with the patients far exceeded her tirades. Each one had a unique and memorable personality. For example, Dick Clark, an elderly retired gentleman who came to the United States from England, was so dignified and proper that he made me feel I was in the presence of a nobleman. A lady, whose name I can't recall, had suffered a stroke and couldn't verbally communicate. However, she could sing "Bubbles, Bangles and Beads" with the sweetest smile imaginable. Another lady suffered from dementia and was constantly wandering out the front door of the nursing home, making her way to the train station and ordering a train ticket to Castle Rock. I'd have to go to the ticket office, tell her we were so glad she'd arrived in Castle Rock and walk her back to her room.

I had so much fun interacting with those old folks that there were times Mable would appear, bring an abrupt end to our conversation, and send me back to work.

The last two years of high school I worked at Kroll's Grocery. That job was so much fun that I've written an entire chapter on that experience.

I also worked for Ray Moeller, editor of the Douglas County News. I worked one afternoon each week folding the paper right after it was printed. Ray used an old line-o-type machine to make up the pages. That machine sounded like a loud gun as it spit out lines of lead type. The type-set pages were then put together in a press that imprinted each page of copy. The pungent smell of hot ink filled the printing room. I'd grab a stack of printed pages, place them on a large flat table and use my hands to crease and fold each page. When I left work both hands would be stained jet black with printer's ink. It would take several days washing my hands with Lava Soap to erase the discoloration. That position only lasted about six months.

In addition to those jobs I was always expected to help Dad at the funeral home. I creased and folded funeral folders, carried and arranged folding chairs, handed out funeral folders at rosaries and funeral services. Dad sent me through the Cliff Mann School of Floral Design so that I could help create funeral sprays and arrangements.

And, of course, I went on all ambulance and coroner calls that were received when I was at home. I also responded to ambulance calls while I was at school. Dad would call the school when he needed me for an emergency. Oliver Matney, the principal, would pull me out of class, take my books and I'd run out the front door and jump into the ambulance as soon as it arrived. Since I wasn't all that interested in academics, I was always glad when Oliver Matney showed up to release me from class. Many of our emergency calls came in the middle of the night. Mom or Dad would awaken me and I would respond. Depending on the location of the emergency we could be on the road for several hours. Our emergency responses could occur anywhere in a 50-mile radius and the closest hospital was 30 miles north of Castle Rock.

It's probably a good thing that I wasn't interested in sports because I simply didn't have time for those extra-curricular activities.

I've always been blessed with a strong faith in God. I felt close to God when I prayed and I found peace attending church. From a very early age I'd been exposed to a lot of violence and death. My relationship with God helped me find peace of mind, courage and strength.

I was very active in church, serving as an acolyte, a lay reader and I was a member of the Sunday Youth Group. Every Tuesday morning, I served as an acolyte at the 6:30 AM Mass. Fr. Pitkin and I were usually the only people who attended that service. We would go to the Castle Café after Mass, eat breakfast and talk. At some point, Fr. Pitkin began urging me to consider the priesthood. That did appeal to me. Fr. Pitkin gave me a book titled "Journey to Priesthood" written by Bishop William Sheridan. I read the book and began praying for God's guidance.

My parents weren't real keen on the priesthood. They wanted me to attend a two-year college, go to Mortuary School, and work at the funeral home. They were willing to pay for my education as long as I continued to work for them. That meant I'd work each summer being "on call" 24 hours a day for two weeks and then have 2 days off, returning for another two weeks of "on call" status. This arrangement would last all summer. Then, if I didn't attend a college where I could live at home, I would be expected to return home every Friday evening by 5 PM and be "on call" until the following Monday morning at 6 AM during the school year.

I applied to several Colorado colleges and, to my surprise, I was accepted by the University of Colorado. It was a surprise because my high school grades weren't great. Additionally, the required recommendation from my principal stated that he thought I'd only be an average student at best!

I choose the University of Colorado because it had a great reputation and the campus was stunningly beautiful. The main campus sits at the base of the foothills in Boulder, Colorado. When my mother and I visited C.U., we drove there on the Boulder Turnpike, a toll road between Denver and Boulder. The first view of the campus occurred as we crested a hill about 4 miles east of Boulder. The massive rock formation known as the flatirons formed the backdrop to the town, and the many dorms, classrooms and administration buildings, all built with matching sandstone walls capped with red tile roofs in Italian Renaissance style, dominated the valley. I was impressed.

During the fall of 1961 I moved into room 313 in Willard Hall. I declared a major in history because I thought that would be valuable if I was going to attend seminary. The only class I ever flunked was the history class I took during my first semester. What a shock.

I had never really studied when I was in high school. I did read assignments and prepare for tests, but I never applied myself. It wasn't that I didn't care about studying, I simply didn't realize what I had to do to get good grades and no one every taught me. College courses were a lot more difficult than the classes I took in high school.

I didn't flunk any classes the second semester at CU; but, my grades were so poor that I was placed on academic probation. I ended that first year very discouraged. For the first time in my life I feared I would not be able to complete college. Before returning home, I changed my major to undecided. I also came to the conclusion that God wasn't calling me to the priesthood.

I spent the summer working for Dad, driving the ambulance and assisting at the funeral home. My social life consisted of occasional dates with a CU nursing student who lived 17 miles from Castle Rock on a ranch near Elizabeth, Colorado. Norma Anderson and I would go to a movie or go bowling on the weekends I wasn't on call. It was a busy summer filled with work, church and an occasional date.

When I returned to school I applied myself and it paid off. I made the Dean's Honor Roll every semester from then until I graduated in 1966 with a Bachelor's Degree in Sociology.

A Fight in the Front Seat

"When you and I stand strong together no one here on earth can stop us."

Rahul Singh

I was at home on Christmas Eve during the second year I was enrolled at the University of Colorado. At approximately 2 PM the Colorado State Patrol dispatcher requested our ambulance respond to a one car roll-over accident on I-25 a mile south of the Lincoln Parkway. My brother, Tim, and I took the call.

I drove and Tim was the attendant. When we arrived at the scene we saw a car sitting upright about 200 yards east of the highway. The vehicle was a convertible and its top was either down at the time of the accident or it had been torn off as a result of the accident. A small crowd was gathered around the car and Colorado State Patrolman William "Bill" Schilling was walking from the vehicle to greet us as we parked.

As we stepped from the ambulance Bill told us there was one patient lying in the back seat of the vehicle with a possible broken back. He turned and ran back to the car while Tim and I got the stretcher. Suddenly we heard Bill yelling and someone else screaming cuss words. We put the stretcher down and ran to the convertible in time to see Bill trying to restrain a very drunk man from entering the back of the car where the victim was laying.

I grabbed the drunk man's right arm, twisted it behind his back and applied pressure. Bill did the same with the man's left arm while Tim grabbed the man's legs and, squeezing them together, and lifted him off the ground. The man violently resisted. He was twisting and turning, screaming and cussing. Bill kept telling him to settle down. As we moved him away from the car Bill jerked the man's arm upward and I heard his arm break. The man screamed and then went limp.

Bill told Tim and me to take the man to the ambulance and place him in the front passenger's seat. I thought that was just going to be a temporary holding place for the man until we could remove the injured patient from the convertible. We placed the man in the seat, fastened the seat belt around his waist, and removed the ignition keys. The man leaned on his left side with his head almost in the driver's seat. His yelling had been replaced with pain-filled moans.

We returned to the convertible and carefully removed the patient with the broken back. As we were carrying him to the ambulance Bill told me to go to Swedish Hospital in Englewood. He also said the drunk was to remain in the front seat of the ambulance and he would follow us to the hospital. The patient was in serious condition so we were given clearance to run with red lights and siren.

When I got into the ambulance to drive the drunk was still laying on his left side. He'd quit moaning and appeared to be asleep. Tim sat in the back next to the patient. I eased onto I-25 and within minutes we were traveling at 90 MPH. Bill remained several car lengths behind me with both of us using our emergency equipment.

I turned onto the exit ramp at Hampden Blvd. and traffic cleared for us as be began moving west bound. The drunk hadn't moved or said a word; however, as I turned onto Hampden he sat up and began staring at me. Several blocks later I turned the siren on as I approached the intersection of Hampden and Happy Canyon, a dangerous intersection where five streets converge. My attention was directed at the heavy traffic when suddenly I realized the drunk had doubled up his right fist and was getting ready to slug me. I yelled to Tim. He jumped from his seat and dove half-way through the open sliding glass window that separates the driver's compartment from the back. Tim said: "Oh no you don't!" Placing his right arm around the drunk's neck, Tim straightened the drunk up and pulled him back toward the sliding window. The man couldn't move and there was no way he could hit me in that position.

All this happened as we went through the Happy Canyon intersection and approached Colorado Blvd. The traffic was so heavy that I was weaving back and forth between lanes with my siren screaming. Bill could see the commotion but there was absolutely nothing he could do except stay close to us. Minutes later we arrived at the hospital.

The emergency entrance was on the west side of the hospital. Ambulances had to back down a ramp into a basement garage. Bill backed his patrol car down the ramp, ran to our ambulance, opened the passenger door and took custody of the drunk. Tim and I removed the patient from the back, lifted the stretcher to the ground and wheeled him into the emergency center.

The emergency center was very busy. A nurse told us they had been expecting us and she directed us to a bed. Each bed in that area was separated by hanging curtains and we could see another State Patrolman standing next to a patient in the bed next to the one we had been directed to. As we were placing our patient on the bed the patient in the bed next to us began calling that state patrolman filthy names.

We had no more than gotten our patient transferred to his bed when a fist fight broke out between the state patrolman and the patient he was watching. For the second time our patient was threatened by physical violence that erupted unexpectedly.

Once again, the Andrews duo jumped into battle. We assisted the patrolman by grabbing the violent man's arms and legs. I had hold of one arm, the patrolman had the other and Tim, again, had the legs. A slight problem developed this time. In the struggle the man's legs got between Tim's legs and he kept trying to kick Tim in the groin. Now Tim was yelling! Within seconds the exam room was filled with people. Someone produced a restraining jacket and it was placed on the man. He was then lifted to a gurney, strapped in place and moved to a secure room.

Before we left the hospital, Officer Shilling found us and told us that the first drunk did have a broken left arm, and he was driving the convertible prior to the accident. He would be facing felony charges for DUI and assault.

Tim and I had a lot to talk about as we drove home. We were grateful we had safely delivered our patient and that we didn't suffer any injuries. We also discussed ways Tim could better grab and hold a drunk's legs. It was a Christmas we will always remember.

What Am I to Do?

"My advice to you is to get married. If you find a good wife, you'll be happy, if not you'll become a philosopher."

Socrates

It all began in the fall of 1963, during the third year of my studies at the University of Colorado. Mike Mead was my roommate and we were living at the Skyline Motel near the campus. Mike was engaged to Susie LaVeau, a CU student living in Libby Hall on the main campus. Susie's roommate was Carol Robinson. Mike and Susie would often double-date with Carol and her boyfriend, Pete Varney. Mike, an extrovert, shared more than I wanted to hear about those double dates. Those two couples enjoyed going out together.

The first time I met Carol, she, Pete, Mike and Susie were eating hamburgers at Tulagi's, a popular bar located near the campus. I had just finished a beer and was on my way to study. It was good to put faces on the names I'd been hearing Mike talk about. Other than that, we didn't talk long enough to form an impression.

It wasn't long after that Carol and Pete ended their relationship. Carol began casually dating and was invited to attend a woodsy, which was an informal drinking party. After that party, she, and the friends she was with, were involved in a minor accident. She injured her knee but didn't realize how serious it was until the next morning. Needing a ride to the Wardenburg Student Health Center, she called Mike. I answered the phone, listened to her problem and offered to give her a ride. That was the second time we'd met. In the brief time we were together I learned that she had graduated from South High School in Denver, her parents lived near Washington Park and she was majoring in journalism. She was easy to talk to and seemed to be a pleasant person.

I was still driving home every weekend to work for my father. With the weekend's committed, there was little time for me to date. Mike, the extrovert, was concerned that I wasn't as socially involved as I ought to be. So, he and his fiancé, Susie, kept after me to invite Carol on a double date. I finally consented. Plans were made and the four of us drove to Denver and see the movie, "Chalk Garden". I drove.

After the movie, as we were searching for a place to eat, I had to yield right-of-way for an mbulance on an emergency run. It was my Dad transporting a patient to Children's Hospital.

I said: "I know who that is and where they're going!" Carol, being the journalist, said: "Well, let's go meet him and find out about his call!" We did and Carol was impressed.

The next time I encountered Carol was at Mike and Susie's wedding. Carol was a bridesmaid and I was an usher. The wedding rehearsal was fun and we enjoyed each other's company. After the wedding, I invited Carol on another date.

Since I could only date every other weekend, we didn't have many dates that summer. I hadn't clearly communicated my work schedule to Carol, so she drew the conclusion that I must be dating another person as well. It wouldn't be until much later that she realized I was committed to a 24 hour two-week on-call job.

With Mike and Susie married, both Carol and I needed to move. We both moved to the Kittridge Complex, which contained new dorms for men and women. Since we ate all meals in the same cafeteria, we saw each other daily. We began studying together and casually dating during the week. I really enjoyed being with Carol. We had fun together and so many common interests that we never ran out of things to talk about.

Finally, one Thursday evening after a date, we were sitting in my car and Carol said: "I love you." My immediate response was: "I love you, too." Then came the shock! Carol said: "That means we are going to get married." There was silence. A real long pause. Finally, I said: "I'm going to have to think about that." It was a long, quiet walk back to Carol's dorm. I gave her a kiss and told her I was going home the next day, but I'd let her know when I returned to Boulder on the following Monday.

Carol's breakup with Pete was difficult. She had come to the conclusion that she wasn't ready for marriage. She was an excellent student having graduated 9th out of a high school class of 908. At the University of Colorado, she was inducted into Mortar Board, a senior women's honor society, as well as Kappa Pau Alpha a National Journalism Honor Society. She had considered joining the Army to travel the world using her journalism degree. That is, until she met me. The opportunity arose, she proposed, and I hesitated. Oh my.

As for me, I still had another year of school to complete. I had declared sociology as my major. I still had no idea what I was going to do with a bachelor's degree in sociology. The only job I had was working for my father to pay for my education.

I've told people I love them all my life. I told my parents I loved them. I told my sisters I loved them. There were old folks at church and the nursing home I'd told "I loved you". And I meant it. But I'd never had anyone respond with a proposition of marriage.

Carol spent her weekend wondering what in the world I was thinking. I spent that weekend thinking.

I didn't share my struggle with anyone. I thought and stewed and contemplated and by Sunday night I had made up my mind. I did want to marry Carol and spend the rest of my life with her. My only concern was that she might have changed her mind.

When I returned Monday, I found Carol and accepted her proposal. She was delighted. I was relieved. And that was the beginning of a relationship that would last more than 50 years.

Forming a Close Bond

"Love is a combination of respect, friendship, understanding, communication and companionship."

Whittney Roach quotes

Carol and I at our wedding shower in Castle Rock.

Carol and I were in love when we got married. We were attracted to each other, we enjoyed spending time together, and we loved to talk. We enjoyed talking to each other on our first date. We could and we did talk about anything and everything. We shared many common interests like current events, our families and our future plans. When we disagreed on some topic we would discuss the differences until we had no more to say. Then, we'd move to a new topic. From the very beginning of our relationship verbal communication was central.

Neither one of us had a job when we returned from our short honeymoon. Within a week, Carol was hired by the Longmont Times-Call newspaper as a staff reporter for a short time. That job came about after one of their reporters was injured in a traffic accident. Carol was delighted to be a working journalist; and, I was relieved to know our first month's rent would be covered.

It was the summer of 1965 and it would be three months before my classes would resume. I soon had a job with the Boulder Ambulance Company working as a driver/attendant. That didn't last long because the hours were long, the pay low and the owner was dishonest. I quit and went to work for the Neusteter's clothing store as a stock clerk. I quickly discovered I didn't enjoy stocking shelves. Finally, I was hired as a part-time patrolman with the University of Colorado Police Department.

In the fall, I returned to the final year of classes. We were both busy, but we were able to find time to be together every day. We spent that time talking. Our verbal communication was fun, comfortable and safe. Neither one of us felt judged for our opinions or convictions or thoughts. We found that we could trust each other to keep confidences. We began to share problems we were facing and together we would find solutions. If we were facing a major decision we'd verbally explore all the options until we decided on the path we'd take.

Neither one of us had ever been in a relationship where verbal communication was so pleasant and rewarding. The more we talked, the more we were revealing ourselves, our beliefs, and our convictions. The trust level between us grew. For my part I was more and more impressed with Carol's intelligence and wisdom, her love of God, and her commitment to our future.

The first trauma we were exposed to involved my brother-in-law Russ's parents. He grew up in Pierce, Colorado. After Cindy and Russ married, Russ's parents often spent time in Castle Rock and my family would visit them in Pierce. I grew to love them and called them Uncle Fred and Aunt Sara. Neither of them were in good health and in the summer of 1965 Uncle Fred was hospitalized. Aunt Sarah would drive to the hospital for visits. One day she took the wrong exit ramp. Realizing her error, she stopped and then began backing down the ramp. A car entering that ramp rear-ended Sarah's car and she was killed by the impact.

Cindy called us as soon as she and Russ were notified. Carol and I drove to Pierce to be with them. We helped them notify Russ's family and then we called members of my family. Carol was the person who notified my mother of the death. It was so sad. But I came away from the experience proud of the way Carol handled herself. She was calm, compassionate and thoughtful.

I'm always surprised when a seemingly minor event turns into a learning experience that impacts the rest of my life. We had such an event in the summer of 1965 when we became involved with a high-pressure salesman. Being young and inexperienced, we accepted an invitation to a sales event that included a small gift if we simply sat through the sales presentation. We patiently listened to the high-pressure salesman offer a number of items, including a camera, a vacuum, and a set of waterless cookware. The price of the items was incredibly low, or so he said. He told us we would be given only one chance to take advantage of the offer and we had to make our decision before we left the presentation. It seemed so good. How could we resist? We couldn't and didn't. We didn't have the cash but that was no problem because the salesman was able to give us a loan, at high interest, that we could pay off within a few months. We signed the papers and walked out with several boxes of things we hadn't realized we wanted or needed.

The next day brought buyer's remorse. We sat, surrounded by pots and pans asking ourselves, "what were we thinking?" As it turned out we did use the cookware for many years. And we never forgot the experience. We never again sat through sales promotions that offered gifts. We never called back after receiving a recorded message that we'd won a free cruise. And we walked out on any salesman who had the gall to tell us we had to make an immediate decision or lose the opportunity to purchase something.

Shortly after our marriage a major flood caused devastation on Colorado's front range. A massive rain storm in southern Douglas County caused creeks and rivers to flood, washing out highway bridges, destroying homes and businesses. Castle Rock suffered major damage from flooding on East Plum Creek and Seller's Creek. East Plum Creek ran along the west edge of a forty-acre parcel of land that my father was developing into a business district. The flood destroyed all the utilities, streets, curbs and gutters that had been installed. My father had no flood insurance so those losses cost him thousands of dollars.

Television and radio news reports first alerted us to the storm. Carol and I left for Castle Rock as soon as we could. We arrived within hours after the flood hit. My parents were out of town on a short trip. My brother was actively involved in rescue efforts that put him in direct contact with many people stranded by the flood. Being a good Samaritan he invited about twenty people to spend the night in in my parent's home. Caring for those unexpected guests was a major task. Carol went to work feeding people while I created sleeping space and listened to the stories folks had to tell. My parents arrived the next day. Dad and I had to walk to the project area because the flood had washed away a bridge dividing the town in half. When dad saw the damage, he broke down and cried. That was one of the few times I ever saw him cry and it brought me to tears. We returned to the funeral home where other members of the family were gathering. It was an emotional time, and Carol's connection to my family grew as a result.

I quickly came to realize that I had married an amazing woman. As an only child, Carol had no brothers or sisters; so, she did all she could to establish close relationships with my siblings. Her efforts to be a loving member of my family were welcomed and she was quickly accepted into the fold.

That was just the beginning of the life events we would face together. Some were trivial, some were major and some were life changing. From the very beginning we encountered those events as a team with both of us using unique gifts that complimented us as a couple. And the love we shared grew and deepened.

The Boulder Police Department

The First of Three Great Careers

"Passion is the difference between having a job and having a career"

Anonymous

Carol graduated from CU the day before our marriage. She had a degree but no job. I, too, was unemployed. As soon as we returned from our honeymoon we both began a job search. We had enough money to rent a one-bedroom apartment, the rest of it went to buy groceries. We needed jobs!

The first place I sought employment was Boulder Ambulance Company. They hired me but the job didn't last long. The manager was young, irresponsible and undependable. The shift assignments were made at the last minute, the manager was seldom available, and the staff was poorly trained. I worked one month, picked up my pay check, and quit.

Next, I found employment stocking shelves at Neusteter's, a clothing store located near our apartment. What a boring job! Surely, I thought, I could do better than that.

By this time, Carol began working as a writer for the University of Colorado News Service. The News Service was CU's public relations office, providing news releases and in-depth stories to the general news media. Carol was one of three writers. She was assigned to produce stories that promoted the accomplishments of faculty, staff and students in the Arts and Sciences departments at CU.

Carol's employment success inspired me to consider working at the university. By the time we were married I had 8 years of emergency ambulance experience and as many years responding to coroner investigations. I enjoyed working with law enforcement personnel and I valued the personal relationships that developed as a result. So I went to the University of Colorado Police Department and applied for a part-time position. Chief Dick Stratton interviewed me and offered me the job. I accepted.

In 1965 the State of Colorado offered no training for police officers, there were no professional standards, and the infamous Miranda Decision hadn't even been rendered. CUPD required its officers to pay for their own uniforms and purchase their own revolvers.

The department consisted of a chief, half a dozen full time officers and a small number of part-time officers who were also enrolled students. I quickly discovered that part-time employment meant we worked 40 hours a week but didn't receive health insurance and retirement benefits. I didn't care. I was delighted to get paid doing something I'd wanted to do for years.

I was assigned to work with and was trained by Ed Anderson, a third-year law student and part-time officer. He was an excellent instructor. He taught me the importance of knowing the law, treating people with respect, and projecting "calm confidence" regardless of the situation one found themselves in. Night after night we would walk the entire campus encountering students, visitors, faculty and staff.

As I gained experience I was given more responsibility and trusted to work by myself. I was assigned to either swing shift or night shift, the busiest times of our day. Those shifts also enabled me to continue attending classes during the day.

The more experience I gained the more I enjoyed the job. Every day was a different experience. I loved the excitement and I felt confident dealing with the situations that arose. CU football and basketball games gave me experience with crowd control and traffic direction. I learned how to investigate traffic accidents and take criminal reports. I gained experience interpreting and applying the law. And I really enjoyed working with the full- and part-time officers.

It was fast becoming time for Carol and me to make a decision about our future. I was scheduled to graduate in the Spring of 1966. Carol really enjoyed her work. Her boss and the other writers were a pleasure to work with. She was getting involved in church and had even volunteered to teach a church-school class. She wanted to stay in Boulder.

I became aware of an opening at the Boulder Police Department. I obtained an application, filled it out and was scheduled for an interview. I went knowing that there were no college graduates on the department and I was the only graduate being considered. I remember the police chief, Myron Teagarden, telling me he preferred hiring stable, hard working farm boys rather than men with a college degree. I told him that I was stable and hard-working. I was hired.

Now we had to inform my parents of our decision. They owned the funeral home in Castle Rock; and had purchased a second funeral home in Canon City, Colorado. In addition, both locations included an ambulance company, a monument business, and apartment houses. To add to that, the Canon City Mortuary included a cemetery. My parents were expecting me to return to Castle Rock and manage that mortuary and the associated businesses. Neither Carol nor I were interested.

We invited my parents to dinner in our Boulder apartment. We sat down to eat shortly after their arrival. As we were eating I began to share our plans for the future. They listened quietly. When I told them I'd been hired by the Boulder Police, they both got up from the table, picked up their coats and walked out of the apartment with only half their meal eaten. It was painful and ugly. They were so mad that over the next 9 years neither one of them ever asked about or commented on my work or accomplishments on the police department. My mother was so ashamed of what I did that she wrote our relatives simply telling then "John works with the law."

On September 1, 1966, I began work as a patrolman on the BPD. I worked a rotating shift that changed each month. We would work day shift the first month, then graveyard shift the next month and finally swing shift. Then it would start all over again. I did that for 2 ½ years and never got used to it. At the beginning of each month I had diarrhea.

Working weekends and rotating shifts had an immediate impact on our social life. The only people who had time off when we did were other police officers and their family. Carol worked Monday through Friday on an 8 to 5 schedule. When I was working swing shift I would still be asleep when she went to work; and so I wouldn't see her until I arrived home at 10:30 or 11 at night. Graveyard shift gave us several hours in the evening after she arrived home and before I left for work at 9 PM. We both enjoyed day shift.

We spent quality time with one couple who weren't in law enforcement, Dave and Kathy Van Liere. They lived near us, and we often got together to play bridge. There were times they would come over at 11 PM, after I got off duty.

For the first 2 ½ years on the department I worked in the patrol division for Lieutenant William Pohorlak and Sergeants Hap McDowell and Ralph Ruzicka. I was one of 10 patrolmen. Our detail worked so well together that we could anticipate each other's response in an emergency. It felt good being part of that team.

In 1968 the State of Colorado created the Colorado Law Enforcement Training Academy. I was one of the first officers from our department to attend the three-week academy. That experience exposed me to proper methods of traffic and criminal investigation, search and seizure laws and practical methods of effecting an arrest. I was grateful for the knowledge and I would later use some of the instruction techniques when I became an instructor.

A position opened in the detective bureau and all officers with at least 2 years' experience were eligible to taken the written examination and undergo an oral exam administered by the department command staff. I took the exams, passed and was promoted.

I was assigned to investigate armed robberies, burglaries and arson. Gaynor (Shorty) Walker was my partner. Shorty was assigned CU campus felonies and sex crimes. We worked the same shift, but we only worked together when one or the other had an arrest or search warrant.

Detectives rotated monthly from day shift to swing shift and then back to day shift. We were considered on call from 10 PM to 2 AM when we were working swing and, on call from 2 AM to 6 AM when working days. The department did not have a crime scene unit. The on call or on duty detective was required to process all crimes scenes.

Shortly after my promotion, I was again selected to attend special courses at the Colorado Law Enforcement Training Academy. I attended a one-week class in burglary investigation, a one-week class in fingerprint identification, and another week in crime scene processing. I learned how to dust for latent finger prints, to measure, sketch and photograph scenes; and, how to collect evidence.

I was fascinated by all I had learned and when I returned to the department I loved putting it into practice. Shorty didn't like that detail work so he was more than happy to have me process the crime scenes that became our responsibility.

The Boulder Fire Department had one man who was responsible for arson investigations. He could investigate the scene but he had no law enforcement experience. I was selected to assist him when an arson investigation was initiated. If a suspect was developed and there was probable cause for an arrest, I would help put the case together and make the arrest.

Our detective bureau had two full time narcotics officers who worked closely with federal DEA officers. The narcotic officers were so busy that they produced no-knock search warrants daily. Most of those warrants were executed after 10 PM. All detectives working the swing shift were required to stay after 10 PM and assist the narcotic officers when a narcotic warrant was pending. That meant that Shorty and I often had to work over-time. We would participate in the forced entries, help make the arrests, then process the scene and collect the evidence.

The Viet Nam War was raging and CU became a center for anti-war demonstrations. Students for a Democratic Society (SDS), the Weathermen and the Black Panthers were established on campus. As the anti-war movement intensified the University and businesses like banks began receiving bomb threats. The city did not have a bomb squad. Fire Lt. Rod Wood and I co-authored a letter and sent it to our respective chiefs urging them to take the proper steps to establish a bomb unit. Within a short time, my chief, Don Vendel, called me into his office and informed me the bomb squad would be formed under the authority of the police department and I had been selected to be a bomb technician. I was told I'd be sent to the Redstone Arsenal in Huntsville, Alabama, for training.

I did attend bomb school. When I returned, I was given permission to select a second officer to assist me. I asked detective Charlie Nay and he accepted. He, too, was then sent to bomb school. We were given a truck to equip, and we built a trailer that was designed to carry explosives. The city provided us with an explosive magazine at the city yards. We were authorized to purchase a large explosive magazine located outside the city limits. Charlie and I were given hazardous duty pay in addition to our regular salary.

I was in charge of the bomb squad for 5 years. Working on the bomb squad was not a full time responsibility. Charlie and I were on call 24/7 to respond to all calls where live explosives were found or to scenes where bombs had detonated. We were not required to respond to bomb threats. We averaged 100 calls each year during the 5 years I was in charge.

The most serious situations occurred in 1972 when 6 people were blown up in two incidents that occurred over a 48-hour period. Those deaths were the result of the victims incorrectly wiring two bombs that they were going to plant at the sheriff's office and the police department.

In 1973 I was promoted to the rank of lieutenant and assigned to the office of the chief of police. I worked as the chief's administrative assistant, writing the department's rules and regulations and department policy. When the city council authorized the formation of an animal control unit I was given the responsibility of purchasing the equipment needed, hiring the animal wardens, forming department policy and the operating procedures for the unit, and training the personnel involved.

Up to this point all our officers were being trained at the Colorado Law Enforcement Training Academy. The chief wanted our department to take over the responsibility of training our own officers. At the chief's command, I formed a training office, planned the curriculum, located the instructors and began offering training. At one point the city authorized the police department to hire and train 20 new recruits. I oversaw the 4 weeks of instruction for those officers.

The largest recruit class I trained. I'm in the lower right hand corner.

This recruit class contained the average number of officers I trained. I am standing to the far left.

This recruit class included several of the first female officers hired by the Boulder Police Department. I am standing in the center of the photo.

In 1973 I was honored to be one of two Colorado police officers selected to attend the FBI Academy in Quantico, Virginia. That 13-week academy included several officers from many different states as well as police officers from countries friendly with the United States.

Upon return from the academy I was transferred into the patrol division as a shift commander. I was responsible for the supervision of 2 sergeants and 22 officers who all worked on rotating 10-hour shifts. During swing shift and graveyard shifts I was also responsible for the supervision of the dispatchers and clerical staff.

I was promoted to the rank of patrol captain in early 1975, shortly after the city hired a new police chief. That promotion placed me 3rd in command of the department. As the year progressed under the new chief, I came to the conclusion I could not in good conscience support his leadership. I did not trust his decisions, and I felt that he often acted in ways that were detrimental to the department. A police union had formed and the chief's decisions created an atmosphere that helped the union gain more and more strength.

I resigned from the police department in December of 1975. The following chapters contain stories of my experiences in my first career…Law Enforcement.

Shakin' Doors

"Any man who has had the job I've had and didn't have a sense of humor wouldn't still be here"

Harry S. Truman

The third shift of the day ran from 10 PM to 6 AM and everyone called it graveyard shift. I have no idea where that term came from or who first used it, but it is very descriptive. A graveyard is a quiet place, void of human activity; it can be a spooky place filled with frightening possibilities. By 2 AM, after the bars have closed and the patrons had either found their way home or were securely behind bars in the county jail, Boulder's streets were deserted, quiet and void of activity. It did resemble a graveyard.

The dispatcher provided the only human sounds in a patrol car. At least every 30 minutes he was required to announce the radio station call letters and do a vehicle check. He would say: 'KAA620, Boulder, Colorado – 0300 hours – radio check – car 20". The officer in car 20 would respond: "20 – OK". The radio check would continue until the dispatcher received a response from each officer. Then, if there was no activity, the radio would fall silent for another 30 minutes.

It was tough to stay awake and alert. Lots of strong, black coffee helped, but the best defense was to do something physical like shaking doors.

Graveyard shift actually began at 9:30PM when the shift commander conducted inspection. He would read a report that contained a description of the most recent stolen vehicles, wanted people, business and residential burglaries, and potential problems. The officers would then be personally inspected to assure they were properly equipped, all leather shined and bullets in their belt pouches. (That was a constant problem because officers who smoked often carried their Zippo cigarette lighter in one of their bullet pouches!) Finally, each officer was assigned a car and a district to patrol. Boulder was divided into 7 districts and each district contained businesses such as gas stations, restaurants, real estate offices and the like. After the bars closed and things got real quiet, an officer was expected to get out of his car and shake doors of each business in his district. Shaking doors had many benefits. The physical activity kept an officer awake, it discouraged burglaries, and it created good will in the business community.

If a business was unlocked and there was no evidence of a forced entry, the reporting officer and an officer who came to assist would enter the business, confirm that no one was present, and call the owner requesting he respond and lock the premises.

Owners usually arrived within a short time of their notification. It wasn't unusual for them to be wearing pajamas and a robe. Their hair was usually a mess and their main concern was to lock the door and get back to bed as soon as possible.

Some officers really enjoyed shakin' doors, others would rather sit in their cars, drinking coffee and eating donuts. I happened to enjoy shakin' doors, and some memorable things happened to me as a result.

Late one night I found the front door of the Masonic Lodge unlocked. Larry Kinion was working the district next to mine and he was dispatched to cover me. Larry, a good friend of mine, had been on the department for a number of years. The first thing he said as he stepped out of his car was: "Only a 'hot dog' would check the Masonic Lodge for an open door." I ignored the comment and suggested he check the basement while I checked the main floor. We entered the building and Larry disappeared down the stairs.

I carefully made my way from room to room using my flashlight instead of turning on the interior lights. When I entered the men's room I shined my light along the wall to my right. I froze and my heart stopped as someone shined a flashlight in my face. Before I reached for my gun I realized I had shined my light on a full-length mirror and I was looking at myself. As I stood trying to regain my composure, I heard a horrible noise coming from the basement. It sounded like a fight.

Thinking Larry was in trouble, I ran from the men's room, down the stairs to the only room that had a light. It appeared to be a dressing room with metal lockers lining the walls. Larry was standing by an open locker near another full-length mirror. He was wearing a huge black ancient ship captain's three-cornered hat that had a stunning white plume rising from the hatband. He had an embarrassed smile on his face and he sheepishly said: "I'm OK"

He explained that he had opened a locker and spotted the hat. He couldn't resist the temptation, so he removed his uniform hat, placed the captain's hat on his head and went in search of a mirror to admire himself. He hadn't seen a metal pipe containing a number of empty coat hangers that was resting on top of two lockers that were opposite each other several feet from the mirror. As he approached the mirror his captain's hat hit the pipe, knocking it and all the coat hangers to the floor. That was the noise that quickly brought me to his side.

With the tension gone, Larry turned to the mirror and said: "We ought to suggest this as department issue for formal wear." We both broke out in laughter. Every time I think of Larry I picture him standing in full uniform wearing that hat with a silly grin on his face. Oh, by the way, he never again called me a "hot dog".

On another occasion, I was on foot patrol in the Hill business district. I found a drive-up window at a pizza restaurant partly open. I notified dispatch and Bill Spotts was sent to cover me. Before he arrived, I was able to determine that all the doors were locked and the only possible point of entry into the business was through that open window. The window wasn't very large. Bill, on the other hand, was large. He stood 6 feet 5 inches and weighed over 250 pounds. I wasn't large; I was skinny, weighing less than 150 pounds. It was obvious I would be the one who would enter the business through that window. Bill offered to support me as I crawled through the window, then I was to open the door and, together, we would check the building. That sounded good to me.

I removed my hat, stuck my arms in the window as Bill lifted and shoved me in. As my hands contacted the inside of the window frame, it felt wet and slick. As my head went through the opening the familiar odor of fresh paint filled my nostrils. Suddenly I realized that someone had painted the inside window frame and the window was left open to help the paint dry. But it was too late. Bill had stuffed me in and, as I struggled to get to my feet, I could see that my dark blue uniform was now covered with fresh white paint. "Aaaaaaahhhhh!" I said. (Actually, I said something else, but I'm writing this for a general audience so I've edited that part.)

I opened the door and let Bill inside. He was no help what-so-ever. He just kept laughing and laughing. The only way we could secure the business was by locking the door from the inside and crawling back through the window. I wasn't about to do that, so we called the owner and he responded with a key. He was no better than Bill. He laughed and laughed.

Bill drove me to the PD where I underwent more humiliation. The shift commander, Lt. Pohorlak, thought it was really funny. As I left the station to go home and change clothes, Lt. Pohorlak's laughter was ringing in my ears. The one good thing about that incident was I never once got sleepy on that shift.'

The number of open doors an officer discovered each month affected his work evaluation. A large number of open doors produced a positive rating. Certain businesses were notorious for having open doors, so they were always the first places officers checked. An old three-story business on Pearl Street had a "dumb waiter" with a door that faced the alley. The door to the dumb waiter was often unlocked.

Early one evening, an unnamed officer assigned to foot patrol in the downtown business district discovered the door to the dumb waiter unlocked. The normal routine was to call the owner of the building and have him secure the door. Instead of following that routine, the officer requested a cover car. When the cover car arrived, the officer removed his hat and crawled into the dumb waiter. It was so small he had to sit with his legs crossed. Facing toward the inside of the business, the officer grasped the rope that was attached to a pulley at the top of the shaft and pulled himself in that dumb waiter up to the third floor. His plan was to open the door of the dumb waiter, crawl out and check the building interior.

The third floor of that building contained a large office. As he opened the double door on the dumb waiter, he found himself facing a group of people who were attending some sort of business meeting. Their conversation stopped when the door to the dumb waiter opened. They couldn't believe their eyes. There sat a policeman, sitting with crossed legs staring out at them. The officer smiled, and said: "Just checking the building". Then he pulled the door shut and lowered himself to the second floor.

The second floor contained a dance hall. Looking through the crack in the door, the officer could tell that the hall was dark. As he carefully opened the door he heard something move. Suddenly he realized it was a dog and it was moving fast toward the dumb waiter. The officer grabbed the double doors and pulled them shut just as the German Shepherd bounded into them. He was barking and growling as the officer quickly lowered himself to ground level.

As he exited the tight quarters he told his cover never to do what he had just done, and then walked off down the alley talking to himself.

I don't remember an officer discovering a burglary in progress by shaking doors. I imagine burglaries were prevented. But I do know that shaking doors has generated many good stories.

The Last Chase

"Change is the law of life, and those who look only to the past or the present are certain to miss the future."

John F. Kennedy

Regis Philbin was the host of the television show "Who Wants to be a Millionaire?" Often when a contestant answered a question, Regis would give them a look that says: "You've just made a mistake." That look makes some contestants feel uneasy while others remained confident of the response they've just made. On August 10, 1967, I was left feeling uneasy about a decision I'd made.

That summer I took the sergeant's written and oral promotion examination and I was successful. My promotion did not take effect until September, and so, on the 10th of August I was still working as a patrol officer on swing shift. Work on the 10th of August began like any other day. Inspection began at 1:30 PM. Corporal Kelly Gaskill inspected our uniforms and equipment, read the latest list of wanted suspects and stolen vehicles, and then assigned each officer to a district to patrol. We obtained the keys to our patrol cars, carried our brief cases and thermos bottles to the parking lot, and cleaned the dirt and debris that had collected in our assigned car during the last 8-hour shift.

At 2:00 PM I notified the dispatcher I was in-service and enroute to district 4, the area I was to patrol. District 4 included the south end of Boulder from Baseline Road to the south city limits. Anyone entering Boulder from Denver or Golden had to drive through that district.

As I entered my district my mind was focused on one piece of information that had been given out during inspection. The military had issued a pick-up request for an AWOL soldier driving a 1960 black Ford sedan with Colorado license MR-8141. The soldier was missing from Fitzsimmons Army Hospital in Denver and the MP's thought he might be headed to his family's home in Boulder. He was described as mentally unfit, armed and dangerous. If the man was traveling to Boulder, he would enter the city through my district.

At 5:00 PM Bill Hull, an off-duty Boulder police officer, spotted the black Ford about 10 miles south of Boulder traveling northbound on Colorado highway 93. Bill drove to the Hummer Club, a notorious bar located near the entrance to the Rocky Flats Nuclear plant and used their pay phone to notify our dispatcher. At 5:02 PM the dispatcher keyed the "major crime alert siren" and notified all patrol units that the suspect was headed our way.

I was at the very north end of my district when the "alert" was broadcast. With adrenalin flowing, I turned south on Broadway at Baseline and kept a sharp eye on the northbound traffic. The dispatcher asked for my location and then he dispatched Officers Kinion and Strasdas to head south and help search for the suspect.

At 5:20 PM I spotted the black Ford stopped at a red light in the right turn lane of Broadway at Table Mesa. I informed dispatch the car had been located. When the light changed, the vehicle made a sharp right turn onto Table Mesa and right again into the Texaco station. When I pulled into the station the Ford drove east toward a vacant lot and then the driver made a sudden U turn and came back in my direction. As we pulled alongside each other the suspect looked straight at me. His expression told me he knew why I was there and he left no doubt he was having nothing to do with me.

The suspect stepped on his accelerator and his tires sprayed gravel all over my car as he fish tailed onto Table Mesa Drive headed east. It took only a few seconds for me to turn my car around, flip on my red lights and siren and notify dispatch I was in a chase. I had a powerful car and in no time I was within a car length of the fleeing Ford. We were traveling at 80 MPH. Table Mesa was a four-lane residential street with a posted speed limit of 35 MPH. With no regard for others, the idiot was determined to outrun the law.

The police radio came alive with voices. Units in the area were giving their location. I was giving our direction of travel and speed. Supervisors were making their presence known. Suddenly we were east bound on the toll road headed toward Denver and my speedometer was reading 90 plus miles per hour.

As soon as we entered the toll road the dispatcher telephoned the tollbooth which was located about 10 miles east of Boulder at the Broomfield exit. The toll operator informed the dispatcher that he would commandeer an 18-wheel truck and have the driver place it across the front of the toll house. The dispatcher told him that wasn't a good idea, but the man was convinced that was necessary to protect his booth from the pending threat. Dispatch notified me of the blockade that was going to be in our path of travel.

At that point a blockade was the least of my concerns. I was having a hard time simply staying on the suspect's tail. He was changing lanes and weaving through traffic. About four miles east of Boulder he moved to the left land and began to slow down. I couldn't tell if he was going to stop or make a U-turn. Suddenly he slammed on his brakes, drove down into the gravel divider and made a U-turn. I was braking hard, trying to stop and get turned, but I was traveling too fast. As my car continued east the suspect's car was spinning onto the west bound lane, again spraying gravel all over the side of my patrol car.

I got turned and began to rapidly accelerate as westbound vehicles were slamming on their brakes and pulling out of our way. I notified dispatch we were headed back into Boulder. Before the dispatcher could respond, Officer Kinion came on the air and said he was westbound ahead of the suspect preparing to be a moving roadblock.

I had a clear view of Larry and the suspect. The Ford was not slowing down. In fact, the suspect never touched his brakes. It appeared he was planning to ram Larry's car. I screamed into my mike: "Get out of the way, Larry! Get out of the way!" Larry moved aside and the suspect passed Larry's patrol unit with only inches to spare.

Larry was accelerating as I passed him, but we left him in our dust since we were again traveling at 95 MPH. Officers Strasdas and Hensley were also westbound ahead of us. Hensley was traveling almost as fast as we were when we passed him. He pulled in directly behind me and followed.

The suspect turned off the toll road onto the exit ramp for eastbound Baseline Road. He was traveling so fast that his car skidded sideways leaving skid marks as he turned. (We would later measure more than 400 feet of skid marks on that ramp.)

Baseline was a straight, two lane highway that carried a lot of traffic. As soon as the dispatcher knew our location and direction of travel he notified the Louisville Police Department that we were headed in their direction. Their police chief was notified and he headed toward Baseline with the intention of setting up a roadblock. He later told us that he was planning to place his patrol car across the eastbound land of Baseline and he intended to use his sawed-off shotgun if the suspect didn't stop.

The suspect almost collided head-on with several westbound vehicles. Then, at Convent Curve, the Ford slowed to 75 MPH and moved into the opposite side of the road nearly colliding with another vehicle. In the 8500 block of Baseline Road I was able to position my unit directly behind the suspect and pulled within one car length. As we passed east and west bound vehicles, dust flew as they skidded into the borrow pits.

Suddenly John Hensley passed me and pulled alongside the suspect's car. I could see John leaning across his front seat with his 357 mag. revolver in his hand, pointed directly at the suspect. Brake lights came on and the Ford pulled onto the shoulder of the road and stopped. John stopped directly opposite from the suspect's door. John was still pointing his gun at the suspect. I jumped from my car, ran to the driver's door, opened it, pulled the man out and threw him on the ground. By the time Strasdas and Kinion arrived, I had frisked and handcuffed the suspect.

The man was obviously deranged. When he spoke he made absolutely no sense. He was screaming threats and nonsense. A search of the vehicle turned up a 12-inch butcher knife. The man was taken to the police department, booked and later released to the custody of the military police.

The chase was successful, an arrest was made, and no one was injured. So, you might ask, what was the dilemma I had with the decision I made? Well, I had made the decision to take the sergeant's examine and I had accepted the promotion, but now I had some doubts. The promotion meant I'd move from the patrol division into the detective bureau. The promotion meant I probably wouldn't be in a position to participate in another high-speed chase. And there was nothing as exciting and fulfilling as a successful high-speed chase. So, on August 10, 1967, I was questioning my decision.

It wasn't until I began working in the detective bureau that my doubts were allayed. I found the excitement I feared losing as soon as I began making felony arrests, participating in "no-knock" searches, investigating burglaries and armed robberies … all of which I could never had done in the patrol division. I even got to participate in a few chases. And there is nothing as exciting as a chase using an un-marked car. That can produce almost as much adrenalin as winning a million bucks.

Attempted Suicide at 913 Broadway

"Courage is not the absence of fear; rather it is the ability to take action in the face of fear"

Nancy Anderson, "Work with Passion"

I was quietly eating my hamburger and fries in a corner booth of the Azar's Big Boy restaurant near 28th and Arapahoe when the dispatcher called me on my pac-set. I'd been anticipating the call. It was the patrol lieutenant's day off and the patrol sergeant had called in sick leaving a corporal as acting shift commander. Being a sergeant in the detective division, I was expected to respond to any major incident if the corporal requested my assistance. Before my food had been served I'd been listening to my pac-set. Patrol officers had responded to a suicide-in-progress at 913 Broadway. Dispatch radioed me about fifteen minutes after the patrol officers arrived at the scene. The message was to "call dispatch" immediately. I was tired and hungry. It was hard to get up from my booth and go in search of a phone.

The dispatcher answered on the first ring. He informed me he'd received a phone call from a woman who identified herself as Susan Scott. She was calling from Hudson, Colorado. She told the dispatcher her estranged husband lived at 913 Broadway and he called her threatening suicide. She felt he was capable of suicide and, she further said, he owned two guns, a Smith and Wesson 32 cal. revolver and a 3006 rifle. Cpl. Longbrook and officers Hanket and Fitzpatrick had been dispatched to the scene. Fitzpatrick was the first to arrive. He went to the front door, looked through the glass window and observed a male sitting at a table talking on the telephone. The male saw Fitzpatrick and motioned for him to wait. The officer tried to open the door. It was locked so he stood at the door watching the suspect talk on the phone for the next ten minutes. Finally, the suspect set the phone down, walked to the locked door and told Fitzpatrick he would not be allowed entry. Fitzpatrick asked if he was willing to talk. The suspect said, "Sure, you can talk to me through the door, but you can't come in here." At that point Officer Hanket joined Fitzpatrick on the porch. When the suspect saw Hanket, he returned to the table, picked up a nickel-plated revolver and yelled to the officers that anyone attempting entry into his apartment would be injured. Fitzpatrick told Hanket to get off the porch and tell the corporal what had just happened. Cpl. Longbrook was standing watch at the back door of the apartment. When Hanket informed him of the exchange Longbrook called dispatch and requested a supervisor.

I told the dispatcher I would respond immediately. I handed the cashier a ten-dollar bill and told her I'd return later for my change. I jumped into my unmarked Ford Mustang and pulled onto 28th street. I radioed dispatch I was in-service and I requested the on-duty detectives to respond to the scene. If I was going to be responsible for the situation I wanted officers who were under my direct command at the scene. It didn't sound like the situation would resolve itself quickly and I was going to release the patrol officers as the detectives arrived.

The apartment was located in a duplex located directly east of a small convenience store. The front porch and door faced Broadway and the rear door was on the west side of the store. Three marked cars were parked in front of the house with their red lights flashing. Officer Fitzpatrick was on the porch crouched below the window of the front door. Officer Hanket and Cpl. Longbrook were standing on the north-west corner of the building watching both the front and back doors.

I parked my vehicle and carefully made my way onto the porch so that whoever was in the house didn't see me. Fitzpatrick, with a gun in his hand, quietly described the suspect and the layout of the apartment. He said he'd tried to talk to the man through the door, but the door was too thick to clearly hear. Fitzpatrick obtained the suspect's phone number and he called him from the pay phone located outside the convenience store. He described the conversation as "mostly one-sided". When Fitzpatrick asked if he could enter the house the man said: "No, and if you try to take me, you'll never get me out of the house alive. I will do anything to stop from being locked up. I trusted the police once and they locked me up. I'm not going to be locked up again. The first one in here is a dead mother-fucker." As Fitzpatrick was talking on the phone, Cpl. Longbrook tried to open the front door. The suspect put his phone down and began yelling at Longbrook. Then the phone went dead. Fitzpatrick again joined Longbrook at the front door. They both tried to get the suspect to talk but he refused to verbally respond.

I told Fitzpatrick to remain at the front door until he was relieved by a detective. Within minutes detectives Spotts, Nay and Coles arrived. I briefed them and told them to relieve the uniformed officers. Fitzpatrick gave me the suspect's phone number. I went to the pay phone at the convenience store and placed a call to the suspect. When he answered, I identified myself and began a conversation that lasted for the next two hours.

It became quickly obvious that the man was angry and frightened. I asked him his name and he identified himself as Richard Scott. He admitted he'd been talking to his wife earlier in the evening. They were separated and things had gotten ugly between them. He told his wife she would never again see him alive and she had no one to blame but herself. He explained he was referring to his plan to leave the State of Colorado. He further said his wife misunderstood and jumped to the conclusion he was threatening suicide.

As the conversation continued, Scott revealed the fact that a Boulder district judge had committed him to the mental ward at Boulder Memorial Hospital earlier in the week. He said he was on out-patient status and scheduled for a psychiatric evaluation in the morning. When I asked why the judge had committed him, he said he'd threatened suicide.

With time, I was able to gain Scott's trust by listening and responding sympathetically. When he volunteered that it was his wedding anniversary, I told him I felt sorry for him. Then

I invited him to tell me about his wife and their marriage. He responded with a lengthy sentimental description.

After we had talked for two hours I told Scott my feet hurt. I explained that I'd been on duty since 2 PM and I was tired. I said I wanted to continue the conversation but I needed to sit down. I offered to remove my gun if he'd just allow me to come into his apartment to continue the conversation. Finally, at 9:30 PM, Richard Scott accepted my offer.

After I hung up I told detective Coles my plans. I walked to the base of the front porch and the door opened. Richard was standing partly behind the door frame with the revolver in his hand. I removed my gun from its holster and placed it on the sidewalk. Richard told me to enter the apartment with my hands visible and in front of me. After I entered the apartment, Coles picked up my gun.

Once inside, detective Nay notified dispatch. Deputy Chief Lowell Friezen and Captain Ted Koznecki were notified and both responded to the scene from their homes.

Within minutes of my entry into the apartment I realized I may have made a terrible mistake. Richard was drunk, very drunk. He kept his revolved pointed at me and told me to pull all of my pockets inside out. He said he wouldn't hesitate to hurt me if I tried to subdue him. The whole character of our conversation was different than it had been on the telephone. He was hostile, threatening and drunk. I told him I needed to let my dispatcher know where I was and asked if I could use his phone. He consented and I made a quick call.

When I hung up Richard told me to sit on the couch and he sat at the table. He called his wife and talked to her for the next 15 minutes. He asked her to tell me the truth about their earlier conversation. She consented and I was handed the phone. She apologized for my situation, then she said her husband had told her he planned to shoot himself and he wanted to be buried next to his grandfather. She was convinced he would have done that if the offices hadn't arrived as quickly as they had. I handed the phone back to Richard. After a few more words, he hung up.

I asked Richard if I could read the court order that had been issued earlier in the week. He told me to remain sitting on the couch and then he handed it to me. I discovered that Larry Hopkins, a local attorney, was representing Richard. I suggested we call Larry and request his help. Richard was open to that but he wanted me to talk to the attorney. I was relieved when Larry answered his phone. I explained my situation and asked his advice. He was quick to say he thought Richard was threatening suicide in order to intimidate his wife back into the relationship. He then talked to Richard. He told Richard he would have to return to the hospital and urged him to hand me his gun. He promised to call Richard's doctor and have him recommend hospitalization over jail. Richard ended the conversation.

From the time I had entered the apartment Richard had been taking nips from a whiskey bottle that was sitting on the kitchen table. His speech was slurred but he did sound coherent. I continually asked him to give me his weapon but he refused.

My shift ended at 10 PM. It was now 11 PM and I was concerned my wife would call the police department and ask why I was late. I didn't want her to find out I was being held hostage, so I asked Richard if I could call home. He handed me the phone and I called Carol. When she answered, I told her I was sorry I was late and I wouldn't be home for several hours. I told her to go to bed and that I loved her.

That conversation seemed to touch Richard. When I again asked him to give me his gun he unloaded all but one bullet and he threw them at me. I saw that as an opening. I asked what he was going to do with the last bullet and he said it was for him.

The phone rang and it was the district attorney. Larry Hopkins had called him and worked out an agreement allowing Richard to be hospitalized rather than placed in jail. Richard demanded to talk with his own attorney again. Hopkins called and Richard agreed to surrender. He hung up and handed me his gun.

I stepped to the front door, opened it and hollered for the others to come in. Almost immediately the apartment was full of police officers. I was surprised to see my captain and the deputy chief. Both appeared relieved I was OK. Actually, they weren't anywhere as relieved as I was at that moment.

I frisked Richard and handcuffed his hands behind his back. He told me I hadn't done a good job of frisking him. He suggested I look in his right boot. I reached into his boot and, much to my embarrassment, I found a switch blade knife.

Detective Coles and I transported Richard to Boulder Memorial Hospital. He talked during most of that trip. He said he had no intention of hurting others, but he did admit he had plans to kill himself. He said he'd purchased the ammunition the day he was released from the hospital. He said he was glad he was alive and no one was hurt. So was I.

The next morning this incident was the lead story on radio station KBOL. I received a Commendatory Critical Incident Report which originated from detective Coles and was reviewed by Captain Koznecki. I also received a letter of commendation from District Judge Horace B. Holmes and a note from Chief Vendel.

Unfortunately, the story doesn't end there. The sad addendum occurred several years later, after I was promoted to the rank of lieutenant and placed in charge of the department's training division.

Detective Harry Coles had received notice he was being transferred from the detective division back to the patrol division. He was to report to the training division prior to the transfer so he could be re-trained on patrol procedures. I assigned Harry to a series of special classes I thought he would find helpful. One of the classes was a crisis intervention course conducted by the Boulder County Mental Health staff. That full day of training included simulated crises situations with mental health staff members assuming the roles of perpetrators and victims.

One of the simulations involved a suicide in progress. Harry handled himself well during the training session. When the role playing concluded all the participants were videotaped as they discussed the exercise. During that discussion, Harry was commended for the way he handled the crisis. He responded by recounting details of the incident at 913 Broadway. He said he'd learned a lot from that incident and it helped him perform well in the training exercise.

That night Harry Coles committed suicide. He shot himself in the head and died instantly. His suicide was a complete shock and surprise. No one knew of his plans and no one was present to help him overcome the demons he had so carefully hidden.

I was deeply saddened when I learned of his death the next morning. I called a member of the mental health staff and, together, we reviewed the video to see if Harry had given us a hint of his pending suicide. He hadn't. There was nothing to suggested he was planning his death. For years, I prayed for the repose of Harry's soul. I know he's in God's love, but his death still haunts me. He knew I would have been there for him, but he never asked. He didn't want to live.

New Life in the Andrews Family

"Your first breath took ours away."

Pinterest

We chose not to have children for the first two years of our marriage. We felt we weren't emotionally ready to have a family and we needed to adjust to our new life. Carol was enjoying her work at the University. I was busy completing my last year of studies and working part-time as a police officer on the campus police. After graduation and soon after being hired on the Boulder Police Department, we began looking forward to having children.

In the spring of 1967 Carol became pregnant. We were living in a 12 by 60 foot Marlette mobile home in a mobile home park in northeast Boulder. Our home had two bedrooms. We quickly began gathering all the items we needed to outfit our second bedroom for the new baby. Medical science hadn't advanced to the point we could have known the baby's sex so all the items were appropriate for either a baby girl or a baby boy.

The two of us have carried on a constant conversation since the day we began dating. So, it was natural that we talked and talked as we prepared for the birth of our new child. Our baby's name dominated our conversation until we finally settled on two names, Christina Ann Andrews, if it was a girl; and, Douglas Raymond Andrews, if it was a boy. We choose the girl's name simply because we liked the sound of it. The boy's name was chosen to honor both of our fathers. Douglas was in honor of my dad; Raymond honored Carol's dad.

Carol's pregnancy developed without any complications. In time she became round, firm and fully packed. She was beautiful and her inner joy would shine forth when she smiled. Finally, very early on the morning of January 14, Carol went into labor. "Very early" means "in the middle of the night!" I was working graveyard shift at the police department, riding as the second man in a two-man patrol car. My partner, Jerry Hardkopp, was driving down Arapahoe Ave. when Lt. Bill Pohorlak radioed us informing me my wife was in labor and I was needed at home. Jerry got so excited that he pulled into the intersection of 24th and Arapahoe and drove in a circle twice. I asked him what he was doing and he said he couldn't decide whether to take me home or to the police department. I suggested he take me to the police department so I could get my car.

Carol's doctor practiced in Denver. The delivery was to occur at St. Luke's hospital. When I arrived home, Carol had everything packed, I changed clothes and we drove to Denver.

Our son, Doug, has been late all of his life. His birth was a precursor to that characteristic. He didn't make his presence until 24 hours after Carol got settled in Saint Luke's maternal ward. Her labor and the delivery took forever. It turned into a painful ordeal. At one point, she was finally given a hand-held medicine dispenser. All she had to do was to grip the device and she was automatically given a measured amount anesthetic to relieve the pain. I can still picture her lying in bed asleep, suddenly awaken, grab that device, administer her anesthetic and then fall back asleep. This went on and on and on.

Carol's parents knew we were in the hospital and they wanted to come; we asked them to wait until the birth occurred. They honored our desire for a while; but Carol was in labor so long they finally showed up. We endured the ordeal until the morning of January 15 when Doug finally made his appearance.

I chose not to be in the delivery room. Instead I sat in the waiting room, chain smoking cigarettes. Right after the delivery a nurse informed me I was the proud parent of a healthy baby boy. She led me into the recovery room where I was reunited with Carol and got to meet my son. Carol looked relieved and happy. Doug looked great. I was excited. The thing I remember most about Doug was the size of his feet. Damn they were big! It was another precursor. Doug would eventually grow to be six feet nine inches tall!

Both sets of grandparents were delighted to see, touch, hold and welcome Doug into the family. Both grandfathers were delighted that Douglas Raymond would carry their name. I even received a telephone call from my cousin in Iowa, Bud Whitmore. Bud was my dad's sister's son. Bud told me he was glad that our son had the same name he had. I apologized to Bud saying we hadn't named our son "Bud". Bud told me that the name "Bud" was his nick name. His given name was Douglas Raymond Whitmore! That was news to me. Much later, when Carol and I began doing genealogy we found that there are a number of other people named "Douglas" and "Raymond" in our family!

Larry Kinion, a friend from the police department, holding Doug!

Doug holding his newborn brother Eric

Carol quit work at the University to devote her time to being a mother. She had hoped we could have two or three children. Her plans were to return to work after they were all in school. She thought we could even have a female college student live in our home and help care for the children after she returned to work. Those plans were never realized.

During the four years between the birth of our first son, Doug, and his brother, Eric, Carol had two miscarriages. Each one left us disappointed and in grief. We began to wonder if we might not be able to have more children. She eventually returned to work part-time. Finally, in the spring of 1971 Carol conceived and that pregnancy presented no problems.

We had moved into a house in south Boulder. Every back yard in the neighborhood was enclosed with high board fences. Doug made friends with several boys his age; and they quickly learned how to crawl over the fences into each other's yards. When we would share our excitement about a new baby, Doug would suggest we adopt one of his friends instead.

January 7, 1972, Carol was very pregnant and we were anxious for the delivery to occur. That evening Carol prepared a wonderful roasted duck dinner and we ate it by candlelight. We went to bed early that night. A little before midnight Carol woke me with the good news that she was in labor. We called the doctor, got dressed and drove to Boulder Memorial Hospital. Carol was assigned a room. A nurse examined her and helped her into bed. We played two handed bridge while we waited for the doctor to arrive. When he did appear, he examined Carol and told us the baby would arrive soon.

Since I was not in the delivery room when Doug was born, I had made it known I'd do the same when our next child was born. After the doctor examined Carol he turned to me and asked me if I wanted to gown up and share the experience with my wife in the delivery room. Much to my surprise I said "Sure." Carol was astounded and pleased.

Carol was prepped. I was gowned. We entered the delivery room with the doctor and one nurse. I stood next to Carol's head and held her hand as the delivery began. Carol had been given a spinal block so, unlike her first delivery, she experienced little pain. In no time, Eric made his entrance. The doctor told us we had a healthy baby boy. As soon as he was cleaned up we got to hold him.

I have to admit that the experience was one of the most awesome events in my entire life. I have to describe the event as holy. Both Carol and I felt the greatest peace and joy as we shared that time. It was so emotionally powerful that neither of us has ever forgotten it.

We were still holding on to the name, Christina Ann, if our new child was a girl. We had chosen the name Eric Trent if the baby was a boy. Eric Trent was not a name connected to anyone we were related to or knew. We chose that name because we liked the sound of it.

When I returned to work at the police department one of the reserve police officers, Eric Gotzmer, approached me and asked if we had named our son after him. I had to explain that we really liked the name, Eric, but we hadn't named our son after him!

A few days after the delivery I brought Carol and Eric home. I was a burglary detective working swing shift and I wasn't given any time off to help with the new child. After I went to work that afternoon Boulder was the target of a terrible wind storm. The wind was so bad that Carol took both children to the basement in case windows broke or the roof was damaged. Our neighbors, Mary and Clarence Woods came to our house to check on Carol's safety. They were so concerned they suggested she and the children come to their home during the storm. Carol accepted their offer which necessitated numerous trips up and down our basement steps as well as up and down the steps to the Woods' basement. All that work such a short time after giving birth exhausted Carol. It would take many days for her to recover.

Two births. Two boys. Our family had taken shape.

Eric giving his dad a kiss!

A Lady with a Knife

"Don't ever trust a lady with a switchblade knife"

John Andrews

It was a cool, cloudy fall Sunday evening. It was early enough that wasn't entirely dark, but late enough the city's street lights had come on. The janitor at the Boulder Medical Center had been working all day scrubbing and polishing floors, emptying trash and cleaning counters. He was bone tired and about to call it a day when he heard glass breaking somewhere on the bottom floor of the three-story building. He ran to the nearest stair well, flew down the steps and as he stepped into the long hall that led to the rear entrance he was met by a woman who was headed in the direction he had just come from. He told her to stop. She told him "…to go to hell" and disappeared up the steps. He grabbed the first phone he could find and called the police department.

I was a lieutenant in the patrol division and that evening I was the shift commander responsible for the supervision of a detail of men consisting of one sergeant and ten patrolmen. My sergeant was working the desk which meant he was busy supervising the dispatchers, records clerks and overseeing the officers as they booked the prisoners they had arrested. I kept busy driving a solo cruiser covering calls and supervising the officers on the street.

The quiet of that Sunday evening ended when the dispatcher triggered the warbling siren that signaled a felony-in-progress. The shrill sound was followed with the words: "Burglary in-progress. Boulder Medical Center. Broadway and Arapahoe. Cars to cover." In rapid succession four officers responded. The dispatcher acknowledged our response, then he informed us the janitor was the reporting party, he would meet us at the rear door on the east side of the building and there was at least one female suspect inside of the building on the second floor.

Officer Olguine, a young rookie, was the first to arrive at the scene. He parked on the west side and positioned himself so he would watch both doors on the north and west sides. The general-north car, general-south car and I arrived within seconds of each other. We all parked in the east parking lot. I told the officer driving the general-south car to remain at the south-east corner of the building and make sure no one escaped from those sides.

Officer Lloyd Durfee and I made contact with the janitor who was standing with his back against the wall next to the east door. The door was open, the glass in the door was broken and glass fragments covered the newly polished floor. The janitor was visibly shaking and he began talking so fast that I wondered if his mind would keep up with the words that were flowing. He told us that he was so startled by the woman that he couldn't describe her. He just knew she didn't belong in that building, he had no idea who she was, and he didn't know if there was anyone with her.

Lloyd and I were probably as tense as the janitor but no one would have guessed that. Our training taught us how to control our emotions and we were projecting a command presence. However, it wasn't every day that an officer arrives at a reported burglary-in-progress, has a witness who can verify a suspect is present and have graphic evidence of a forced entry. With the building secured so the suspect couldn't escape, our task was to locate and arrest a burglar who was possibly armed. I know that I could feel my heart beating in my throat.

Using my pac-set I notified dispatch that we had officers posted outside the building and officer Durfee and I would search the building interior. Since the woman was last seen running up the steps we decided to start on the second floor. We found the stairs and cautiously made our way up the steps. As we were about to enter the wide second floor hallway we heard a loud noise that sounded like heavy equipment hitting the floor. Both of us unsnapped the safety strap on our holsters and entered the hallway. A reception area was located near the far end of the hall. It contained a long counter with several desks and filing cabinets behind. Our suspect was standing behind the counter throwing everything she could find on the floor and against the wall. In her fury, she'd tossed a large typewriter into the hall, followed by staplers, tape dispensers and metal filing baskets full of lab reports and letters. She was in the process of ripping out a telephone as we approached her. She was so absorbed in the destruction that she wasn't aware of our presence.

I yelled: "Freeze!" She spun around, pulled a switch blade knife from her pocket and said: "Fuck you ass hole. Don't come near me!"

At that point I wasn't about ready to 'come near her'. She was standing behind the counter near a desk. She appeared to be in her early 30's, stood about five feet two or three and probably weighed less than 120 pounds. Her hair was a mess. She was wearing light blue slacks, a white blouse and a red jacket with a non-descript logo on the upper left side. Her eyes glistened as if she had been crying or was drunk.

As we stood staring at each other, officer Durfee positioned himself behind me with his back against the wall so he had a clear view of me, the woman and the hall to our rear. He notified dispatch we were in contact with an armed suspect. Dispatch acknowledged the message and asked for a description. As soon as officer Durfee completed his description, the dispatcher said he had just received a missing person report from Boulder Memorial Hospital, Ward B. Ward B was a locked ward where violent mental patients were held. The description of the missing person fit our suspect.

While officer Durfee and dispatch were communicating I slowly began moving toward the end of the counter. I kept my eyes on the suspect and I kept talking to her in a low soft voice.

I told her I wasn't going to hurt her but she had to drop the knife. She didn't seem to hear a word I was saying. Instead she kept yelling at me to …stay away or she would kill me! As I came around the end of the counter she moved to the second desk and with one quick sweep of her hand she knocked another typewriter onto the floor.

The sound seemed to startle her and I made my move. My plan had been to grab the hand holding the knife, brush it aside and pin her to the floor under my weight. I lunged. She moved her hand and I missed it. So much for my plan. However, I was moving so fast and I weighed so much more that she did that I knocked her down and was able to pin her to the floor. That is, I pinned everything but the arm holding the knife. Lloyd had followed me around the counter and he was able to step on her hand and neutralize the knife. Lloyd and I were both yelling and the suspect was screaming. I'm sure we were heard blocks away.

Lloyd replaced the knife with a handcuff, helped me lift the woman to her feet and we cuffed her other hand behind her back. A quick search of her clothing turned up nothing else, no more weapons, no ID, nothing. She continued to fight and scream as we took her to the cruiser.

A psychiatrist from Boulder Memorial drove into the parking lot as we were bringing our prisoner out. He called the woman by name and she immediately responded in a calm clear voice. He told her he was disappointed with her but he was glad she was safe and OK. He asked us if we could return her to Ward B. "Sure", I said, "that's where she would end up anyway."

We were later able to determine that her car was parked in the parking lot at Boulder Memorial Hospital. She didn't have a key, however it was unlocked and she got her jacket and the switchblade knife and then began her adventure. Her primary physician practiced at Boulder Medical Center and she went to the Medical Center seeking her doctor and hoping to find drugs. The center was closed so she "opened" it and was extremely frustrated when she couldn't find either her physician or her drugs.

That woman was the only female I physically fought during my 10 years on the police department. I'm glad I won.

Years later at a police department reunion I ran into Lloyd. The very first thing he said when he saw me was: "Lieutenant, do you remember that crazy woman we fought in the medical center?" I said: "You bet I do!" And we both shook our heads.

Busting a Speed Lab

"Relax; the handcuffs are tight because they're new. They'll stretch out after you wear them awhile."

Author unknown

Speed. Meth. Crystal. Names for a drug that came into popularity in Boulder in the early 1970's; so popular and so easily obtained in Boulder that the hippies called the place "Crystal City".

Meth amphetamine was manufactured from common chemicals anyone could purchase over the counter. Once all the chemicals were obtained the process of preparing, mixing and cooking those chemicals took about six hours to complete. It wasn't illegal to possess the chemicals needed to produce meth amphetamine. However, meth amphetamine was illegal to possess. Narcotic officers not only had the difficult task of identifying suspects who had the chemicals in their possession and the ability to "cook" them; they also had to have some idea when the suspects would begin the process of mixing the chemicals so that arrests could be made soon after the "cooks" had prepared their "stew".

I had the privilege of participating in one of the very first successful raids of a meth amphetamine lab in the State of Colorado. It all began in the summer of 1969 when one of our narcotic officers received information that some people were purchasing the ingredients needed to manufacture speed. He confirmed the information and identified the suspects. One of the suspects was a chemist which meant he had the knowledge and skill to cook the ingredients.

Forest Service sign at Mount Alta picnic ground

At that time the Boulder Police Department had only two detectives assigned to investigate narcotics so federal narcotics officers were often called upon to provide additional manpower and resources. Since speed was new on the scene and few meth labs had ever been raided the federal narcs were more than happy to assist.

An informant was quickly found. He was someone who knew the cook and he had a pending drug charge that gave him the incentive to snitch, hoping to have his charges dropped. The informant was able to pinpoint the date and time the portable lab would be set up but he wasn't able to determine the location.

The day the lab was to be set up five undercover federal narcotic officers arrived early in Boulder. Using four vehicles they began their surveillance. The game of cat-and-mouse continued until 4PM that afternoon when the suspects drove to Mount Alto, a mountain park located in the foothills west of "Crystal City". The suspects parked their vehicles at a picnic site and began unloading Bunsen burners, test tubes, Pyrex beakers and a large amount of chemicals.

The road leading to the picnic site was an old abandoned rail road bed. At a point near the picnic tables the road was cut into the side of a hill. A rock and dirt wall lined one side of the road and the other side was a cliff. The road was so narrow that it would only accommodate one vehicle at a time. Mount Alto was a perfect spot for the clandestine operation because the suspects could block access to the lab by parking one of their cars on the road. At the first sign of a raid the suspects could flee by running into the woods that surrounded the area.

Officers parked some distance away and hiked to a spot they could continue their surveillance. During the early evening hours more suspects arrived bearing additional equipment and chemicals. It began to look like a major operation.

The narcs stayed in contact with their informant who was able to continue providing information as it developed. The narcs learned that a van containing one person and a guard dog was going to be parked on the road leading to the lab. The person in the van was going to be armed with a shot gun. The cook wouldn't begin working until 9 PM when the last of the chemicals arrived. That meant the chemicals the lab was producing wouldn't be illegal until about 3 AM.

I was a burglary and armed robbery detective working the 2 PM to 10 PM shift. All detectives working that shift, regardless of their assignment, were held over to assist with the raid. When my shift ended, I was allowed to go home to change into clothing suitable for the raid. When I returned, I joined all the other investigators, we were briefed, and given assignments. My assignment was to accompany the raiding party.

At 1 AM I was one of a dozen officers who drove into the foothills in four different vehicles. We parked in some campground miles from Mount Alto. We all sat or stood around a picnic table and made the final plans for the raid. Each officer's assignment was coordinated so the raid would occur at exactly 3 AM. Some of the officers were to stay with the vehicles, others would hike through the woods above the van, and still others were to wait until the van was secured and enter the site along that road. My assignment, along with one other officer, was to surprise the person in the van, disarm and arrest him. As soon as the plan was finalized we drove to a spot about one mile from the lab.

Paul and I were the first to move out. We walked along the old rail road bed turned road to the point the road became one lane. The moon was out, but it was very difficult to see more than ten feet in front of us. It was 2:30 AM and we had 20 minutes to get to the van. At first we walked single file next to the dirt and rock wall. We stopped as soon as the van became visible. From that point on we quietly crawled on our hands and knees.

Lookout vehicle where Paul and I arrested man and woman

My adrenalin was flowing. I had visions of someone jumping from the van with his shot gun blazing or being attacked by a vicious dog. Every noise we made increased my adrenalin.

As we got close to the van we began to hear a squeaking sound. It was impossible to see inside the front window, but the van itself seemed to be gently rocking. My first thought was that the guard was moving around in the van to either get his shot gun or release the dog. Yet, nothing happened.

Paul and I were able to crawl to the passenger side of the van without any response from within. We caught our breath, holding our revolvers in one hand and our flash lights in the other. Paul nodded his head, grabbed the handle of the sliding door and yanked it open. We both turned on our flashlights. The sight we saw would have been funny if it hadn't been such a tense situation. The dreaded guard was lying on top of a young woman who was naked from her waist down. The young man's pants were down around his ankles. We caught the couple in the act of sexual intercourse. There was no dog in the van.

I placed the barrel of my gun against the man's temple and quietly told him to "freeze and don't say a word." Paul placed a handcuff on one of the man's wrists, pulled the other hand behind the man's back and finished handcuffing him. We then cuffed the woman. The man quietly asked if he could pull up his pants. "Hell no," Paul said, "don't you move." Then Paul signaled the officers to move down the road past the van to begin the raid. I guarded the couple as the rest of the officres quietly moved past the van.

At exactly 3 AM the raiding party descended on the lab from two directions, surprising the four people who were busy "cooking". The timing couldn't have been better. The over-the-counter chemicals had become the illegal drug, speed. The suspects were so surprised that no one offered resistance.

Meth lab set up on picnic table

As soon as the suspects were restrained and the chemicals secured, several officers rejoined me at the van. The guard and his girlfriend were allowed to dress. The suspects were placed in different cars and transported to the police department. I finished my duty that night by helping inventory the contraband and equipment which had become evidence.

During my career, I made a lot of arrests but this was the only arrest where the suspects were so "down and dirty".

Michael Louis Donelson

"So much in life depends on attitude. The way we choose to see things and respond to others makes all the difference."

Thomas S. Manson

On August 22, 1969, a rather small article appeared in the Boulder Daily Camera. The headline read: "Persevering Police Catch Two Burglars Red-Handed". The story that followed told of the arrest of Michael Donelson, age 21, and an unnamed juvenile male. The young burglars were arrested inside Renalde, Crocket and Kelly Bit and Spur Company as they were attempting to break into the company safe. That small story was only part of a much bigger story…a story I will never forget.

In 1968 I was promoted to the rank of sergeant and assigned to the detective bureau. My responsibility was to investigate burglaries, armed robberies and arsons. My partner, Sergeant Gaynor Walker, was assigned to grand theft investigations and sex crimes. Sergeant Walker stood 6 feet 7 inches tall and weighed close to 300 pounds. He responded to the nicknames "Shorty and "Tiny". I preferred "Shorty". The two of us worked the same hours each day but our work time was spent investigating different crimes. We actively assisted each other when one of us obtained a search warrant or had an arrest to make.

Being only six feet tall and weighed about 145 pounds, I appreciated Shorty's help. And, the fact he had lived and worked in Boulder for many years was another bonus. Shorty had developed a number of reliable informants and they provided us with the latest information on the street.

Boulder was experiencing a high crime rate and 1969 was a banner year for residential and business burglaries. We were averaging almost one a day, which was a lot for a community of less than 100,000. During the summer of 1969 the number of business burglaries increased dramatically and many of them shared the same MO. The burglar forced entry through the rear door or a broken window. Cash, electronic equipment, keys and tools were taken. And if the business contained a safe, the burglar would attempt to force entry by crudely beating on the hinges, knobs and handle. It was apparent the prolific burglar was using his victim's safes to learn the skill of safe cracking.

August 1969 Shorty and I were assigned to the day shift which began at 6 AM. Almost every day I began the shift by responding to the scene of a newly discovered burglary. Since our department was too small to have a crime scene unit, it was the responsibility of the on-duty detective to process fresh crime scenes and collect evidence. We would photograph the scene, prepare a detailed sketch and collect evidence such as fingerprints, fibers, tools and tool marks. By the end of that month I had responded to so many burglaries that I was intimately aware of the burglar's MO. I could almost predict what a crime scene would look like before I arrived.

I also had a good idea who was working so hard to hone his safe cracking skills. Mike Donelson was my suspect and Shorty agreed with that hunch. Mike had been contacted in the business districts numerous times by officers on the night shift. The patrolmen would note the time and location he was contacted, the clothing he was wearing, his mode of transportation and companions. Then they would send me the information on a suspicious person card. Mike preferred wearing dark clothing and he had a habit of carrying a backpack. None of the officers ever had enough probable cause to search the backpack, but some of them asked to examine the contents. Mike always refused to cooperate.

Mike was tall and skinny. He had a sinister look about him and he was not friendly. He drank beer at Walt and Hank's Tavern in downtown Boulder and he moved from motel to

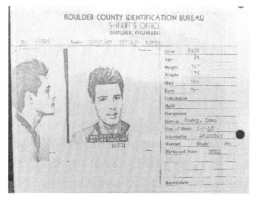

Mike Donelson's booking sheet

motel. He had a live-in girlfriend whose name was Kay. There were rumors that Mike was Kay's pimp, but those rumors were never substantiated.

One morning I arrived at work and was immediately notified that I had four burglary crime scenes waiting to be processed for evidence. All four scenes were located in downtown businesses and two of them involved safes that had been badly damaged. One of the businesses, Der Wienerschnitzel drive-in restaurant was missing cash receipts and a quantity of pennies that the night manager had hidden inside a cigar box in the refrigerator. Another business, the Coca Cola distributing plant, had suffered the loss of a large ring of vending machine keys.

From 6 AM until almost 11 AM I drove from scene to scene, interviewing victims and collecting evidence. The victims were angry and stressed, the scenes were large and each took a long time to process. It was hard work and it did not produce the kind of evidence to prove who was responsible and the theft of vending machine keys was serious because Mike would begin using them to gain entry to vending machines throughout the city.

My frustration and concern prompted me to do something I had never done before. I drove to Mike's last known address, the El Rancho Hansen, a cheap motel located on East Arapahoe Ave. The manager confirmed my suspicion, Mike was staying in unit #5.

I wasn't sure how I was going to proceed. With no plan of action but lots of bravado, I knocked on the door of unit #5. Kay opened the door. She immediately recognized me because I had arrested her several times in the past. She looked like she was either on drugs or just woke up.

"What do you want?" she said.

I told her I wanted to talk to Mike.

She quickly responded, "He's not here."

"Then", I said, "you won't mind if I search your room." With that I took hold of the door, opened it wide and stepped in. At first Kay didn't know what to do or say. In shock, she stood and watched me as I began walking around the room and searching through dresser drawers. I found an empty cigar box in the wastebasket, a quantity of pennies and the missing vending machine keys on top of the dresser in plain view. I took the keys, the pennies and the cigar box and started out the door. Kay claimed the pennies were part of her coin collection. I ignored her and left.

I knew I had conducted an illegal search and seizure. I did not have probable cause to believe those items were in that motel room; and I did not properly inform Kay of her right to refuse a search. But I was able to confirm my suspicion that Mike was the burglar responsible for our crime wave. And it wasn't like he would come and claim that property.

I drove directly from Mike's room to the district attorney's office and met with an assistant district attorney who handled many of my burglary court cases. I was suffering from conflicting emotions. On the one hand the illegal search left me feeling like a criminal, like the burglar I was trying to arrest. On the other hand, I was thrilled to have just solved a crime and I desperately wanted to find a way to make that illegal search legal. I explained all that to Bill and he laughed. He said there was nothing I could do to "right the wrong" and I should be satisfied with the recovery of the stolen property and the fact I now knew the identity of our criminal. As I was leaving his office he cautioned me not to conduct another illegal search.

Shorty's informants provided us with all sorts of interesting tidbits of information during the next week. They heard that when Mike returned home and discovered the vending keys missing he was furious. He accused Kay of being an informant and then he beat her up. Fearing I would return with an arrest warrant, Mike packed all their possessions into his car and they moved out of town. I didn't need informants to know he'd left. The drastic drop in the burglary rate revealed his absence.

These events encouraged me to re-examine all the evidence I'd collected from the burglaries I suspected Mike had committed with the hope I could connect the evidence to Mike. Unfortunately, there was no smoking gun. Mike hadn't left any fingerprints, there were no tools to match to tool marks and we didn't have one witness that could place Mike at any of the scenes.

Around 5 PM on Tuesday, August 19, Shorty received a telephone call from one of his informants. He ended the conversation, hung up the phone and let out a yell that could be heard a block away.

He said: "You won't believe this. Mike Donelson had been drinking beer at Walt and Hank's and has been overheard planning to burglarize Crocket Bit and Spur!"

I could believe it and it was music to my ears.

Shorty picked up the phone, called Crocket Bit and Spur and caught the owner before he left for the day. He asked if we could meet him at his office. Then he hung up, looked at me and said: "Come on, we have some business to take care of!"

Renalde, Crockett and Kelly Bit and Spur Company was located one block north of the police department. The company, which functioned in an old run-down building, manufactured expensive silver bits for horse reins and attractive cowboy spurs. The rear portion of the business contained all sorts of large machines used to cut and stamp the silver metal. The front one-third of the building contained offices. The main office, which contained an upright, old-fashioned safe, had a large picture window facing Pearl Street.

We walked to the business and entered the rear door next to the alley. No one was in the machine shop as we walked through it to the office. The owner greeted Shorty like an old friend. They exchanged pleasantries, and then Shorty informed the man of the pending burglary. The owner shook his head as Shorty talked. The man told us his company had just received a large quantity of silver and a successful burglary would leave them with a huge insurance claim. He also said that everyone who worked there knew that the silver had arrived and had been placed in the safe. Many of his employees drank beer at Walt and Hank's after work. We all agreed that Mike Donelson had probably overheard employees discussing the arrival of the silver.

We asked the owner if he would give us a key to his business and allow us to spend the next few nights inside. He thought that was a great idea and suggested a tour of the plant. He showed us the two rear entrances and we walked among the metal stamping machines. The hardwood floor was dirty and the heavy odor of machine oil filled the air. One door led from the machine shop to a public hallway and on out to the front entrance. The other door led to a small office used by the company secretary. That office had another door that led into the owner's office that contained the safe.

Shorty began to walk into the owner's office, but before he entered he stopped in his tracks. "SHHHH!" he said as he stood in place. There, standing on the outside sidewalk, with his face cupped in his hands, looking into the office was Mike Donelson. His younger brother, David, was at his side. They had no idea anyone was in the building as they cased their next burglary. We stood, frozen in place, as they talked and motioned to each other. Finally, they walked off in the direction of Walt and Hank's Tavern. That encounter delighted us and it gave us even more confidence that our information was correct. The owner wanted to know if this experience was common. Shorty told him it was as unusual as a Baptist receiving communion at the Catholic church.

Shorty and I returned to the police department and notified our lieutenant and captain of the circumstances. Lt. Ruzicka suggested we go home, eat dinner and get a thermos of coffee. Shorty and I agreed to meet at 9 PM and go to the business together.

I was so excited I was back at the PD by 8:30 PM. I checked out two sawed-off 12-gauge shotguns, a box of double aught shells and a pack set. I notified the shift commander and the dispatcher that we would be on a stakeout. Shorty arrived just before 9 PM. We were both wearing dark clothes and our hands were full as we walked to Boulder's next burglary.

We entered the rear door, placed everything except our guns on a workbench and made a thorough search of the building to make sure Mike hadn't arrived before we did. Then we found several chairs, set them among the machines and settled in.

Window where burglars entered the building are to the right of this truck

By 3 AM we had drunk all the coffee and both of us were dead tired. We had worked the entire day and then began the stakeout. Once inside the building we maintained complete silence and we sat in total darkness. All I wanted to do was lay down and go to sleep. Finally, Shorty broke the silence.

"I'm going home." He said.   "I'm not." I replied.

"Do as you please." And with that Shorty took his shot gun and left. At dawn, I left the building and drove home. I slept until late that afternoon and then went to work. It was Shorty's day off, but he had called and left a message for me to call him at home. When I called he told me he was planning to help with the stakeout but a prior commitment would prevent him from helping until midnight. I was still disappointed with his performance on the previous night. I simply said: "Do as you please."

About 9 PM, as I was gathering my equipment, patrol officer Bill Spotts stepped into the detective bureau and asked how things were going. Bill was a friend who I had known and worked with since joining the department. When I told him I was going on a stakeout, he asked if I needed help. "Sure" I said.

Bill's shift didn't end for another hour. Since there were plenty of officers on the street he asked his shift commander if he could park his patrol car and assist me. Permission was granted and it only took a few minutes for Bill to change clothes and join me.

I gave Bill the shot gun Shorty had used, and we began walking to Crockett's. I filled Bill in on the details as we walked an asked if he had ever been inside the bit and spur company.

This window was the point of entry for the burglary

"No" he said, "you can give me a tour when we get there."

We stepped up onto the loading dock, I unlocked the rear door and we entered. I shut the door and locked it. We moved into the middle of the machine shop and, as I was about to describe the layout, we heard a rear window break. We squatted down and froze in place. Our eyes were still adjusting to the dark so it was hard to see what was happening. I could barely make out two figures

109

standing on the loading dock. They must have entered the alley just after we entered the building.

One of the figures reached through the broken glass and unlatched the window. Suddenly a backpack appeared and it ended up on the workbench directly below the window frame. Then both people crawled through the window. When they spoke it was in whispers too low to hear.

I couldn't believe what was unfolding in front of me. Bill had no idea how the building was laid out and we hadn't talked about what we would do if the burglary occurred. My immediate concern was to remain hidden. We didn't move. We tried to control our breathing so as not to be heard. I braced myself to make an arrest if the burglars discovered us.

I was fairly confident that the two people were Mike and his brother, David. They made no effort to search the machine shop. One of them picked up the backpack and they both quietly made their way to the door that led into the front hallway. After they entered that door we were surrounded by a deafening quiet.

I was so full of adrenalin that it was extremely difficult to remain still. If I gave Mike time to work on the safe before I arrested him that would establish his motive for the forced entry and it would help tie him to the other burglaries. So, we didn't move. Bill knew that I was in command and he patiently waited for my direction.

My greatest fear was that something would startle Mike and David and they would escape. I couldn't imagine anything more embarrassing. The thought of them escaping increased my adrenalin and I could hardly control my desire to make an arrest and end the suspense. My knees hurt and my heart was beating so fast I imagined the drunks at Walt and Hank's could hear me.

Finally, we heard metal striking metal. Mike was back at work trying to learn how to crack a safe. Now it was my turn to act. I whispered to Bill: "Follow me and yell as loud as you can." We carefully stood with our shot guns in hand. As the blood returned to my legs I began yelling and running toward the open secretary's door. The noise cut through the dark like a train rumbling through a tunnel.

The only thing standing between the burglars and us was a closed wood door. I hit the door with my left shoulder hoping it would burst open. No such luck. The door held and I bounced back. However, Bill, who stood six foot five inches and weighed 250 pounds, was right behind me and he was moving fast. He hit me and drove both of us right through the door. The crashing sound and wood splinters filled the air. And there in front of us was one of the most beautiful sights I have ever beheld. Mike Donelson was kneeling in front of the safe with a large ballpein hammer in his gloved hand. David was standing at his side.

Bill and I leveled our shot guns and told those boys to "Drop the hammer, stand, put your fucking hands on the wall!" Both immediately obeyed.

I didn't find any weapons when I frisked Mike. When I finished I handcuffed his hands behind his back. He was wearing gloves and I was in such a hurry that I didn't have him remove them.

David didn't have any weapons either. Once he was searched and handcuffed I told both of them to kneel on the floor and face the wall.

Bill turned on his pack set and notified dispatch that we had two burglars in custody and we needed a car to meet us in the alley to transport the prisoners to the police department. Three patrol units and a patrol sergeant arrived within minutes. Everyone was excited and wanted to be part of the arrest.

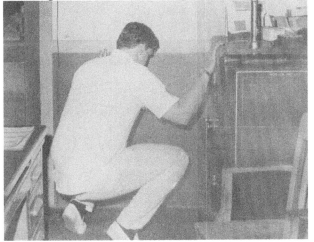

I took Mike by the arm and lifted him to his feet. As he moved something caught my eye. He still had a tiny flashlight in his gloved hand. In the excitement neither Mike nor I realized it was there. I took it out of his hand and searched him again.

I decided not to inform him of his constitutional right to remain silent because I had all the evidence I needed. However, out of curiosity, I asked him what he was thinking

Bill Spotts kneeling just as Mike Donelson was kneeling when

we entered the office.

when he heard Bill and me running and yelling. Mike shook his head saying: "I thought David was making that noise and I told him to shut up." Both of us laughed as he and his brother were escorted to a patrol car.

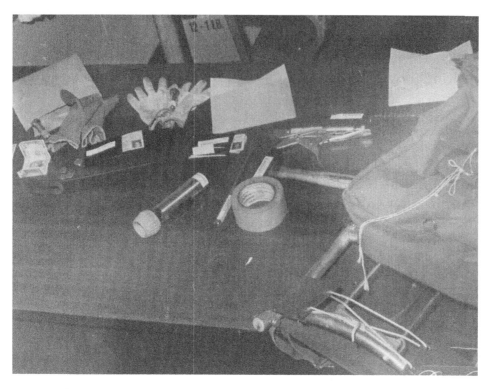

Contents of Mike Donelson's backpack

After Thoughts

Mike subsequently admitted his guilt in court and, much to my disgust, was granted probation. Within a short period of time he violated his probation by fleeing the state. He quickly became involved in a string of crimes including burglary, auto theft, armed robbery, rape and kidnap. He was arrested in Texas and returned to Colorado. His probation was revoked and he was sent to the Colorado State Penitentiary in Canon City.

This entire ordeal was a watershed experience for me. Mike was a dangerous criminal. I had worked hard to arrest him. Seldom does the State have such a strong case as the one Mike Donelson faced. My first reaction was one of defeat when the judge granted Mike probation. But the more I reflected on the events the more I came to the conclusion that the judge's response reflected on the judge, not on me. There was nothing I could do about Mike's sentence. My job was to perform the best investigation I could and then let the chips fall where they may. I actually came away from this situation committed to excellence. The experience instilled within me the desire to always do my best, and to judge myself by my efforts rather than the actions of others.

The experience was a watershed on another level. It marked my maturity as a burglary detective. To my knowledge that arrest was the very first time in the history of the Boulder Police Department that officers arrested burglars in the very act of forcing a safe open in a business. Granted it involved teamwork. Shorty, though he was not present for the actual arrest, had developed the information; and Bill ably assisted me making the arrest. But it was my persistence and efforts that held it all together.

I received two commendations for my efforts and I consider that investigation and arrest one of the highlights of my law enforcement career. I felt the arrest deserved more than one small article in the Boulder Daily Camera.

We are all God's Children

"What the world really needs is more love and less paperwork."

Pearl Bailey

I was a lieutenant in the Training Division. That position gave me the luxury of working regular hours Monday through Friday. One Friday afternoon at 4:45 PM as I was preparing to leave work, a desk clerk entered my office and asked if I would be willing to give a visiting law enforcement officer a tour of our building. That was the last thing I wanted to do at that time of the day, but I said I would. The clerk looked relieved. She thanked me and said she'd asked several other command staff officers and none of them were interested.

I followed the clerk to the front desk where I was introduced to a very black man who identified himself as Mike Ogutami. He was short and stocky, well- groomed and dressed in a suit and tie. He told me he was a police commissioner from Nigeria, Africa. He was visiting his children who were attending the University of Colorado and he wanted to tour our police department. Since it was so near quitting time I launched right into the tour. Mike asked lots of questions and he wanted copies of all our paperwork. He had a camera and he took pictures of each room, the patrol cars and the booking area. We finished the tour in about forty-five minutes. Mike shook my hand, thanked me profusely, and we exchanged business cards.

I did enjoy the experience; after all, it's not every day an American policeman gets to spend time with an African policeman. During the tour Mike made comments that left me with the impression law enforcement in Africa was quite different from law enforcement in America. He seemed more interested in our "tools and equipment" than information about policies and procedures. I kept his business card as a souvenir of the experience, never thinking I'd ever see or speak to the man again.

At 5:30 AM several months later Carol and I were jarred awake by the telephone. I answered the phone. The woman's voice on the other end sounded like she was talking through a megaphone. With a foreign accent the woman asked to speak to John Andrews. I told her that was who she was speaking with. She then said she was a transatlantic operator with a call from Nigeria from a Mike Ogutami. Then I heard "Hello John, this is Mike. Can you hear me?"

"Yes, Mike." I said. I was still groggy and my mind was struggling to locate Nigeria, identify Mike Ogutami, and wake up all at the same time.

Mike said: "I ask as one police officer to another, will you help me?"

Suddenly I realized who Mike Ogutami was. I said: "Yes, Mike. I will try to help if I can. What is the problem?"

"My son is in my daughter's room on the University of Colorado campus and he is threatening to kill her. I told him not to harm her. I also told him I was calling you and asking you to go talk with them. I told them I am giving you my authority. You are now their father and they are to obey you. Please hurry."

I asked what the disagreement was about and he told me it involved a car. Then he gave me his daughter's room number in Cockrell Hall and again urged me to hurry.

I hung up, jumped out of bed and quickly got dressed as I relayed the details to Carol. I told her I'd call her from the girl's room just as soon as I assessed the situation. Then I rushed to my car and headed toward the campus.

Thoughts were spinning through my head. To begin with, I had deliberately chosen not to notify the police department. A call to the dispatcher would automatically result in marked patrol cars responding with red lights and siren. It would also force me to file a criminal complaint. I wanted to avoid all that. But the closer I got to Cockrell Hall the more I questioned my decision. I didn't know these people and I didn't have a clear understanding of the situation. The young man could be armed. How did I know if the young man and his sister would respect and obey me solely on the word of their father? And all this was occurring in the early 1970's when race was an explosive issue. How could a white police officer expect to establish rapport with feuding black siblings? In spite of the questions I chose to continue on the path I was following.

I parked, walked to the room and knocked on the door. A beautiful young black lady opened the door and invited me in. I introduced myself and she said she was expecting me. The center of the room was filled with luscious, tall green plants. Several rubber tree plants with leaves reaching toward the ceiling formed a canopy over the other plants. In the middle of all the vegetation sat a young black man. In solemn tones he said he was Mike's son. He was casually dressed and he looked tired. He wasn't holding a weapon, much to my relief, and his clothes didn't appear to be concealing a knife or gun. Both of them spoke with the same foreign accent their father had.

I told them their father had asked me to respond, to act on his behalf, to examine the circumstances and to help find a resolution to the problem. They both acknowledged that their father told them the same thing and they said they were willing to respect me as a father substitute. Before we went any further I asked for the phone and I called Carol. I told her everything was OK and I'd call again in 15 or 20 minutes.

I hung up and asked the young man to explain the situation. Before he could speak his sister said her brother was threatening to kill her because she wouldn't let him use her car.

Her father had purchased the car for her as a reward for good grades. Her brother was doing a poor job academically and Mike was not going to give him a car until his grades improved. The young lady said her brother had forced his way into her "nest" and demanded the car keys. She refused and called her father who in turn called me.

Finally, the young man spoke. He said the car belonged to both him and his sister. She interrupted calling him a liar. I stopped the conversation and, in a stern voice, told them we would discuss this in a civil manner. They both agreed, leaving me feeling that they did accept my position as a surrogate father.

The young man then explained that in Nigeria women are not allowed to own cars and they are completely sub-servient to men. Therefore, his sister was culturally required to give him the car keys or suffer the consequences. The consequences were that he would either kill her soon in America or, for sure, when they both returned home to Nigeria.

I asked the young lady for the title to the car. The title she produced was in her name alone. I told her brother that American law was clear. His sister was the sole owner of the vehicle and she alone had the right to deny him access. His response was: "Then I will kill her."

I told him that just because he was a foreign student didn't mean he was immune from punishment for committing a crime; and the punishment for killing someone in America was very severe. He said he would kill her anyway, if he didn't do it soon, he would do it when they both returned to their native land.

His sister was as stubborn and determined as he was. She was not going to give in to his demands. He was not going to get her keys or drive her car.

Both of them were willing to discuss the matter for as long as it took so we talked and talked and talked. We talked so long that I lost my ability to be creative and I kept repeating myself. We also talked so long that I had to call the police department to notify them I would be taking a personal day off.

Finally, I thought of something that would at least inject a new element into the mix. I asked for the name of their foreign student advisor. They both shared the same advisor, a faculty member who had been born and raised in Nigeria. I called his office. When he answered I identified myself as a police officer. I told him where I was and I asked him to join me as soon as he could. He was there in no time at all. It took a while to bring him up to speed but once he was on board he became a strong advocate of my position. In fact, he informed the young man that unless he gained control of himself his advisor would have him expelled from school and deported.

When those threats changed nothing, the student advisor and I stepped from the room and had a private discussion. We both felt the situation was so serious that the only course open to us was to send the young man back to Africa. I located a phone and called Mike. He listened patiently as I explained the situation. He said he was sad things could not be worked out but he agreed that it was best that his son return home. He promised to wire airfare to the student advisor as soon as the one-way airfare was purchased. He thanked me and hung up. The student advisor called a travel agent and was able to arrange a flight that would leave within twenty-four hours.

We returned to the girl's room and informed them of our plans. The young man was even angrier, but he was willing to do as he was told. I was surprised but I suspect that his response was culturally conditioned. When he first met me he said he accepted me as his father and he was honoring that. He even accompanied the student advisor home and agreed to stay with the advisor until he got on the airplane.

Sadly, he told his sister she was as good as dead. He said her return to Nigeria would seal her fate. She didn't show outward signs of fear, but all of us knew his threat was real. We three men left a little after noon. The young lady was alone, in her nest, sitting in the midst of her plants.

The next day the student advisor took Mike's son to the airport and placed him on the plane. He called me when he got back to Boulder. He thanked me for all I had done. I silently marveled at the way a black professor and a white police officer had been able to co-operate to resolve a potentially explosive and racially charged situation. That occurred at a time American race relations were stormy, at best. That black professor felt so positive toward me that he and his wife later invited Carol and me to attend a party at his home for Nigerian students.

Mike phoned me as soon as his son arrived home. He thanked me and said his son was still angry, but he was also glad to be home. Several weeks later I received a thank you letter from Mike. He was deeply grateful and mentioned the fact that my help was proof of the bond that exists between police officers. I think a deep bond also exists between parents. It's amazing to find that African families can have the same problems American families have.

I have always liked black people. I was raised to respect black people. I've even felt a kinship to black people because an ex-slave black man, Uncle Ben Franklin Robinson, raised my father. I was glad I was able to help; after all, we are all God's children.

Nichols Hall Commandos

"Luck affects everything. Let your hook be always cast in the stream where you least expect it, there will be a fish."

Ovid

I love reading graffiti whether it's on the wall in a rest room, carved in a tree, or written on a desk. Most graffiti are nonsense but there are times it can be delightfully funny or full of wisdom. The reward of those infrequent gems keeps me reading whatever graffiti I come across. And once, in May 1969, I came across some graffiti that led me to a band of burglars. Let me set the stage.

On May 18, 1969, Harold Campbell, a University of Colorado food service employee, reported a burglary in the kitchen of Farrand Hall. The university police took the initial report. All felonies occurring on the campus fell under the jurisdiction of the city police so the university police asked dispatch to have a Boulder police detective respond. My partner, Shorty Walker, was the detective assigned to investigate all campus felonies: but, since he was on vacation I was given this particular case. When I arrived at the scene I was told that 200 sirloin steaks valued at $123 had been stolen. (Imagine, 200 sirloin steaks costing only $123! My how the economy has changed.) It appeared that the burglar had used a key to gain entry to the kitchen because there was no sign of a forced entry. None of the windows were broken or forced and none of the doors showed any sign of damage. I inspected the refrigerator, took photos of the scene and interviewed Mr. Campbell. He couldn't offer any helpful information and he didn't have any suspects in mind.

Most crimes committed on the university campus were committed by students. If a student was responsible for this burglary then, it seemed to me, the theft of 200 sirloin steaks would present an immediate problem. The burglar had to either eat the loot or have some sort of refrigeration so the meat wouldn't spoil. With that in mind, I returned to the police department and searched the files for anything that might relate to this case. In no time I found a criminal complaint that detailed the theft of a small refrigerator from the Ketchum building on the campus. The refrigerator was taken six days prior to the Farrand Hall burglary. I thought the two thefts could be related. I filed the information in the back of my mind.

The university campus was honeycombed with connecting tunnels containing steam pipes that provided heat to each building. All doors leading to the tunnels were secured with locks that required special keys that were only carried by campus plumbers and security officers. The day after the steak thefts, a university plumber discovered a broken door latch in the frame of the door leading from the Farrand Hall kitchen into the steam tunnel that ran beneath that building. He discovered the broken latch when he unlocked the door from the kitchen side to repair a small leak in the steam pipes. That broken latch was not visible in the kitchen. Since the plumber didn't know about the burglary, he didn't report the broken latch to the university police until the next day, May 20.

University police officers Fred Gerhardt and Don Beach took the report and immediately called me. Together we interviewed the plumber, examined the door and determined that the door had been forced open from inside the tunnel. After the burglary the perpetuator left the scene through the same door. Damage to the latch was such that the burglar was able to shut and lock the door from the tunnel side.

After photographing the damaged latch, we entered the tunnel and began a search for evidence. Walking through the tunnels was a miserable task because the tunnels were narrow, the steam pipes made them hot and humid, and the dirt floors and open grates designed to ventilate the tunnels made the environment dirty. About fifty feet down that miserable tunnel I saw something that made the effort worthwhile. It was an important clue. Carved into the bricks that lined the tunnel was this piece of graffiti.

May 3, 1969

"Nichols Commandos"

Jack Jahn & Co.

John Leventhol

Gary Beardsinorta

CSU bun Clem Schaeffer

Another fifty feet into the tunnel we discovered a large metal screen door standing open and the padlock that normally secured the door was lying on the ground. The screen door had been pried open. In order to arrive at the spot on the wall where the graffiti had been written the parties responsible had to either pry the screen door or force the locked kitchen door. With their names "written on the wall", Jack, John, Gary and Clem were now prime suspects in the steak burglary.

I spent the rest of that day confirming the addresses of the suspects, checking their criminal records and searching criminal complaints for possible related crimes. I found that none of the suspects had a criminal record, and Jack and John each occupied different dorm rooms in Nichols Hall.

The following morning, May 21, I went to Nichols Hall hoping to contact Jack Jahn. When no one responded to the knock on his door, I went to John Leventhol's room. As I approached the door I could hear voices and laughter inside. I knocked on the door and someone inside yelled: "Who's there?" I responded" "John" (everyone knows a John!) In a confident voice the person inside hollered: "Come on in."

So I did. What I saw as I entered the room was candy to my eyes. The walls of the room were lined with street signs and a small white General Electric portable refrigerator was sitting on the floor under a window. I identified myself, flashed my badge and asked the two young men to identify themselves. One of them was John Leventhol and the other was a visitor from down the hall. I placed John under arrest for investigation of possession of stolen property – the street signs. I told the visitor to leave. As he was walking out the door I frisked John, handcuffed him and informed him of his right to remain silent. While he was contemplating his situation I asked him where he had obtained all the street signs. Without hesitation he said they belonged to his roommate, Gary Wuetig. I asked him where the refrigerator came from; and, again he implicated his roommate, Gary. He said Gary had recently purchased the "fridge". I asked if I could have a look inside the "fridge" and he said: "No!" He did tell me that his roommate, Gary, was visiting a friend in a room in Brackett Hall.

I didn't have a radio (pac-set) so I used the phone in the dorm room to call the dispatcher and request assistance. Minutes later university officer Fred Gerhardt arrived. I quickly briefed Fred and told him to seize each of the street signs and the refrigerator, place them in his patrol car and take them to the Boulder Police Department.

John Leventhol, still in handcuffs, and I walked to room #224 in Brackett Hall. Again, I knocked on the door and Michael Wedman opened it. I asked if Gary Wuetig was in the room. "Yes", he said. I then identified myself as a Boulder detective; then, holding John Leventhol's arm, I stepped into the room and asked the only other person present if he was Gary Wuetig. He said he was. I placed him under arrest and handcuffed him with cuffs I'd borrowed from Officer Gerhardt. At this point I spotted a stop sign hanging on the door room wall. I asked Michael Wedman if we were standing in his room. "Yes", he said. I told him he was under arrest for possession of stolen property. I didn't handcuff him because I was fresh out of cuffs. But I did inform both Gary and Michael of their right to remain silent.

I then turned to Michael and asked where the stop sign had come from. "From a street corner in Littleton, Colorado," was his reply.

So, at this point I was standing in a dorm room with three people under arrest, two wearing handcuffs and one unrestrained. I still didn't have a pac-set; so again, I used the telephone in the room to call for assistance. While we were waiting for other officers to arrive, I noticed a new Sony Solid State TV sitting on a chair. I asked Gary where the TV came from and to my surprise he said: "I stole it from a Howard Sound store."

The three suspects were transported to the police department, again advised of their rights and then interrogated. Each of them had a different story to tell. As with almost all criminals, the truth didn't come to the surface without a lot of conversation. In the end, each of them admitted participating in the theft of the street signs, taking part in the theft of the TV from Howard Sound as well as a stereo from Montgomery Wards. Each of them admitted they, along with others, had entered the university steam tunnels on multiple occasions.

No one admitted to the theft of the refrigerator. John claimed he bought it three weeks prior to his arrest from another student after seeing an ad in the paper. That was a lie. The serial number on the refrigerator matched the stolen refrigerator, and the theft of that "fridge" had only occurred six days earlier.

I never did locate the stolen steaks. However, I did locate and arrest the remaining "Nichols Hall Commandos". I recovered additional stolen property and I filed felony charges against each of the individuals I arrested.

The success of this investigation came as a result of my inability to ignore graffiti. If you write it on a wall, I will read it.

Childhood Memories – Not Mine, Theirs

The next best thing to the enjoyment of a good time,

is the recollection of it."

James Lendall Basford

We had fun with our children as they grew up. Doug and Eric were not alike. Their outlook on life, the way they approached new events and adventures, and the decisions they made were unique to their personalities. That's what made them so interesting.

After Doug was born I often worked a rotating shift. Working one month on morning shift, the next month on graveyard shift and the third month on afternoon shift was hard on the family. Each shift changed the time I would sleep and which meals I'd be able to eat with the family. I think Doug and I enjoyed graveyard shift the most. I would go to work after Doug went to sleep and arrive back home about 6:30 AM. Doug would get up, meet me in the kitchen and we would quietly share breakfast together. It was special for the two of us to spend that time talking and eating.

Doug standing in front of the TV we enjoyed watching together.

I usually arrived home from swing shift between 10:30 and 11 PM. The family would all be in bed asleep. One night I got home late, changed for bed and decided I'd check to see that Eric was sleeping soundly. I tip toed barefoot into his dark room. As I reached the side of his bed I stepped on something warm and soft. Whatever it was oozed between my toes. I checked Eric. He was OK. Then I walked into the bathroom to find that our dog, Woofer, had pooped in Eric's room and I'd stepped in his mess. Yuck. Yuck. At least I didn't holler and wake everyone in the house!

While we lived in Boulder, Doug was old enough to appreciate his dad's job. He liked climbing in the police car when I was home for a meal; and he was proud when his dad showed up in uniform at school. And he liked listening to my stories about the bomb squad. All that impressed him enough that when he joined the Marine Corps he wanted to go to Explosives Ordinance Disposal training.

Eric had a tricycle, but he was more interested in his big brother's bicycle. He would pester Doug for a ride. One morning Doug finally gave in and offered his brother the opportunity to join him on a ride around the block. Try as best they could, neither boy was able to safely position themselves. The ride never materialized.

Carol and I have been "Rail Buffs" for many years. We really like to ride trains, especially trains pulled by steam engines. We had taken the Durango and Silverton train and knew that there was a guest ranch that could only be accessed by riding that train. We booked a week at "Awe Wilderness Guest Ranch" for us and the boys. We drove to Durango, loaded our gear on the train and rode it to the siding next to the ranch. We had rooms in the bunk house, all the meals were prepared by their staff and served family style, and we had the pleasure of watching the train pass the ranch twice a day. There were scheduled children's activities every day, so Carol and I had some quiet time we could share alone. I took my service revolver and we were able to practice on their outdoor range, we hiked and also did some fishing.

One afternoon all four of us were on a wood suspension foot bridge as we were returning from a hike. We were startled by the loud sounds of a large animal running toward the bridge. It was a horse. It ran onto the bridge and passed us galloping at full speed. The frightening experience took our breath away. That was the most memorable part of that wonderful vacation.

The four of us also took day trips riding the train behind Union Pacific's 4-8-8-4 steam locomotive. One trip was from Denver to Julesburg and several others were from Denver to Cheyenne, Wyoming. I tried to interest Doug in steam engines; but he preferred diesel to steam. Eric enjoyed model trains more than the real McCoy.

Carol read books to the boys when she put them to bed. Doug enjoyed fantasies and fairy tales so much that he took up reading books almost as soon as he had mastered the skill of reading. Doug read his way through adolescence and into adulthood. No matter where we went or what we did as a family, Doug was present with his attention riveted in a book. Science fiction novels became his favorite reading material. He's probably read every sci-fi book available on the market today.

There were good and bad aspects to Doug's attachment to books. The bad aspect is that he probably couldn't recall many of the family gatherings or travel experiences because he was lost in one of the many novels he was reading. The good aspects were that his reading skills greatly improved his vocabulary and reading helped him pass many boring hours of travel during the twenty-three years he spent in the Marine Corps.

Eric wasn't interested in reading, though he did like hearing his mother read him to sleep. Eric was interested in fishing. He loved to fish and he became a good fisherman. For example, Carol, Eric and I spent a weekend in a cabin near Meeker with Fr. Don and Verlene White when Eric was about seven-years-old. We had taken our fishing poles and Eric and I spent a little time fishing in a stream near the cabin. I got bored and went to the cabin while Eric continued to fish alone. He only returned to the cabin after he caught several fish. He was so delighted with his luck he tried to spend the rest of the weekend with a line in the water.

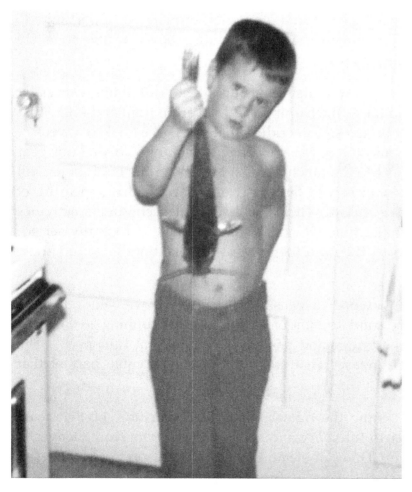

Eric holding a catfish he caught in Washington Park Lake!

Eric was in junior high school when I was attending seminary in Wisconsin. During the summer of my junior year of studies Eric and I spent almost every day in a canoe fishing the lakes near our home. Eric would catch fish while I'd paddle. He still spends his summer fishing and boating in his pontoon boat at Chatfield Reservoir near his home in Littleton, Colorado.

Doug did not like living in a funeral home. The fact that his dad, his grandparents and his aunts and uncle had all lived at one time or another in the same funeral home did not impress him. A lot of the students in his school lived in very nice houses and he was embarrassed his family lived in a business. He did what he could to avoid being associated with the Andrews Funeral Home.

Eric, on the other hand, loved the notoriety of being the undertaker's kid. Eric was four when we moved from Boulder to the funeral home in Castle Rock. In no time his curiosity peaked. He wanted to see the caskets on display, he wanted to see a dead body, and he wanted to know all about death. Carol and I believed it was important to satisfy those requests and help both him and Doug adjust to our unique residence. Eric would accompany me into the casket display room and I'd be inundated with all sorts of questions. "How do you open that thing up?" "Does it have a mattress and pillow cases?" "How does a dead person get inside?"

Eric knew when I'd leave on a death call and he'd watch for me to return. He would watch as I'd remove the body from the hearse and push the covered stretcher into the morgue. He'd ask to see the body. We would only allow that to occur after a body was embalmed, dressed and in a casket.

His curiosity was satisfied after he viewed several bodies. But that wasn't until after we experienced one minor problem involving Eric. He had asked to see a body that was in a casket in the chapel. I didn't realize that Eric had been eating some warm chocolate chip cookies and he had chocolate on his hands. When we got into the chapel, Eric walked to the casket, placed his hands on the linen casket lining and peered into the open lid. It wasn't until we turned to leave that I realized he had left some chocolate stains on the white linen. Carol had a tough time removing those spots.

Robert Frisley was Doug's best friend in middle school. Robert lived about 20 miles south of Castle Rock. He'd often come home with Doug after school and one of his parents would pick him up when they got off work. We had a basketball hoop attached to the back side of the funeral home. Doug and Robert would toss the basketball into that hoop for hours. They would play a game we called "horse". Every time one of them would make a basket they won a letter in the name "horse". The first one to win all the letters would win the game. Sometimes Robert would stay after school and Doug wouldn't be able to spend time with him because of other commitments. Whenever that occurred, Robert would walk into my office and challenge me to a game of "horse". What fun.

One weekend afternoon Doug asked me if I would drive him to Robert's house, pick Robert up and bring him back to spend the night. Robert got his parent's permission and off we went. On the trip back, as I drove down I-25 cars kept passing us, honking and waving. I couldn't imagine what was going on. Come to find out, Robert had a sign that said "HONK AND WAVE" that he would flash to each car behind us. My confusion left those two boys in stiches.

After moving to Castle Rock we became active in Christ's Episcopal Church. We attended services every Sunday and the boys attended Sunday School. Eric learned a lot about the

Lord, about God's love for us, and he was very aware of heaven. It was natural that we talked a lot about heaven since we lived in a funeral home and dealt with death.

Eric often rode with me when I went to cemeteries to prepare monument foundations or set up grave equipment for committal services. Early one morning Eric was riding with me as I drove to Spring Valley Cemetery in rural southern Douglas County. The weather that morning was cloudy with patches of fog. The dirt road leading to the cemetery is fairly straight but it has a lot of hills and short valleys. We would drive into fog as we climbed each hill and then we'd drop out of the fog when we entered the brief valleys. As the trip progressed I thought I'd have some fun with Eric. I told him we were driving to heaven. Eric got really excited. He wanted to know how long it would take. I told him it wouldn't be too long. Then he wanted to know if we'd see Jesus. "Yes!", I said. Then he wanted to know if we'd encounter angels.

It quickly became apparent that Eric believed me and he could hardly contain his excitement. I didn't want to destroy his excitement but I had to find a way to bring him back to reality without disappointing him. Finally, I told him we weren't going to heaven. We were going to Spring Valley Cemetery which was full of people who had gone to heaven. The conversation turned into a wonderful exchange of thoughts about Jesus, angels and heaven.

One weekend members of our church gathered and everyone car pooled to Elitche Gardens amusement park in Denver. Eric was about 5 years old. He and I took a ride on an aerial tram. Each chair on the tram held two people, it moved very slow and it circled the parking lot. As we were drifting along I noticed that Eric was leaning forward over the rail that held him in the chair. I asked him what he was doing; and, in a very calm voice he informed me that he just spit on a fat man. To my horror there was a fat man below us wiping his head. I slapped Eric's mouth and told him never to do that again. Thank God the man never figured out where the drop of moisture came from.

Doug wanted to make some money so he decided to start his own business. Using our power mower, he would go from house to house and ask if he could mow the lawn. He established a few steady customers and made enough money he opened a checking account at the Bank of Douglas County. He called his business "Doug's Lawn Service". He was really excited when he got his box of checks. When I looked at the checks I found that the checks stated simply: DLS. Doug told me he didn't want to write out the full name of his business so he just used the initials instead.

The boys really enjoyed camping. The Great Sand Dunes National Park was the site of one memorable spring trip. Our nephew, Craig Walker, who is the same age as Doug, was along for the fun. We all fit in our large canvas tent. Carol cooked our meals on an open fire. Water was running fast enough in the stream near the dunes that the boys could lie in the water and float downstream. The kids filled the tent with fine sand they picked up in and stream and climbing the sides of the dunes.

We had some backpacking equipment that Eric and I used on a camping excursion we took near Goose Creek in western Douglas County. That camping trip gave us the chance to hike, fish and camp overnight. We packed to the spot we chose to pitch our small tent. It was very cloudy and threatening to rain when we began fishing. Eric caught several small fish. I had no luck. It began to rain so we put the fish on a stringer, laid them in the stream and put a heavy rock on the stringer. By then it was pouring, so we scrambled into the tent.

Did I say that tent was small? It was so tiny we laid on our sleeping bags facing each other and there was no more room. Eric is an extrovert. He talks just to talk. It never stopped raining that day. Eric never stopped talking that day. I have never been so wet and I've never heard a longer monologue than I experienced on that camping trip.

The next morning the rain had stopped when we awoke. We decided to have those fish for breakfast. When we went to the stream we discovered that there was no rock, stringer or fish. We figured they had washed away. Eric kept looking and suddenly he discovered that the stream had risen, covering the rock. The stringer was still under that submerged rock and the fish were still attached! He waded out into the water, retrieved the fish and we had a grand breakfast.

On another camping trip, Carol and I, Doug and Doug's friend Derrick Womeldorf, spent a weekend in a forest service campsite near Silverthorne. Doug and Derrick had just entered high school and both were determined they were going to join the military after graduation. Both boys had camouflage clothes and large hunting knives and they pitched their tent some distance from Carol and me. All night they pretended they were stalking the enemy in the woods. We kept waking up to the sound of those boys running, hitting the brush and whispering to each other. It must have been positive for both of them because later both of them did join the Marine Corps.

Doug learned to drive as soon as he was old enough to get a permit. I would take him on rural roads near home and sit next to him as he practiced driving. Early in his training Eric joined us on one practice drive. I had driven the car to an isolated dirt road west of Sedalia. I didn't think we would encounter any traffic and it was a good spot for Doug to practice driving on a twisting narrow road. I sat next to Doug and Eric was sitting in the back seat. Did I mention that Eric talks a lot? He even talks more when he is nervous. Doug's driving made him so nervous that he simply wouldn't shut up. It not only irritated Doug, it distracted him and he drove the front passenger side wheel off the road. He got the car stopped, but we had one wheel hanging in the air. I never realized Doug knew so many swear words. Doug's response was so effective Eric stopped talking. We all got out of the car and were finally able to push it enough we got traction and the car was back on the road. That was the last time Eric accompanied his brother while he was undergoing drivers ed.

Four years later we were living in the mountains of Colorado. Our home was in Granby which sits at an elevation of 8,500 feet above sea level. That was where Eric learned to drive in the winter of 1988. It snows most winter days in the mountains and so Eric had to master his driving skills on two lane highways that were often icy and snow packed. Eric learned well and became a safe, competent driver. The only problem he had was a lack of experience driving in urban areas. Shortly after obtaining his license, we had to make a trip to Craig, Colorado. We let Eric drive. The trip took us through Steamboat Springs, a town that contained several traffic lights. Having never considered the fact he had no experience with traffic signals we were surprised when he drove right through the first two red lights he encountered. Thank God there were no cars in the intersections and no police officer in sight. And Eric was glad his brother wasn't in the car. These are just a few of the many wonderful memories of living with two boys who filled our lives with unexpected fun and joy.

First Homicide – Alone

"The Pilgrims didn't have any experience when they landed here. Hell, if experience was that important, we'd never have anybody walking on the moon.

Doug Rader

John Kirkland was a young, out of control drug addict who belonged to a band of hippies known as the STP family. He and the STP family lived in tents and slept on the ground in dirty primitive conditions in the mountains west of Boulder. They used and sold drugs; and, when they weren't too stoned to stand, they haunted The Hill, a business district next to the University campus. Every officer on the Boulder Police Department knew John, AKA, STP John, and his friend, Donald Williams, AKA, The Bishop, by sight. In fact, any officer who regularly worked The Hill had either arrested them or verbally encountered them.

My encounter with STP John occurred late in the evening of Saturday, July 11, 1970. He didn't give me any trouble because he was dead. Twenty minutes prior to our encounter, he and the Bishop had crashed a party, gotten into a fight and John was shot dead. Donald Williams, the Bishop, stabbed the assailant with a large hunting knife and then fled the scene. It would take five more days for me to find and arrest him.

The circumstances that led to my involvement in STP John's homicide began days earlier when members of the Boulder Police Department's detective bureau began planning a poolside party. The festivities were to occur on Saturday, July 11, at the Sheraton Inn Motel on 28th Street. All the detectives and their wives or girlfriends were invited. The plans included lots of food and booze. Daily conversation left me with no doubt the party would turn into a drunken mess and I wasn't interested.

As time went on I told my lieutenant, Ralph Ruzicka, that I would be willing to be the on-call investigator for any emergencies that might arise during the party. That was fine with Ralph because my offer relieved him of the responsibility of being on call or assigning someone else to cover calls.

The long-planned event began that hot summer afternoon and it would continue late into the night. I never made an appearance at the party but I later heard enough about it to confirm the wisdom of my choice.

Just because I wasn't partying didn't mean I spent a quiet night at home. About 10:45 PM my home phone rang. It was the dispatcher. His voice was tense and the background chatter between patrol cars told me there was lots of action on the street. The dispatcher said there'd been an armed robbery at a motel on Arapahoe just east of Broadway. No one was injured and the armed suspect left the scene on foot. My presence was needed to process the crime scene, collect evidence and interview the victim. I told the dispatcher I'd be on the air and enroute to the scene with a few minutes. I grabbed my snub-nose 38 revolver and flashlight, jumped into the unmarked car I had brought home, and headed to the scene. As soon as the radio warmed up, I called in-service. The radio chatter left no doubt that The Hill was crawling with hippies and a full complement of foot patrolmen were making their usual contacts and arrests on the street and in the bars.

As I was arriving at the motel another drama was unfolding in the 1300 block of College Avenue. STP John and the Bishop were attracted by the noise of a party in a house just south of the Boulder Theater. Without an invitation, with no knowledge of who lived in the house or who was throwing the party, STP John and the Bishop decided they wanted to attend. Boldly they opened a side door, climbed a few steps and entered the room where the noisy party was in progress.

The renter of the house and the host of the party was a young man whose name was John Coleman. John didn't know his uninvited intruders and he didn't appreciate their rudeness. A confrontation ensued and when STP John and the Bishop refused to leave, John Coleman produced a revolver. A fight ensued. Coleman shot STP John. The Bishop pulled his hunting knife from his belt, stabbed Coleman and then ran out the door he'd entered. Coleman, who was bleeding heavily, staggered out the front door of the house, dropped his gun in the yard, crossed 13th Street and fell to the ground outside his neighbor's house.

Thirteenth and College was teeming with hippies and street freaks and many of them ran to the scene. Foot patrolmen working that area heard the gunshots, saw the commotion and they also ran to the scene. An ambulance was called as soon as Coleman was found.

All this was unfolding just after I had arrived at the motel and walked into the office. The armed robbery scene was under control and quiet. A patrolman briefed me while the owner sat at his desk hand writing a description of the robbery. According to the officer, a lone gunman had entered the office, pointed a small black handgun at the owner and demanded money. The victim opened his cash register, removed a small wad of bills and handed them to the assailant. The thief then backed out the door and fled the scene. The only thing he might have touched was the handle of the screen door when he entered the office. The first officers who responded to the robbery destroyed any fingerprints that might have been left. The robber was described as a young, white, longhaired hippy wearing dirty jeans and a tan short-sleeved T shirt and tennis shoes. There were probably several hundred people fitting that description roaming The Hill.

I began interviewing the owner when the office door flew open and another officer rushed in. He said there had been a fight on The Hill, one person had been shot and another person stabbed. Dispatch was requesting my immediate presence at the scene because there were no patrol supervisors on duty and I was the highest-ranking officer on the street. As I headed out the door the officer handed me his pack-set, and I radioed dispatch that I was back on the air and on my way to the shooting.

My adrenalin peaked as I turned onto Broadway. I had never investigated a homicide and I knew none of the department's investigators would be in any condition to assist me. With my siren screaming, I cleared a path through traffic. The fire department's rescue units had been notified and several of those emergency vehicles followed me up the Broadway hill. We all turned onto College and sent pedestrians scurrying as we passed a popular tavern, The Sink.

My mind was fixed on the importance of securing the crime scene and I was almost overwhelmed by the mob I encountered as I parked in front of the Boulder Theater. There must have been three or four hundred street people milling in the street and in Coleman's front yard. A patrolman and the firemen were assisting the ambulance crew with Coleman and another foot patrolman yelled that there was a dead body in the house south of the theater.

I ran to the house and found a third patrolman standing just outside the room containing STP John's body. I told him not to move, not to touch anything and not to allow anyone into the scene. Knowing that much of that area was under control, I stepped out the side door to begin securing the rest of the scene. I couldn't believe what happened next. There, standing directly in front of me, was a drunken hippy with a loaded 9-millimeter automatic pistol in his belt. In a calm voice, I said: "Hi!" Then, with one hand I grabbed the gun from his belt and spun him around with the other hand. I buckled his legs with mine and he fell to the ground. "Police officer," I said, "you're under arrest." At this point, more patrolmen were arriving at the scene. One of them saw me handcuffing my prisoner and he came to assist. I gave him the loaded 9-millimeter pistol and told him to transport the prisoner to the jail.

With the help of some more patrolmen I was able to clear the two front yards and that part of 13th street that lay between those yards. I directed a foot patrolman to ride with Coleman in the ambulance, to note anything he said, and to collect his clothing as physical evidence.

The scene began to quiet down after the ambulance left and that gave me the opportunity to examine the yard in front of Coleman's house. Much to my surprise, I discovered the handgun Coleman had used lying in the grass. It was amazing that someone in the crowd hadn't seen it and removed it.

For the next four hours, I sketched and photographed the scene, collected evidence and helped the coroner examine and remove STP John's body. It was the detailed work I enjoyed doing, and it was very productive. I recovered spent bullets, blood samples and fingerprints.

Just as I was about to finish processing the scene, Lt. Ruzicka appeared. His eyes were blood shot and his breath reeked of liquor. He appeared angry. He asked me why he hadn't been notified.

"Because", I said, "I figured you were at the party drunk and I felt I could handle the situation myself."

Ralph thought about that for a moment and then he asked what needed to be done next. I told him I was going to take the evidence to the police department and then I was going to try to interview Coleman. Ralph left shortly after that exchange. Instead of thanking me or complimenting me for the work I'd done, he reacted out of his fear that he might be disciplined for his absence from the scene.

Details of the shooting and the assault with a deadly weapon unfolded over the next week. I was able to determine that the hippy I'd disarmed at the scene had nothing to do with the event. He was simply at the wrong place at the wrong time carelessly carrying a loaded weapon. The Bishop hired an attorney and his lawyer brought him to the police department. He claimed Coleman fired his gun so close to his chest that he had some broken skin and powder burns. I transported the Bishop to Denver and had Dr. Orgura, a noted pathologist, examine the alleged wound. The examination proved inconclusive. I jailed the Bishop on a charge of assault with a deadly weapon.

After Coleman was released from the hospital he was transported to the Boulder County Jail and charged with homicide. His attorney asked that Coleman be placed in solitary confinement because there were many hippies in the jail who threatened to harm his client. Coleman never waived his rights to allow me to interview him. He later pled to second degree murder and was sentenced to the Colorado State Penitentiary.

It was a real challenge to conduct this investigation alone. I was proud of the results, but conflicted about my lieutenant's response. Ralph never discussed the case with me, and he was disciplined for his conduct. Eleven days after the homicide another lieutenant, Ted Koznecki, issued me a commendatory critical incident report. That report went to the chief and was placed in my personnel file.

I was also honored by the Boulder Jaycee's when they chose me as the Police Officer of the Month. Not bad for my first homicide investigation – alone.

Burglary at the Raggedy Ann Clothes Emporium

"How sweet it is!"

Ralph Cramden

It's not easy to make a living selling used clothing. The markup isn't large, the clientele isn't looking for really expensive items, and much of the cash receipts has to go to pay the rent, the help and the consignees. Every penny counts so the success of the enterprise can really suffer when some two-bit burglar steals the cash. That's exactly what happened at the Raggedy Ann Clothes Emporium on the night of November 28, 1970. Someone broke into the store and stole $60 of cash from the cash drawer under the counter. Lynne Wiarda, an employee, discovered the burglary when she opened the store for business the next day.

I was working the 6 AM to 2 PM shift in the detective bureau when Ms. Wiarda called the police department. The dispatcher requested my presence at the scene to do a crime scene search. When I arrived I immediately interviewed Lynne Wiarda. She told me the front door of the business was unlocked when she arrived at work. A key was needed to unlock the door from the outside, but anyone could simply turn a knob that unlocked the door from the inside. Unless the burglar had a key, he would have had to force his way in at some other point. I examined every possible location the burglar could have entered including all the windows, each door and the attic. I wasn't able to locate a point of entry. The only physical evidence I obtained were some fingerprints from the cash drawer, some photographs of the business and a sketch of the scene. Ms. Wiarda couldn't think of anyone capable of or interested in committing the burglary. There were no disgruntled employees, angry customers, or suspicious shoppers. I left the scene thinking that whoever had committed the crime almost certainly had used a key.

Shift change in the detective bureau occurred on the first day of each month. So, on December 1, 1970, I reported to work at 1:30 PM. For the rest of the month I would be working 2 PM to 10 PM. The first priority of my day was to brew a fresh pot of coffee. The next task I tackled was a review of all criminal complaints filed during the previous 24 hours. The first thing that caught my eye was another burglary report filed by the owner of the Raggedy Ann Clothes Emporium. The store had again been burglarized sometime after it was closed on November 29 and before the owner opened on December 1. This time the burglar removed $45 in cash and a brown fake fur vest. No evidence was collected because none of the detectives on the morning shift were dispatched to the scene. The patrol officer who took the complaint reported that the owner was unable to name any suspects or provide any leads; and again, there was no apparent point of entry.

The loss of one hundred and five dollars was bad enough, but the owner of the store would also have to pay the consignee for the vest that was missing. The situation was serious. The owner of that small business just couldn't afford to suffer another loss. His profit margin was simply too small to absorb the continued loss of money and merchandise. I felt sorry for the owner, but there was little I could do until I could develop a suspect or a lead.

The break I was hoping for came later that day. About 9:25 PM, just 35 minutes before my shift was to end, I was sitting at my desk completing the day's paperwork when my telephone extension rang. Officer Jim Smith who was assigned to the communications desk was on the other end of the line. He sounded excited as he told me he had just received an anonymous phone call from an adult male who said the Ragged Ann Clothes Emporium was going to be burglarized sometime between that time and midnight. Before Jim could ask any questions, the man hung up.

With no time to lose, I hung up the phone and yelled for my partner, Charlie Nay, to come running. He dropped what he was doing in the back room and ran to my desk. I informed him of the situation and we quickly prepared to respond to the vicinity of the store and begin a stake out. We each grabbed a pac-set and keys to two unmarked police cars. On the way out the door I told Charlie to park somewhere inconspicuous so that he could observe the alley and north side of the business and I would find a spot that would allow me to observe the business entrance and the south and west sides of the store.

The sky was dark and cloudy and the air was cold and breezy. Traffic was light. The business was located near the police department so within minutes of receiving the anonymous call I parked my vehicle in the parking lot on the east side of the old Boulder school administration building. I was less than half a block from Raggedy Ann and I had an unobstructed view of the business. I turned off my headlights and the only noise to break the silence was an occasional message over my police radio.

One minute after parking something almost unbelievable happened. I saw a person open the front door of the clothes emporium, step out, close the door and begin walking toward the street. Adrenalin shot through my body and my heart began to pound with excitement. I started my car and began driving toward the person. By the time I had driven the half block that separated us, the suspect had walked into the Presbyterian Church parking lot directly south of the clothing store. I drove into the parking lot and stopped right next to the person who I could now see was a young male. My unmarked car and street clothes left him with no idea who I was.

"Hi", I said in a friendly voice, "I'm lost can you help me?"

"Sure", the male responded.

I opened my door, stepped out of the car, pulled my badge from my rear pocket and informed him I was Detective Andrews of the Boulder Police. Before he could say anything, I asked him his name.

"Kenney Shuler", he said.

"Where did you just come from?" was my next question.

"Across the street", he said.

At that point I grabbed Kenney Shuler by the front of his coat and threw him across the hood of my car as I was telling him he was under arrest for investigation of burglary. I frisked the young man quickly. He didn't have a weapon, however when my hands reached his coat pockets I could feel a large amount of loose change.

My car was still running and the driver's door was standing open. I grabbed the collar of Shuler's coat and forced him into the driver's door of my vehicle. He landed partly on the front seat and partly on the floor of the front passenger side. I shoved him aside and got behind the wheel. I told Shuler to keep his hands on the dashboard and in my sight. I put my car in reverse and my wheels spun as I backed from the church parking lot into the parking lot just west of the clothing store. I stopped, put the car in park, grabbed my mike and informed Charlie and the dispatcher that I had a burglary suspect in custody and needed assistance at the front of the Raggedy Ann store. Without waiting for a response, I again took hold of Shuler's coat and pulled him out of the car. As we were getting out, the front door of the clothing store opened again and another male stepped out. Now my heart was racing. I threw Shuler to the ground. He landed face down at my feet. I put my foot on the back of his neck, drew my gun and yelled to the male at the door of the clothing store to lay face down on the ground. To my surprise and relief, he did everything I ordered him to do.

Within moments, Corp. Al Staehle and Detective Nay arrived. I told Corporal Staehle to search and handcuff Kenney Shuler as Charlie and I moved toward the other suspect. The quiet night was filled with screaming sirens as Charlie and I frisked and handcuffed the second suspect. Officer Bob Hendry was the next patrolman to arrive at the scene. I had him take custody of the second suspect while Charlie and I entered the store to search for additional burglars.

We didn't find any more suspects, but I was so full of adrenalin that I felt I could tackle an elephant as I stepped out of the store. We had interrupted and in-progress burglary and arrested two felons without injury to anyone. Both suspects were in our custody and it appeared they were in possession of stolen cash. That kind of arrest doesn't happen very often, and when it does those involved feel a deep sense of pride and accomplishment. Frankly there have been few times in my life that I have experienced such satisfying excitement.

Both suspects were transported to the police department where they were photographed, fingerprinted and interrogated. We were able to determine that Kenney Shuler was 14 years old and his partner, the second burglar, was Randy Evans, age 15. Evans had a prior arrest on his record for carrying a sawed-off rifle. Both boy's parents were notified, but only Kenney's mother was willing to respond to the police department. In the presence of his mother, Kenney Shuler admitted that he and Randy had committed all three burglaries. They had used a ladder to gain access to the rear roof of the business and had removed a pane of glass from a second- floor window which enabled them to unlock the window and enter the premises. After each burglary, they had again used the ladder and replaced the windowpane. Both boys were booked into the juvenile quarters of the Boulder County Jail. I was never able to identify the anonymous caller.

The owner of Raggedy Ann's Clothing was delighted to receive some of the cask taken in the earlier burglaries, the stolen vest and the $46 cash found in Shuler's coat at the time of his arrest. I was delighted to have arrested two punks and recovered that stolen property. It just doesn't get any better than that. Like Ralph Cramden used to say: "How sweet it is!"

Bomb Squad

"When you get hungry enough, you find yourself speaking Spanish pretty well"

Josh Gibson on playing baseball in Cuba

It's said that necessity is the mother of invention. That was certainly true in Boulder in 1970.

At that time the United States was deeply involved in a war in Viet Nam and radical groups opposed to the war were active on college campuses. The University of Colorado was no exception. Students for a Democratic Society (SDS), the Weathermen, and the Black Panthers had active support in Boulder. Citizens commonly encountered anti-war rallies, marches and demonstrations on campus and on the streets around The Hill business district.

The rhetoric turned violent. Early in 1970 a gasoline bomb gutted the Air Force R.O.T.C. headquarters in Folsom Stadium. The bombers spray-painted the words "Viet Cong", "Napalm ROTC" and "Imperialism Burns" on the walls outside the damaged offices. The following day an explosion damaged several parked campus police cars. Then in March of 1970 a dynamite bomb blew a 12 X 18-inch hole in the roof of Macky Auditorium causing $5,000 damage. Another explosion damaged the Behavioral Science building on the University campus. Then on the 4th of March the Boulder Police became the next target. Several separate explosions damaged the roof of the police department and a patrol car was damaged when a stick of dynamite was thrown under the vehicle shortly after an on-duty officer parked it at the municipal building.

Officers from the police and fire departments were assigned to investigate the bombings, but neither department had personnel equipped or trained to handle live explosives or bombs. I was a sergeant in the detective division at the time and part of my responsibility was to respond to and investigate all suspicious fires and explosions. The sudden onset of explosions prompted fire Lt. Rod Woods and me to jointly write a letter to both the police and fire chiefs requesting the formation of a bomb squad. Unfortunately, the lack of funds prevented both departments from taking action on the request. However, there was plenty of "action" on the streets as the city continued to experience explosions and bomb threats.

One afternoon a metal film can containing an M-80 firecracker, black powder and metal pellets was confiscated during an arrest on The Hill. Confiscation of the small explosive device prevented the possibility of serious personal injury. Soon after that incident a Boulder police officer observed a hippy place another can in the gutter in the 1100 block of 13th street. The hippy tried to light a piece of paper protruding from the device. The hippy ran when a police officer approached. Fortunately, the device had failed to light. The small homemade bomb was a metal band-aid can which contained 409 grams of #4 shotgun pellets and 42 grams of gunpowder. Had that anti-personnel bomb functioned numerous by-standers would have sustained injuries from the metal shrapnel.

Nationally, Viet Nam War protesters and student radicals were targeting financial institutions. So it was no surprise when bombs were discovered at several Boulder banks. An Arapahoe National Bank employee was surprised when he opened a window curtain and discovered a glass wine bottle filled with gasoline sitting on the windowsill. A can filled with black powder was attached to the bottle with duct tape, and a crude ignition system protruded from the can's lid. Someone had ignited the fuse but it extinguished before the gasoline bomb exploded.

I am examining the bomb. Charlie Nay, Chief Vendel and Detective Tom Blowers are standing around the corner from the bomb.

On May 5, 1971, John Rogers, a janitor at the United Bank of Boulder discovered a brown paper sack sitting on the sidewalk just outside the front door of the bank. When he opened the top of the sack he was shocked to see a clock, wires and a large pipe bomb. He ran to a phone and called the police department. Officers responded and evacuated four city blocks surrounding the bank.

The police dispatcher called me at home and told me to respond to the scene to evaluate the situation. (How dumb, I wasn't trained at that point!) A patrolman was dispatched from the police department with the only equipment the department owned, an old military flak jacket and a bomb blanket designed to lay on top of small bombs. I put the flak jacket on, approached the paper sack and carefully looked inside. My heart stopped. I could clearly see a pipe bomb lying below a battery and a clock. The bomb was armed and wired to blow up. The wiring was simple and it was obvious that all the connections were in place and the device should be functioning. But nothing had happened. I slowly backed away and called the dispatcher on the radio to request the assistance of Jim Jordan, a trained bomb technician for the Colorado Bureau of Investigation.

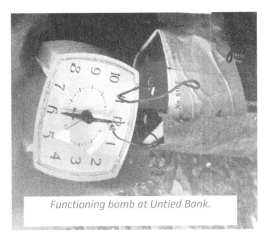

Functioning bomb at Untied Bank.

Agent Jordon responded to the scene. He and I were able to dismantle and examine the bomb. The pipe was filled with black powder and the ignition system had been functioning, but an air pocket between the igniter and the black power prevented an explosion. Had either Mr. Rogers or I moved that bomb before it was dismantled the black powder would have shifted and the bomb would have exploded.

Chief Don Vendel was present at that scene. That incident led to the decision that a bomb squad would be formed under the direction and control of the police department. Chief Vendel selected me to be the first member. I remember being surprised by that choice. I told the chief that I probably wasn't the best choice because I was mechanically inept. In fact, I told him I owned two screwdrivers and I wasn't sure which one was a Philips head. He laughed and walked away. It was obvious I was his choice.

I attended and successfully completed numerous training courses including Improvised Explosive Devices School at the Redstone Arsenal located at the U. S. Army Missile and Munitions Center in Huntsville, Alabama, a course offered by the Alcohol. Tobacco and Firearms Division of the United States Department of Treasury, and a course offered by the Colorado Metropolitan Arson Investigators Association. Shortly after my return from Huntsville, I selected Det. Sgt. Charlie Nay; and, later Officer William Kingston to be trained as bomb technicians.

Upon my return from Huntsville funds were made available to purchase the tools and equipment that was needed. The squad was given keys to a small concrete explosives magazine located in the city yards that was to be used to store dynamite and confiscated explosives.

As the number of bomb incidents continued to increase, so did the need for a vehicle to transport explosives. The cost of commercially-built bomb trailers began around $7,000. There were no funds to cover that expense. Members of the squad began to explore ways to build a home-made bomb trailer. Creativity was born out of necessity. A trailer frame was obtained from a wrecking yard and a Boulder metal fabricating company agreed to donate the labor to build and attach a wooden box to the frame. A Denver aircraft-wrecking yard donated two

Boeing 727 aircraft tires. The tires were placed one on top of the other and held in place with four metal cables. The tires were then filled with sand that was held in place by a cardboard tube. The entire cost of the complete bomb trailer was $150!

A vehicle was needed to pull the trailer. The squad asked the city yards to donate a half-ton Chevy pickup truck that was scheduled for sale at auction. An agreement was reached giving the squad the transportation it needed. A volunteer rescue group, the Boulder Emergency Squad, had a large garage with an empty bay at the city yards. The bomb squad was given permission to store its truck and trailer in the empty bay. All this goes to prove that "if you ask, you shall receive!"

I am wearing the bomb vest and head shield next to our truck

Once word got out that the police department had people and equipment to handle explosives, the calls for assistance began to grow. Over the next two years the bomb squad responded to several hundred calls to examine, remove and destroy all sorts of dangerous chemicals and explosives. Since Boulder County once had many operating mines, dynamite and blasting caps were common items discovered in old homes and garages.

One of the most unusual calls occurred in August 1972 when a curator at the museum on the Colorado University campus discovered boxes containing World War I explosive ordnance. Apparently someone donated the items and they were then stored among other relics and forgotten. Among the items removed by the squad were four live German hand grenades, three boxes of machine gun ammunition, 11 boxes of live rifle cartridges, 20mm anti-tank shells and 75mm time fuse shells. The pins on several of the grenades were in advanced stage of corrosion. Classrooms in several buildings had to be evacuated for several hours while the ordnance was carefully removed. The items were placed in the magazine and US Army ordinance officers from Fort Carson army base responded and disposed of the items.

A Jewish CU student provided the squad with its first exposure to a possible mail bomb. The young man had received a package in the mail from Tel Aviv. He didn't think he knew anyone in Tel Aviv and he feared the package was a bomb. The package was taken to the city yards where it was carefully opened. To everyone's relief the package contained a geometry book that had been sent by a distant relative of the student.

The package from Tel Aviv made the bomb squad aware of its need for some more costly equipment. A portable X-Ray machine was needed to examine closed containers like packages, suitcases and brief cases. Necessity would again generate invention. Charlie and I decided to make a search of the United States government surplus outlet in Glendale, Colorado. To our surprise and delight we were able to find a new military surplus portable X-ray unit. We also obtained film and lead aprons, all for the paltry sum of one dollar.

In 1974 we received a call from the Boulder County Health Department. During an examination of a closet which contained old Civil Defense materials, someone detected an unusual odor. Upon close inspection, they found 666 quarter-pound cans of anesthetic ether. Some of the cans were corroded and leaking small amounts of ether. We examined the closet and decided to move the cans to our disposal site at the city yards. We notified the fire department, and evacuated the building. The fire department responded with several trucks. We informed the firemen that we would remove the cans and place them in the bomb trailer and then transport them to the city yards. We could only safely carry about 100 cans per trip. One fire truck remained at the site and the second truck followed us as we made each trip. The cans were placed in our burn pit at the yards. After all the cans were moved, we burned them. Ether is highly flammable and the resulting fire was impressive.

All my life I wanted to ride on the back of a fire truck. On one of the trips to the yard I asked permission to ride on the back of the fire truck that was following our truck and trailer.

To my delight my request was approved. What fun!

In 1974 the city as again rocked by a number of major explosions. The Koenig Alumni Center on the CU campus was the scene of an attempted firebombing. Several Molotov cocktails were thrown through a window and they failed to explode. Then, within a month, the Boulder Valley Education Center sustained $100,000 damage when an arson fire gutted a meeting room in the center's east wing.

Figure 1I'm placing unexploded dynamite in the bomb trailer at the Courthouse explosion

Two days later, Flatirons Elementary School was the target of a bomb blast that caused $15,000 in damage.

Dynamite explosions also damaged the Boulder County Court House and the University's security offices. No injuries were reported. Those explosions occurred near the time several Chicanos were scheduled to appear in court to answer charges stemming from participation in a disturbance during a speech on the campus.

On the evening of May 27, 1974, the city was rocked by a powerful explosion at Chautauqua Park in which three people were killed. Forty-eight hours later three more people died in another car explosion in the parking lot of the Pudlik Liquor Store. Details of those deaths and the resulting actions by the bomb squad are contained in another chapter of this book.

All three members of the squad were required to be available 24 hours a day, 7 days a week. We all carried pagers, and we were given an extra $100 a month as hazardous duty pay. Each of us were assigned full time responsibilities separate from the bomb squad, but we were expected to set those responsibilities aside and respond to all calls for the bomb squad.

By 1975 the squad was handling so many explosive items that we had out-grown the concrete explosive magazine in the city yards. Newly purchased City of Boulder green belt land had a large explosives magazine we were able to use. The Rocky Flats plant south of Boulder provided us with space for disposal of hazardous material.

Explosives Magazine

Surprisingly, it isn't uncommon for people to forget their suitcases and briefcases when they are out and about. In the mid-1970s Boulder residents were so on-edge that they would call the police when they encountered an unattended suitcase or briefcase. We were called to evaluate the circumstances. Usually we would either X-Ray the item or blow it open with a handy device called a water cannon. The cannon was built by a local tool and die company using plans obtained from the Redstone Arsenal. It used a 12-gauge shotgun shell to propel water at very high pressure. The cannon could be operated remotely, and it was so effective that it often left only debris in its wake. We would load the cannon by placing a condom filled with water into the cavity of the cannon. Every six months we would obtain a purchase order from the city's purchasing agent to buy a box of condoms. Talk about necessity leading to invention!!

A funny incident involving the water cannon occurred when Cameron Bishop, a man who had once been on the FBI's 10 most wanted list for bombing four Colorado high voltage towers, was invited to speak at CU's University Memorial Center after his release from prison. Just before he was to speak the University police were notified that a suitcase had been abandoned at the north entrance to the UMC. They evacuated the area and called the bomb squad.

Charlie picked up the bomb truck and I responded from home. Carol happened to be going downtown so she drove me to the scene. Unknown to me, after dropping me off, she parked the car and joined the crowd of people who were watching the squad from a distance.

Charlie and I examined the suitcase and decided we would open it with the water cannon. It took us little time to get everything set, but finally we were able to discharge the cannon and blow the suitcase apart. Carol had gotten bored waiting for something to happen and she was walking back to the car when the cannon was fired. The stone buildings on campus amplified the loud noise of the cannon. When Carol heard the noise she thought the suitcase had blown up. She ran back to the scene to see if Charlie or I had been injured. She was relieved to see that we were safe and had successfully destroyed the suitcase that only contained clothes.

On September 4, 1975, the Louisville police department called us to one of the most dangerous situations we ever encountered. A woman living in Louisville sold a large rabbit hut to her neighbor. As the neighbor began to move the old hut he discovered it contained 100 pounds (192 sticks) of crystallized dynamite. The date on the dynamite was November and December of 1947!

When sticks of dynamite sit for long periods of time without being moved, their nitro glycerin seeps out of the sticks, dries and crystals form between the sticks and any surface the sticks rest on. In this situation, the bottoms of both boxes were lined with crystals. If the fragile crystals break the dynamite explodes.

After the discovery, the neighbor called the police who in turn called in several "powder monkeys" (explosives experts) from Explosive Fabricators, a Louisville Company that used explosives to manufacture metal products. They took one look at the boxes and refused to provide any assistance due to the danger involved. They suggested the Boulder bomb squad handle the mess.

Charlie, Bill and I responded with the truck and bomb trailer. We decided the best method of destruction would be to burn it. However, we couldn't burn the dynamite at the scene because the heat from the fire could cause the nitro to explode. We had to transport both boxes out of town to a site that provided protection in case of an explosion.

We selected a site near town. We knew we couldn't use the bomb trailer to transport the dynamite because it would provide such a rough ride the crystals would fracture and explode. We decided to use Charlie's convertible. I sat in the back seat with the top down. Together, Charlie and Bill carried the first box of crystallized dynamite and placed it in my lap. My lap provided the box with a soft cushion and I had absolute control over its movement. Charlie then drove me to the site where we had prepared a burn pit. Louisville police stood guard at the site while we returned and repeated the process with the second box. Once both boxes were in place they were torched. The fire completely consumed the boxes and the dynamite was safely destroyed. You can imagine how relieved we were when that task was completed.

Of all the different responsibilities, I fulfilled on the police department, working on the bomb squad was by far my favorite. Each call required creative thinking, ingenuity and resourcefulness. No one, **and I mean no one** ever second-guessed us and we could depend on complete privacy as we worked. It was a dream job for an introvert! And there is no doubt that our work saved lives and property.

Six Killed in 48 Hours

"I've developed a new philosophy, I only dread life one day at a time"

Charlie Brown, Charles Schulz's "Peanuts"

On the night of the Chautauqua bombing, Dave and Kathy Van Liere were visiting us at our home on South 43rd Street. We'd had a pleasant evening, and as Dave and Kathy were preparing to leave our conversation was interrupted by the sound of a loud explosion. We all commented on the noise, but almost immediately, the conversation returned to the farewells we were exchanging

Moments after the Van Lieres drove away the telephone rang. The Boulder police dispatcher hastily told me that a car had exploded near the auditorium at Chautauqua Park and I was to respond to the scene immediately. I told the dispatcher to notify my partner, Det. Charlie Nay, tell him to get the bomb truck and meet me at the scene. I changed into my bomb squad cover-alls, grabbed my flashlight and snub nosed revolver, and drove to the scene.

As I pulled into Chautauqua Park I could see flashing red lights on a number of police cars and fire trucks parked on the southwest side of the old Chautauqua auditorium. Search lights

from the fire department aerial truck were trained on what was left of a sedan. The vehicle's roof and doors were missing and there was debris scattered in all directions around the car.

I notified the command officer at the scene that I had arrived and I told him that no one was to go near that vehicle until Charlie and I had completely searched it for unexploded bomb material and additional explosive devices. He assured me that no one had approached the car and nothing further would be done until our search was complete.

Car destroyed by bomb explosion

Charlie, arrived minutes later. We both put on flak jackets and helmets. Then we carried our tool kit to a spot near the vehicle. As we were doing this the fire department began moving all of its trucks away from the vehicle. I went to the fire department's commanding officer and asked him to leave the aerial truck in place so the search lights would illuminate the scene. He said no because he couldn't place his men in such

144

a dangerous position. He said that if another bomb detonated it would severely damage their truck and equipment. He apologized, then he ordered all of his trucks pulled back 500 feet from the vehicle we were about to search.

Well, that felt dark and lonely. The only light Charlie and I had to conduct our search was our flashlights. I was angry, but deep down I thought the fire commander's decision probably made sense.

As we approached the car we could detect several distinct odors. The acrid odor of detonated explosives hung in the air, gasoline from the vehicle's fuel tank was evident as was the smell of dead human bodies.

Car destroyed by bomb

When I mentioned the odors to Charlie he said: "Smells like hell, doesn't it?" He meant that both literally and figuratively. There was a trail of blood that went in a northwesterly direction from the passenger door. Charlie shined his flashlight on the trail of blood. About 50 feet from the car, his light illuminated a human leg. This was the first confirmation that someone had died in the explosion. We stepped to the west side of the car and stood still as we shined our flashlights through the car. Among the debris on the vehicle floor were several human feet. This told us that more than one person had literally been blown to bits.

We spent the next hour carefully sifting through the debris in and around the car. It was clear that the explosion had occurred in the front seat of the vehicle. The roof had been blown up and back. The doors had been blown out, and the front dash board had been blown forward. We located six human feet. Some were in the floorboard, one was west of the car and one east of the car. The upper portion of the bodies had been blown out of the car to the north. All this information told us that there were three people sitting in the front seat. The explosive device had been sitting in the lap of the center person when it detonated.

We did not find any additional explosive devices or undetonated explosives. When our search ended, we turned the scene over to the detectives so they could process it for physical evidence. One detective was assigned to debrief Charlie and me.

It was a real relief to have that search completed. I remember feeling the tension leave my body as the detective began the interview. Charlie had an odd sense of humor that came to the surface when he was under stress. When the detective interviewing us said: "I understand you found six human feet. Are you sure we only have three dead bodies?" Charlie answered: "Yea, we found six feet. Four left and two right feet." The detective sat in silence for a moment. Then he rose to inform his commander that there were four dead bodies. Charlie grabbed his arm. "I'm kidding, he said, "three left feet and three right feet."

Det. Capt. Kelly Gaskill would later speculate to the news media that the three people, a man and two women, were assembling a dynamite time bomb when the device exploded. Deputy Chief Lowell Friesen described the scene to reporters saying: "The floorboard went south, the seats went north, and the car doors went east and west." He told the news media that human remains were found more than 100 yards from the point of explosion.

Charlie and I were released from the scene at 4AM. We went home exhausted. We got several hours of sleep and then we both had to work our regular patrol shifts the following day.

When that shift ended at 10 PM, I was tired. I remember getting ready for bed as soon as I arrived home. As I was sitting on the edge of the bed taking my sox off when another loud explosion rocked the city. Carol was in the bedroom with me. I looked at her and said: "Damn, here we go again!" Sure enough, the phone rang moments later. Dispatch informed me that another car had blown up. The vehicle was in the parking lot just north of Pudlik's Liquor Store on 28th Street. I was told there were dead bodies at the scene, fire and police units were enroute, and I was to respond immediately.

When I got to the scene I was told there were three dead bodies in the vehicle and one person had been taken by ambulance to Boulder Community Hospital in very critical

Second car destroyed by bomb

condition. The explosion had badly damaged the vehicle and the interior had sustained fire damage. The Burger King and Pudlik's Liquor had been evacuated so that the bomb squad could make a search of the scene for additional explosives and explosive devices.

Charlie arrived at almost exactly the same time I did. He went to the rear of the car to begin a search. I went to the front of the car. Again, we had to use flashlights because the fire department would not provide lighting and the explosion had blown out all the streetlights.

It was dark, quiet and eerie. Just as I reached the front of the vehicle the car battery shorted, causing the horn to blow. I froze in place thinking another bomb had exploded. After I caught my breath I disconnected the battery to stop the noise.

This search, too, took about one hour and turned up one item of interest. We found an unopened gas can just west of the car. We used our equipment to remotely jar the can. Nothing happened indicating the can was safe. We turned the can and the scene over to the detectives to begin their crime scene search.

People throughout the city were frightened. From 11:30 PM that evening until 10:30 AM the next morning, Charlie and I were dispatched to six different locations to investigate suspected explosive devices. Numerous businesses received bomb threats. Even the firemen at the 30th and Arapahoe station requested a search of their vehicles for bombs. It was a wild and exhausting night for the bomb squad.

It was difficult to identify the victims of the two explosions because of the massive injuries and dismemberment that occurred. But as identities were made it became apparent that the victims were active in Chicano organizations that championed radical Mexican-American issues. The three dead bodies in the Chautauqua bombing were identified as Reyes Martinez, an activist attorney, Una Ashley Jaakola, 24, and Neva Arlene Romero, 20, daughter of the mayor of Ignacio, Colorado. The investigation revealed that all three were sitting in the front seat of the vehicle with Martinez in the driver's seat, Miss Romero seated in the middle holding the bomb, and Jaakola to her right.

The vehicle involved in the second explosion was registered to an employee of the Platte Valley Action Center in Denver. The owner had lent the vehicle to another employee who was the 1972 LA Raza Unida candidate for the University of Colorado board of regents. Those three victims were identified as 31-year-old Florencio Granado, 24-year-old Heriberto Teran, and 20-year-old Francisco Dougherty. All three men had recently moved to Denver from Laredo, Texas. The fourth victim who survived but was severely injured was 23-year-old Antonio Alcantar of Denver.

Investigators later determined that the occupants of both cars brought the bombs to Boulder. The explosions occurred as someone in each vehicle was attaching the detonating device. Both times they incorrectly wired the bomb and it exploded.

The intended target was unknown; however, it appeared that the target was probably either the police department, the sheriff's office or the county court house. Some time prior to the explosion four Chicanos had been charged with the disruption of a speech by Texas Representative Henry Gonzales at the University of Colorado. One man had his charges dismissed, a second who was sentenced to 60 days appeared in court just one day after the explosion in Chautauqua Park. The second bomb went off on the night before one of the defendants was originally scheduled to go on trial. Reyes Martinez, one of the Chautauqua Park victims, was an attorney in the case. All the victims knew each other.

Two days after the second explosion a Colorado State Patrol officer stopped a young woman for a minor traffic violation on the Boulder turnpike at Broomfield. During the stop the officer informed the woman she was going to be arrested. She asked permission to retrieve items from her car. With permission, she walked to her car, got in and drove off. She was chased to the exit ramp at 28th street and Baseline where Boulder Police had established a roadblock. Her vehicle was stopped and she was arrested.

The woman was verbally abusive and insisted that her car not be searched. An officer spotted a kitchen-timing device in the back seat. The woman's place of employment indicated that she probably knew the people who had died in the two fatal bombings. Officers at the scene requested the bomb squad respond to conduct a vehicle search.

Charlie and I were briefed when we arrived at the scene. The situation forced us to conduct our search from a distance using ropes and pulleys. Though both of us had been trained to conduct a search that way, we had never actually done it. We organized our equipment and began the detailed and time-consuming work. As time passed a crowd gathered on the 28th street bridge and along Baseline. Television news crews arrived and began photographing the scene.

Charlie and I Remotely opening car

We successfully gained entry into the car and checked the interior. Then we remotely removed the rear seat so we could gain entry into the trunk. Slowly and carefully I crawled through that opening and entered the trunk. The space was small and cramped. Using a flashlight, I could see everywhere except the wheel well where the spare tire usually sits. The tire was missing. I slowly reached into the wheel well and when my hand touched something it began to hiss loudly. It sounded like a dynamite fuse had been lit and was burning. Unable to see what it was, I wasted no time backing out of the trunk. Unfortunately, I was wearing the cheap surplus military flak jacket and it got caught on the metal attachment that held the back seat in place. I couldn't move.

I hollered for help. Charlie leaned in and dislodged the jacket, then both of us scrambled out of the car and ran to our truck. Our actions startled the crowd that was watching from a distance. When the spectators saw us running, they, too began to run.

Nothing happened. We returned to the car. This time we opened the trunk with a key and found the source of the noise. I had touched the base of an up-side-down aerosol can causing the spray head to function. The noise I heard was the spray from a can of carpet cleaner.

The search ended with nothing unusual found. That week ended with approval for the bomb squad's request for a bomb suit, a portable generator and equipment to light a bomb scene. It also ended with some extra time off to catch up on a lot of lost sleep.

A Rough Ride on the Way to the Funeral Home

"There is a time for departure even when there's no certain place to go."

Tennessee Williams

Myron Teegarden, long-time chief of the Boulder Police Department, interviewed and then hired me in 1966. Starting pay was $490 a month and no one received overtime pay. Carol had to work to supplement my salary. All patrol officers had to endure frequent (monthly) shift changes that created stress on family life. About half of all the officers were divorced. In spite of all that, there was nothing I wanted more than to work on the police department.

Don Vendel was appointed police chief in 1967. He had a wonderful reputation as a hard-working, highly respected investigator. Men on the department looked forward to his promotion and there was a lot of genuine excitement when it occurred.

It was common knowledge that Don Vendel was a committed Christian. There was no problem with that until he imposed his moral standards on his officers. Sylvia Pettem, in her book *Behind the Badge,* (p214) summarized the situation saying: Chief Vendel was "a highly religious and moral man who expected his officers to follow his own strict code of conduct. While the average residents of Boulder could frequent the newly opened bars, Vendel opposed drinking and wouldn't even allow his officers, off-duty and out of uniform, to go in a bar within the Boulder city-limits. The only permissible alcoholic drink was with a meal in a restaurant with family and friends."

"In addition, Vendel prescribed a strict code for his officers' hairstyles, and he prohibited any officer from living with a woman out of wedlock. Instead of changing with the times, Vendel turned back the clock to Victorian and turn-of-the-twentieth-century values. His police officers were regular middle-class working people, and they didn't like being denied their personal freedoms." (p214)

It became common knowledge that many of the officers were upset with the requirements the chief imposed, but that didn't bother me. I respected Chief Vendel. I was glad he had replaced Chief Teegarden and I felt comfortable working under Vendel's code of conduct because I never participated in conduct that would have violated the rules and regulations. I believed he was doing all he could to professionalize the department.

Within 2 ½ years I was promoted to the rank of sergeant. Several years later I was again promoted. I had gone from being a police officer on the street to a felony investigator to an administrative assistant to the chief of police. In 1973 the chief nominated me to attend the FBI National Academy in Quantico, Virginia. I was selected and was one of two officers from Colorado to attend the 93rd Session. Upon my return I again found myself in the patrol division, this time as a command officer.

During those years, Boulder experienced major changes that affected the city's crime rate. The hippy scene grew and with it came drugs and street crime. It was not unusual for more than 1,000 "street freaks" to congregate in The Hill business district every afternoon and evening. The situation became so serious that a police substation was opened in The Hill mall in April of 1971. It was not unusual for the afternoon shift to include 7 two-man foot patrol teams, a scout car and a paddy-wagon just to patrol The Hill. One month after the sub-station opened an all-out riot followed the arrest of fourteen people on The Hill. The Denver Police sent its helicopter, and our officers were only able to bring order after all the department's tear gas was expended.

The Viet Nam war expanded and so did student unrest. In May of 1972 3,000 students blocked U.S.36 near the campus, and all of our officers again found themselves engaged in a riot. "In September 1972, a city-sponsored study called the Summer-Hill Report identified two groups of people in The Hill neighborhood. They were either "transients on the road to maturity," or "street people on a path to self-destruction" according to Pettem. Burglaries, armed robberies, and the sale and use of drugs increased and impacted the city.

During those busy years "an era of infighting crept into the Boulder Police Department." The Boulder Police Benefit Association, which for years had been a social club, became a union that "represented the police in collective bargaining and in handling disputes with management" she said. The BPBA began actively opposing departmental rules, regulations and policies and provided officers with representation when they were accused of misconduct.

Chief Vendel continued to enforce his code of conduct which led to the firing of several officers. Then, "in 1974, Chief Vendel was investigated by the U. S. Department of Labor for allegedly misusing a federal grant for surveillance of his own officers. Supposedly, the money bought an agent whose duties were mainly confined to internal police spying" Pettem wrote. He was cleared, but the allegations only fueled the animosity between management and the officers.

When I was functioning as an administrative assistant to the chief, I was once ordered to conduct surveillance on a command officer the chief suspected to be involved in a violation of the department's code of conduct. I worked that unsuccessful surveillance for less than a week. That experience gave me an appreciation for the difficulties faced by internal investigation units.

An attorney who represented the union conducted an inquiry into the internal affairs of the police department. In the attorney's report to City Manager Archie Twitchell, he wrote that the Boulder Police Department 'has been a rigid, virtually dictatorial system lacking in communication, openness, consistency and predictability, and is infected with fear, mistrust, and an Orwellian big-brotherism. Boulder was experiencing frequent anti-war demonstrations, the crime rate was extremely high, and the city was full of drug addicts.

There was tension on the street and there was tension within the department. It was a tough environment to work in and being a supervisor made it even more stressful.

When Vendel retired in November 1974, he was quoted saying, "It was a good job which had its aches and pains. But you get to a point when you just don't enjoy it anymore." I had to agree.

There was a lot of speculation about who would replace him. I remember many conversations with other members of the command staff. We were all hopeful the new chief would be someone who could bring peace and unity to the department. We were in for a disappointment.

Rather than replace Vendel with someone from within the department, John Barber, campus chief of police at the University of California at Santa Cruz was hired. Barber had once served in the Los Angeles County Sheriff's Department. Instead of bringing peace and unity to the department, Barber brought confusion and disorder. Again quoting Sylvia Pettem's book, "As 'Mr. Nice Guy,' Barber tried to establish an easy-going and relaxed atmosphere in the department. He tried to be everybody's friend." We didn't need a friend, we needed a professional leader.

Barber participated in a number of out-of-town conferences. "He was often criticized by the union for attending three-day seminars that turned into two-week absences."

That wasn't all he was criticized for. Many were critical of his failure to delegate authority. "In an interview … with *Boulder Monthly Magazine*, former chief Teegarden was asked about the city's problems with the police department. 'It started with that nut Barber, the way he dealt with the BPBA,' Teegarden stated, 'I heard the news one morning that the union had presented demands or something of the sort regarding shift changes or the like. Barber just accepted their demands and might as well have said, 'You run the department.' The damn fool, no wonder they're having problems. A police department is a quasi-military organization. You just can't do that," Pettem wrote.

But that is what he did and his actions left me more and more dissatisfied with my work. I wanted out. Carol and I spent time every day talking about the mess and exploring future work options. Police departments do not have lateral entry options. If I quit the department I would have to start all over again in a new department. I wasn't interested in that option. A sociology degree didn't provide me with credentials employers were interested in; I'd need at least a master degree to find employment. I felt like I was between the proverbial rock and a hard place.

Faith Provides the Answer

"Faith is more than thinking something is true. Faith is thinking something is true to the extent that we act on it."

W. T. Purkiser

Where was God in all this? To begin with, God was not in the picture. When I joined the police department church attendance became less and less important to me. When I worked graveyard shift I would arrive home at 6:30 AM too tired to go to church. When I worked day shift I was usually scheduled to work on Sunday.

Work became so important to me that it became my god. It provided me with the status I wanted. It was my identity. If someone were to ask me who I was I would reply: "I'm a policeman." I would not have replied: "I'm a Christian." My work gave me pleasure, success and confidence. I'm ashamed to say that nothing was more important than my work; not God, my wife, or my family. But all that was about to change.

At times the stress at work was almost unbearable. It left me feeling there was no one I could turn to for guidance. The situation was beyond my control and I had no confidence the future would be any better. I began to pray, asking God for help.

Carol was active in St. Aiden's Episcopal Church. One Sunday she came home excited about a diocesan weekend retreat scheduled to occur at the YMCA camp in Estes Park. She asked me to attend it with her. I consented and we went. The conference was designed to renew and deepen one's faith in God. Bishop William Frey and Fr. Terry Fullum were the featured speakers. The worship and music was led by a group called The Fisher Folk. It had been years since I'd opened myself to God. I was inspired by the teaching, the worship and the beautiful music. I returned home glad I'd gone

Several months later, Christ Episcopal Church in Denver planned a Renewal Weekend and someone who met us at the diocesan renewal conference suggested Carol and I as discussion group leaders. We were surprised when we received the letter requesting our involvement. We discussed it and decided to accept. The weekend was to begin Friday afternoon and continue through Sunday afternoon. Leaders were invited to sleep in the homes of church members. When we accepted we informed the church we would be driving back to Boulder each night.

Friday evening began with a potluck meal followed by an excellent presentation by Lyn Alexander, a Canon City businessman. He talked about his commitment to the Lord, explaining that he had given his business to God. He treated his business as if God owned it and he was working for the Lord. He said he didn't make a decision without first praying for guidance. I'd never heard anything like that. I was impressed and I left that presentation thinking that if I owned a business that is the way I would operate.

After the presentation, we were introduced to Bob and Robin Holmes and told that we would be staying with them at their house for the night. What? We were planning on going home. As it turned out, Bob was the Englewood Chief of Police. I didn't know him, but I did know who he was. We accepted the invitation.

Bob and Robin were new in their commitment to the Lord. They were trying to find ways to live out their faith just as we were. After we arrived at their home we found that we had so much in common that we talked until after mid-night. We shared our Christian faith, our love of the Lord and our desire to lead Christian lives. The rest of the presentations and the following night with the Holmes was a blessing.

Shortly after that weekend my father called and told me the funeral home in Castle Rock was going to be sold and he wanted to offer it to Carol and me before he placed it on the open market. My parents had two funeral homes that were located 90 miles apart and they had reached the age that it was just too difficult to run two 24 hour-a-day businesses. I told him I would pray about it.

We talked and we prayed and then we discussed it some more. We even bought a pad of newsprint, placed it on a stand and wrote list after list of the pros and cons of quitting the police department and buying the funeral home. Finally, we came to the conclusion that if the Lord wanted us to make that change we had to step out in faith and begin the process of purchasing the business. We felt that if that was the way we were being led then doors would open to help us accomplish that. Everything we did to enable the purchase seemed blessed as matters at the police department only got worse.

We drove to Castle Rock and spent a weekend with my parents discussing the details. They set a reasonable price on the business which included a home for us to raise our small family. The purchase included the monument business and an established pre-need funeral trust account. My father owned four apartment buildings and several houses in Castle Rock, and I agreed to manage those properties. We ended the weekend by signing an agreement to purchase the business.

The following Monday morning I walked into Chief Barber's office and gave him notice I'd be resigning in two weeks. He was shocked, but he accepted my resignation. As I walked out of his office I encountered a CU business professor who had been providing training to our command staff. When I informed him I had resigned he invited me to join him for coffee. We went to a coffee shop near the department. When he asked me why I resigned I cried. It was the first time I had cried in 10 years. I was so embarrassed I excused myself and drove home.

My resignation was effective in early December 1975. We listed our house for sale. Two weeks after resigning we moved to the funeral home in Castle Rock. We arrived believing we were where the Lord wanted us to be. We were determined to do as Lyn Alexander had done, to dedicate our life and work to God. We saw the funeral home as a lay ministry to people in grief.

Adjustment to our new life wasn't easy. While I had grown up in the business, I had never had any formal training. I wasn't licensed. I had never made funeral arrangements with a family. I had to establish working arrangements with each of the cemetery organizations, the excavators who opened and closed graves, the clergy in each different congregation in both Douglas and Elbert counties, as well as the many musicians who provide music for funeral services. There was so much more I needed to learn and it would all take time.

I observed my father make funeral arrangements with the first family that had called for our services after purchasing the funeral home. After they left he verbally told me the procedures I was to follow when a family wanted to purchase a monument, then he left. That the extent of his instruction.

Terry Payne, a young licensed funeral director, worked for the funeral home. I hired him. He was our only full time employee. I had to depend on his knowledge.

The next five months were a blur of activity. I met a lot of the clergy who served churches in Douglas and Elbert counties; I was deputized a deputy coroner and began responding to coroner calls, and I did my best to adjust to life at the funeral home. I was even trying to remember to pray for God's guidance with every decision no matter how large or small.

Carol became aware of another weekend spiritual retreat called a Cursillo. This Episcopal retreat was to be held in May at the Bethlehem Retreat Center in Broomfield, Colorado. She urged me to consider going. We called my parents and they agreed to come to Castle Rock to take care of our children and watch the business.

When we arrived at the Cursillo we found that men were to be housed with men and the women were housed with women. I was surprised to find that Bob Holmes, the Englewood Police Chief was my roommate. We also discovered that an Arapahoe County Sheriff's Investigator and his wife were members of the Cursillo staff. They had specifically chosen to attend that weekend to support Carol and me. One of the lay leaders for the weekend was a Colorado State Patrolman. Throughout the weekend, I kept finding myself identifying with those police officers. I felt I was one with them. I was a policeman. I didn't feel like the owner of a funeral home. As the weekend progressed I began to think I had made a big mistake. I couldn't understand why, if I quit my job believing I was doing what the Lord wanted me to do, I was feeling so bad about no longer being a policeman. Saturday night I shared those thoughts with Carol. She couldn't help.

Sunday morning during the Mass I believe God spoke to me. God told me it didn't matter that I was in grief over the loss of my identity. He said that hurt was temporary. It would heal in time. He said that what mattered was the fact I was doing His will. It was critically important that I recognize God's will and do it.

I cried during the Mass and I cried on the way home. In spite of the tears, I couldn't have been more at peace. I left that Cursillo assured of God's love, convinced I'd made the right choice and ready to move ahead with our new life.

One week later, Bob Westdike, the Boulder City Manager, telephoned me. He told me that he was going to ask Chief Barber for his resignation that night and he asked me to return to Boulder as the Acting Chief of Police. I told Bob I would pray about that and call him early the next morning. I did pray. It was a surprisingly easy decision. I phoned Bob and turned down the job.

Andrews Funeral Home

George Carter

"Be thankful for all the difficult people in your life, and learn from them. They show you exactly who you do not want to be."

Unknown

George Carter was unpleasant, rude, cantankerous, impatient, inconsiderate, self-centered, and down-right nasty. Oh yes, and he was something else, he was our neighbor. In fact, we had paid good money to give George a home next to ours. You see, George lived in the house located next door to the funeral home in Castle Rock. His house was included in our purchase of the funeral home. George went with the deal. He'd been living in that house and paying rent to Dad for more than six years.

My first face-to-face meeting with George set the tone of our relationship. We'd moved into the funeral home and spent the first month unpacking and getting settled. I hadn't met George yet but circumstances were such I arranged to meet him. George had been paying $100 a month rent the entire time he lived in that house. Having just purchased that home, I found that $100 dollars a month wasn't enough to meet my expenses. So, I called George and asked if I could collect the rent in person.

"Sure", he said, "come on over." When I stepped out our back door he was standing by the fence waiting for me. "Hello George", I said, "I'm Doug's son, John, and I bought the funeral home and your house from Dad and Mom." "I know", he said as he handed me his check and started to walk back to his front door. "Wait a minute, I need to talk to you." I protested. "Probably going to rise my rent, aren't you? Well you can go to hell. I pay a hundred dollars a month. It's always on time and that's all you're going to get." Then he turned and disappeared into the house.

You can only imagine the emotions that began to build within me. I had just resigned from the Boulder Police Department. I had been a commander in the patrol division with forty men under me. People listened to me, they did what I said and if they didn't they suffered the consequences. How could I ever allow that skinny, 83-year-old man to respond to me with such contempt?

I found Carol and tried to remain civil as I described the encounter with George. She bit her lip to keep from laughing as I finished the story. Then she said: "That's a tough one." As she went back to work I swear I heard a snicker.

On the first of each month for the next year and a half, George would call and tell me his check was ready. We'd meet at the fence and he'd hand me a check for $100 with a notation written in the lower left hand corner: "rent paid in full". I had told him the rent was $135 a month. So, I would accept his check and hand him a receipt that acknowledged the $100 check with a notation written in the lower left hand corner: Rent $135 … with a current total of the unpaid rent to date. He'd smile. I'd smile. Neither one of us spoke.

Rent wasn't the only problem. George had five dogs. The dogs spent most of their time in the house, but three times a day they would accompany George when he drove to a local restaurant for his meals. George would open his door and the dogs would rush into the yard and each one would bark as loud as they could. Whenever we had a funeral that was held in our chapel the grieving family parked their cars in our driveway. If George happened to open his front door when grieving family members were getting into or out of their vehicles, the dogs would bound to the fence barking and everyone's focus would immediately shift from grief to terror. It was annoying. It was rude. And it was George.

One afternoon when things were quiet I heard gunshots. I ran to the back door in time to see George firing his shotgun into the trees. "What in the hell are you doing?" I yelled.

"Shooting the damn birds!"

"You can't do that!" I said.

"The hell I can't!" he said as he fired again. "They are eating the food I put out for the squirrels. I'll kill every last one of them!" And that's what he tried to do. Thank God that happened only once.

That following winter we had a terrible snow storm. We woke up to find drifts four feet deep in the back yard. Since I was managing my father's four apartment buildings I was responsible for snow removal. I had a cup of hot coffee, dressed, grabbed a snow shovel and began clearing snow. While I was shoveling snow, I thought it would be nice to stop by George's house and let him know that all the roads in town were closed, that he wouldn't be able to drive to a restaurant. I knocked on his door. He opened it and stood looking at me. "George" I said, "all the roads are closed and none of the restaurants are open. Do you have food to eat?"

'Yeah" he said and begun to shut the door.

"Don't go out in this weather, you'll just get stuck." I said as the door slammed in my face. I went on shoveling until I was too wet and cold to continue.

A while later I was standing in the bedroom changing my clothes when I caught sight of George walking out of his house. Damn, I thought, he's going to try to walk to a restaurant. Sure enough he slowly made his way through the snow until he reached the street. About ten yards into the street he fell down. Ha, I thought, it serves you right. The snow was so deep I couldn't see him, but it became obvious he wasn't getting up. In disgust I pulled my cold, wet jeans back up, put my wet boots back on and went out the back door. He was still down. As I approached I found him struggling to get up but he was too weak and, alone, he couldn't get the leverage he needed to stand on his feet. "Are you OK?" I asked.

"Yeah", he said, "on my way to get some breakfast."

"George, I told you the City Hotel and the B & B are closed. Why don't you come to our house and I'll ask Carol to fix you something to eat?"

"OK" he said.

I helped him to his feet and we made our way to the back door without speaking another word. We stomped the wet snow off our clothes and stepped inside. Carol had been watching the situation unfold and she was full of smiles.

"Hi George." She said, as if his presence in our home was an everyday event.

"Carol" I said, "George would like some breakfast."

"How about some fried eggs and toast, George?" she said without missing a beat.

Without any hesitation, George responded: "I'll have scrambled eggs and bacon."

Carol prepared a wonderful breakfast. With hardly any conversation at all, George consumed everything on his plate and emptied two cups of steaming hot coffee. Then he grabbed his coat and, with my help, he made his way back home. There was no "thank you" or "that was nice" or "I appreciate your hospitality". Like I said, George was rude.

The last day of George's life was memorable. It was almost noon on a warm, sunny day. George was observing his lunch-time routine. He and his five barking dogs came out of the house, he opened the front gate and the dogs, still barking and yelping, ran to the driver's side of George's car. He opened the door and the dogs piled in. Then, he slowly got into the driver's seat, shut the door, started the car and died.

Our six-year-old son, Eric, was playing on the lawn across the street and he had been watching this scene unfold. Somehow Eric sensed that something was wrong. He walked over to George's car, looked at George as the dogs barked; and then he came to the back door of our house and rang the doorbell. I went to the door and Eric said: "Dad, Mr. Carter just died." At that point in his young life he had seen dead bodies. He was an observant child and he was not joking. I believed him. "Where is he?" I asked.

"He's sitting in his car, Dad."

I thanked Eric, told him to find his mother and I quickly made my way to the driver's side of George's old Dodge. And, sure enough, the car was running, the dogs were barking and George was dead.

That strange situation presented me with a real dilemma. I was the Douglas County Coroner. All I need do was pronounce the old man dead and take his body down my driveway to the morgue. But, I felt uncomfortable doing that. Others needed to be involved.

While I was considering my next move, Carol and Eric appeared. I told Eric he was correct; Mr. Carter was dead. That left Eric feeling very proud of himself. It left Carol and me amazed at our son's ability to observe and respond to his immediate surroundings.

I suggested we all return to the house while I make a phone call. We did and I called Mark Stover, a paramedic with Care Ambulance Company. I asked him to respond, to confirm my observation and to help me move George to the morgue. I also notified the sheriff. They all responded. Mark and I moved George while the sheriff took responsibility for the dogs.

Unfortunately, several of the dogs got loose in the process. Several sheriff's deputies chased them through the neighborhood and were finally able to corral them. No doubt, George would have enjoyed the scene.

Later we were surprised to find that George had a son. We weren't surprised to find they had a rotten relationship. George's son wanted us to handle his father's funeral. After walking through his father's house, he took a few items of sentimental value and declared the rest unsalvageable. It was too much for him to clean up. He apologized for the mess in the house. He asked me to clean the house and said I should keep anything I wanted in return for my time and effort.

The house was a mess to say the least. It took weeks of effort, 16 trips to the dump, and many gallons of Pine Sol to rid the house of the odor of dog pee. We found a pie tin full of dead mice in George's freezer. Apparently he was contending with the rodents and he was saving the dead mice to show me.

An unusual problem quickly developed as we cleaned George's house. The mice fled. Needing a home, they made their way into our house. Almost overnight we began hearing mice in the heating ducts, finding droppings in the kitchen, and spotting the rodents as they scurried across the floor at night. We set traps everywhere. At first we only caught the adults, ten in one day. When the babies were left they began hunting for food in the daylight. Over and over again we would hear a trap and find another victim. It was awful. Finally, we were able to rid our house of the pests. My Aunt Hazel was visiting Colorado at the time. When she heard of our dilemma, she called and told us to put steel wool in all the possible entry holes in the foundation of the house. What a great idea, and it worked.

We were able to salvage several pieces of furniture which helped offset George's unpaid rent. We obtained two ornately carved end tables, an overstuffed chair and an old oak accented sofa. We had the chair and sofa reupholstered. Those pieces adorned our home for years. They were small but attractive reminders of an awful neighbor.

Paul Barnes

"It is by chance that we met, by choice that we become friends."

Henri Nouwen

Paul Barnes was a cattle rancher who lived near Franktown when I was growing up. He was a tough cowboy who lived a very rough life.

The first memory I have involved a memorable ambulance call to the Barnes ranch. Paul had been drinking heavily and decided to commit suicide. He placed the barrel of a shot gun in his mouth and pulled the trigger. Fortunately, or unfortunately, Paul was so drunk that he moved as he pulled the trigger and the blast removed his upper lip, nose and the front of his forehead. When my dad arrived at the scene in the ambulance he found Paul lying on the floor in his kitchen with Sheriff John Hammond sitting on top of him. Paul was thrashing about making loud noises. Blood was everywhere. Sheriff Hammond was using all his strength to keep Paul from hurting himself even more. Dad, his attendant and the sheriff placed Paul on a stretcher, tied his arms, legs and waist with restraint straps, and placed him in the ambulance. What followed was a very wild, loud and fast trip to a Denver hospital.

Paul recovered from the suicide attempt sporting new features on his face. In fact, the surgeon did such a good job that one might not notice the scars it they didn't look too close.

The second early memory I have of Paul Barnes involved the death of his wife. For some unknown reason, Mrs. Barnes had dyed her hair bright red several days prior to her death. She was disgusted with the results. Not wanting anyone to see her, she resolved to stay on the ranch until her hair grew back to its natural color. Her plan went astray when she suddenly died of a heart attack. I remember going with Dad to the Denver hospital to pick up her body. We encountered Paul there. He asked Dad to dye his wife's hair back to its original color before he placed her in a casket. Dad told him that her hair wouldn't look like it had in the past. Paul didn't care as long as it wasn't bright red.

Then Paul made a curious comment. When Dad asked him how he was feeling, Paul said: "I don't feel good enough to be shot!" What a statement from a man who knew what it was like to be shot.

John Hammond was the person who brought Paul Barnes back into my life. Let me set the stage. It was now the late 1970's. John Hammond was no longer the Douglas County Sheriff. He was probably in his late 70's. He had continued to maintain a relationship with Paul, who was now in his 80's. Paul no longer owned his ranch. In fact, Paul had lost all of his money and he was living in a Denver nursing home.

I was managing Dad's four apartment houses. One afternoon the office door bell rang and when I opened the door, there stood John Hammond. He asked me if I had any apartments available. I told him I had a buffet apartment on the ground floor of the Waldron building which was just south of the funeral home. John said that would work. I asked him if it was for him and he said: "No. It's for Paul Barnes." He went on to tell me he had driven to Denver to visit Paul at the nursing home. When he walked into Paul's room Paul announced he was moving out. He had all his clothes in an old cardboard egg crate, and he asked John to drive him to Castle Rock. John told me Paul was in his car. He also said Paul had no furniture so I'd need to find him a table, a chair and a bed.

John went to his car and returned with Paul at his side. Paul was wearing a soiled dirty old cowboy hat, cowboy boots and jeans. He looked like a man who needed nursing home care. He was old. He needed a shave and his clothes were wrinkled and dirty. In spite of that, Paul was one happy man. He told me he got a monthly Social Security check and he'd pay the rent next month when his check came. I was trapped.

I found an old recliner, a kitchen table and a matching straight back chair and a bed for Paul. Carol located some sheets and a blanket and we made his bed. He was as pleased as he could be when we left him standing in his new home.

The next morning and every morning thereafter until Paul died, he came to my office door and rang the bell. When I answered the door, he would hobble in and find a seat. I was now Paul's best friend. He would talk about whatever was on his mind. Over the next 18 months we discussed ranching, cattle, the condition of the banking business in Douglas County, the weather, the best drinking whiskey and a myriad of other topics.

At first Paul was a pain in the neck. He had a habit of showing up at the worst times. He didn't seem to understand that we were running a business, and he didn't have a clue he was bothering us. However, as time went on, I came to enjoy Paul's visits. He had a wonderful sense of humor and the more I listened to him the more I learned about cattle ranching.

One morning Paul arrived just after I'd picked up the mail. My bank statement contained another one of Paul's checks that was returned because of insufficient funds to cover the amount he'd written. I gave Paul the check and asked him what he was going to do about it. He dug into his pocket and handed me his checkbook, saying: "I'm going to give you my check book and you can take care of my bills from now on." I discovered that Paul had never kept track of how much money he had in his account. He simply wrote checks when he needed something, never mind if he had money in the bank or not. I told Paul I would help him if he gave me his Social Security check and if he only purchased items with cash. From that point on Carol and I helped Paul manage his funds.

Late one evening the office door bell rang. Carol and I were in bed. I opened the door and there stood Paul. He was rubbing his chin and dancing up and down. He asked me to scratch his chin. "What!" I said. "Rub my chin." he said. It turned out that Paul had some sort of rash on his chin and it was driving him to distraction. I had him come in and sit down and I sought

Carol's help. She got a bottle of calamine lotion and rubbed that into Paul's chin. That was the relief he needed. He finally went home with our lotion in hand.

As noted earlier, Paul had a habit of being in my office at the wrong time. The best example of that occurred one morning when Bye Southers, a Vietnamese woman, arrived to view her deceased husband. I was talking to Paul, who was sitting on the office couch, when I noticed Bye's car pull to a stop in front of the office. Vietnamese women grieve differently than American women. They express their emotions by wailing. I could hear Bye wailing as soon as she opened the door of her car and the office window wasn't even open. Paul, who was hard of hearing, hadn't noticed anything.

As soon as I opened the office door, Bye entered and sat down next to Paul. She was wailing so loud I'm sure the curtains on the window were shaking with the sound vibrations. And Bye was so deep in her grief she never saw Paul.

I'll never forget Paul's reaction. He looked at Bye, then turned to me with his mouth wide open. The only thing on his mind was to get as far away from her as he possibly could. He tried to stand up, but his legs were too weak and he fell back onto the couch. He tried again, only to fail again. Then he looked at me and said: "HELP!" I could hardly keep from laughing. I gave Paul my hand and as soon as he was on his feet he was headed out the door.

During the last months of Paul's life, he became very depressed. He would talk about his desire to die. At first I humored Paul to change the subject. Later, I just patiently listened to him. Most of Paul's friends were dead, he no longer enjoyed life and he was often in physical pain.

One day Paul bought a quart of whiskey at the drug store, walked to his apartment and consumed the entire bottle. The next morning, he tried to go for a walk. He made it two blocks before he fell. I became aware of the situation when I heard the ambulance go in service on my police scanner. They were given enough information by the dispatcher that I knew they were going to pick up Paul. I prayed that God would help Paul die. He was transported to Swedish Hospital in Englewood where he died the next day.

Paul had pre-arranged his funeral with us. I picked Paul's body up, brought him home and embalmed him. When I took custody of Paul's body I made sure I got his clothes and cowboy hat. As long as Paul lived in our apartment I can't remember seeing him without that hat on.

Paul's pre-arrangement called for us to have him in a casket so that his friends could see him and pay their respects. There was to be no funeral. He was to be cremated and his ashes scattered.

Paul's body laid in his casket in our chapel for several days. I had placed his cowboy hat on the lid of the casket. The only person to pay their respects was John Hammond. After spending a few minutes with Paul's body, John asked me what was going to be done with Paul's hat. I told him it was going to be cremated with Paul's body. John thought that was a real waste because the hat was a "seven star Stetson", the most expensive Stetson made. "Yes," I said, "but it's part of Paul."

Carol and I came to love Paul and he had become a part of our family. I couldn't imagine taking him to the crematory without some sort of service. So Carol joined me as I recited the Burial Office out of the Book of Common Prayer. We both cried.

Richard Creer

The service we render to others is the rent we pay for our room on earth.

Wilfred Grenfell

Richard Creer was a tenant who rented the upstairs rear apartment in the old Waldron building across the street from the funeral home. He was divorced with grown children living nearby. Richard was a quiet man who always paid his rent on time and never caused a problem. We did suspect that he might have a drinking problem because he'd have a heavy scent of whiskey on his breath when he'd pay his rent after work each Friday.

One evening when I was chairing a Castle Rock Planning Commission meeting, Carol received a telephone call from the tenant who lived in the apartment directly below Richard. The caller complained that water was dripping from the ceiling in his kitchen. Carol said she'd look into the problem right away. Knowing that water had to be coming from either a broken pipe located between the floors or from Richard's bathroom, she decided to check with Richard first.

Richard didn't answer his telephone, so Carol went to his apartment and knocked on his door. There was no response. Carol could hear sound from a TV set, so she knocked again. Finally, the door opened and there was Richard, naked except for a short dirty T shirt.

Carol, being the composed and focused lady she is, asked Richard if he knew anything about a water leak in his bathroom. Richard mumbled something unintelligible. Carol pressed the point and then told Richard she was going to check his bathroom. She stepped around him, walked to his bathroom and found the floor covered with water. He had turned on the tub faucet to fill the tub and forgot about it. Water was cascading over the side onto the floor.

Carol turned the water off, pulled the plug and mopped the standing water from the floor with a bath towel. Without a word, Richard had returned to his chair in front of the TV. As soon as Carol finished, she told him that the water was leaking through the floor into the apartment below his and then she left.

As soon as I got home, Carol told me all that had happened. She said she had no doubt that Richard was very drunk. We decided I would check on him the next morning.

Early the next day I went to Richard's apartment. The TV was still on and loud enough I could hear it in the hall. I knocked on the door. When it opened, Richard was still naked except for his T shirt, his eyes and skin were jaundiced, and his stomach was swollen and extended. The odor of alcohol hung in the air.

I looked Richard in the eye and said: "Richard you don't look well. I suspect that you're an alcoholic and you look seriously ill. Do you want help?" To my surprise, he said: "Yes." When I suggested that he go to a drug and alcohol treatment center, and he said he thought that would be a good idea and asked me to help.

At that time there were no alcohol treatment centers in Douglas County so I used Richard's Denver phone book and called Denver General Hospital. The receptionist told me there was one bed available in the detox unit. She explained that it would be filled on a "first come – first served" basis. Since I was calling before noon she thought we had a chance of admitting Richard. But, she cautioned, I was to hurry.

Before I hung up I told her Richard was weak and he had the shakes. I asked for advice. She suggested I give him a can of beer and, she added, it might help if he had a second can as we drove to Denver. I followed her advice.

While Richard drank his first can of beer I rummaged through his dresser and found some clean clothes. I had to help him dress and tie his shoes. Then I steadied him as we walked down the steps to my car. The trip to Denver General took no time at all. Richard hardly spoke. He was too busy concentrating on his brew.

I drove to the emergency entrance, found a wheel chair and pushed Richard to the admitting office. I asked if there was an available bed in the detox unit and was told there was one. You can't imagine the relief I felt. I have no idea what I would have done next if Richard had been denied admittance.

The admitting clerk began asking Richard all the standard questions and surprisingly he was able to answer for himself. I stood at his side silently thanking God for His help. Suddenly my silent prayers were interrupted when I heard the clerk ask Richard for his religious denomination. Before he could answer I thought: "This will be interesting … he's probably never set foot inside a church." Richard said he was an Episcopalian. What? I was stunned. Embarrassed. I returned to my silent prayers but this time I was asking the Lord's forgiveness for my negative judgments.

Once he was admitted he thanked me and I left him in the capable hands of a nurse from the detox unit. The following day I called to check on his condition. I was told he had been moved to the VA hospital. When I called the VA hospital the unit clerk said Richard was doing as well as could be expected.

Three weeks later Richard Creer died of cirrhosis of the liver. During that time, he had dried out and was able to spend some quality time with his children. His funeral was held in our funeral chapel.

I can't help but think that the Lord was part of all that had happened. I imagine Richard would have died a few weeks earlier, alone, in his apartment, if he hadn't forgotten to turn off the bath water. Instead, Carol encountered him and urged me to check on his condition. I'm so glad I did. I do think that the events that followed made a difference during the last few weeks of his life.

Erwin and Betty Brietweiser

"Blessed are they who have the gift of making friends, for it is one of God's best gifts. It involves many things but above all, the power of getting out of one's self, and appreciating whatever is noble and loving in another."

Thomas Hughes

Erwin and Betty were much older than I was, they had lived in Douglas County for many years. They had known me all my life. Both were born in Germany and immigrated to the United States. They never had children and their only relatives lived in the "old country". Erwin was a short thin man who spoke English with a noticeable German accent. He had a cheerful disposition, a quick smile and he loved to talk.

They had lived for many years near the Curtis ranch just north of Saint Philip-in-the-Field Episcopal Church on west Plum Creek. Erwin was a rancher of sorts. He raised foxes and sold fox pelts that were made into expensive clothing. It was work Erwin enjoyed and over the years he told me many stories about the care and feeding of his foxes.

When the fur industry began to lag, Erwin could no longer make enough money to support his ranch. He sold all his foxes and the pens they were raised in and moved into Castle Rock. He and Betty lived in a rented duplex about one block from the funeral home.

Erwin owned an elaborate spray paint outfit and he enjoyed painting. Offering to use his own equipment, he obtained a job painting highway bridges for the Douglas County road maintenance department. He painted the metal bridge supports and railings on bridges from one end of the county to the other. Finally, with years of bridge painting under his belt, Erwin retired.

Carol and I moved to Castle Rock after Erwin's retirement. Soon after we were settled in he dropped by to welcome me back home. We had fun reminiscing, and from that time on, Erwin got into the habit of stopping by for a visit several times a week. Our conversations centered on a myriad of topics which included the weather, the joy of walking, the benefits of a daily steam bath, a diet of fruit and nuts, and the care of foxes. I looked forward to our visits and I learned a lot from Erwin.

At some point in Erwin's life he purchased a steam box and set it up in his basement. One day he invited me into his home to show me that steam box. The contraption looked like an old iron lung that polio victims had to use during the polio epidemic in the 1950's. It was a rectangular metal box about seven feet long. The lid was curved and attached with hinges along one side. The bottom half of the box rested on top of metal legs about four feet high. Erwin would fill the bottom about half full of water. An electric motor ran a heater that would warm the water until steam would rise. Once steam appeared, Erwin would lie naked on wood slates that sat several inches above the hot water. As soon as he was comfortable he would pull the lid down. His head was the only part of his body that would remain outside the steam box. Erwin was convinced that his daily steam bath was one of the healthiest things he did. He thought I'd enjoy an occasional steam bath and he often invited me to join him. I never did.

Erwin claimed that a daily steam bath offered the cure for the common cold. He said that his colds never lasted more than a week and he credited his steam bath for that miracle. I would counter Erwin's claim by saying that most colds never last more than a week. He didn't think I knew what I was talking about and he never accepted my argument.

Erwin once told me that he had written me into his will. He said that at the time of his death I was to take possession of that steam box. I was honored by his thoughtfulness and I really didn't know how to respond other than to thank him. I have no idea what happened to that steam box because I received nothing from his estate after he died. Frankly, I was glad because I didn't have the space to store that rusty old piece of equipment.

Erwin couldn't have weighed more than 110 pounds. His diet of fruit and nuts kept him thin. I don't think he ate any red meat or fish. He just ate fresh fruit, dried fruit and nuts. He believed his diet was another reason he was healthy. His physical health was so important that he regularly went to a chiropractor to have his hair analyzed. He was sure that any imbalance in the condition of his hair would reveal any health problem or need to supplement his diet. Since the condition of his hair never changed, he was confident he was eating right. I thought all that was nuts and I told him so. He'd laugh and tell me that I'd be convinced otherwise if I would consent to having my hair analyzed. I never did.

One afternoon Erwin told me that he wanted to make arrangements with me for his and Betty's cremation and pay for it in advance. He said that he didn't want to pay cash, but rather he wanted to trade his elaborate spray paint equipment for the cremations. He knew the cost of two cremations and he believed his paint equipment was of equal value. Since I managed four apartment buildings and two houses in addition to the funeral home, I thought I could probably put that equipment to good use. State law prohibited me from drawing up a contract based on an outright trade so I simply purchased the equipment from Erwin and he returned that money to me and it was placed in a pre-need funeral account. That barter turned out well because I did use that equipment. It also marked the only time I accepted anything other than money for our services.

For years Erwin and Betty took a daily walk that averaged five miles. They had numerous places in and near Castle Rock that they loved to hike. Erwin often stopped at the funeral home after hiking and he would describe the wild animals they had spotted, the singing birds they had heard and the condition of the vegetation. I did accompany them on several hikes and I was amazed at their vitality. They would maintain a steady pace and a lively conversation. When they purchased a mobile home on the west side of town and moved in, they continued to hike until Betty became too weak and lost interest. The loss of her companionship on those walks was a source of disappointment for Erwin. On more than one occasion he told me how he tried to convince her to join him and his sorrow when she declined.

Betty was 10 years older than Erwin and she suffered from a number of ailments. One afternoon Bud Curtis called me with some distressing news. He said he'd just talked with Erwin by phone and Erwin said Berry was very sick and near death. Bud asked if I knew anything about the situation. I was really surprised and I told him I didn't but I would drive to the trailer park and check on them. I jumped in my car and drove to their home. When Erwin answered his door I asked him how Betty was feeling. He thanked me for stopping by and then he said he was afraid Betty was near death. He invited me in as he continued to talk. He said Betty had been unconscious for several days. I asked him if I could look in on her and he said he'd appreciate my doing that.

I found Betty lying under the covers of their bed. She was unconscious but her vital signs were strong. She had a solid heartbeat, good color, and her breathing was deep and steady. I asked Erwin if he had called a doctor.

"No," he said. He didn't like Betty's doctor and he was so sure she was in her last hours of life that he hadn't considered calling the doctor. And, there was one more important matter. Betty had made Erwin promise that he would never allow anyone to attach her to machines in order to keep her alive. He was afraid that if he called the doctor he wouldn't be able to fulfill his promise to his wife of 60 years.

I told Erwin that I thought Betty had suffered a stroke and I didn't think she was dying. That information stunned Erwin. He asked me why I didn't think she was dying.

"Erwin," I said, "Even though she's had a stroke you've taken such good care of her and her body is so strong that, in spite the fact she's unconscious, her vital sights remain solid. She is not near death." I went on to say that while I shared his conviction that Betty shouldn't be kept alive on machines, I did feel it was important that a physician examine her. Betty's doctor was our family physician. I told Erwin that I had a good relationship with the man and I would urge him to refrain from using any life support machines. With tears in his eyes, Erwin asked me to call that doctor. I picked up the phone and dialed the number. An answering machine greet me with the message that the doctor was on vacation and I was given the name and phone number of his back-up physician.

Now the situation was even more complicated. I did trust the first doctor but I didn't have the same trust for his back-up. Again I sat down with Erwin and we discussed the matter. I told him I was acquainted with a young doctor who was an active Christian. He had a good reputation and was a person I suspected would honor Erwin's request to avoid life support. Erwin felt we should call the man, so I telephoned him at his home. He listened to the circumstances and said he would immediately drive to Erwin's home and examine Betty.

His careful examination confirmed my suspicions. Betty had suffered a stroke. The doctor urged Erwin to have Betty transported to the hospital in Englewood, but Erwin wasn't ready to take that step. He wanted to wait until the following day. The doctor patiently listened to Erwin and then he said he would do whatever was necessary to comply with Erwin's wishes.

Erwin was exhausted. He'd been giving Betty kind attention ever since she suffered the stroke. The doctor urged Erwin to find someone to help care for Betty through the night. He said he didn't know of anyone who could help, and then, he turned to me and asked if I knew someone. That was a question I'd been mulling over in my mind.

"Yes", I said, "I think I do." Carol Bryden, a member of Christ Episcopal Church in Castle Rock, and an RN who worked part time at the Silver State Nursing Home, was the person I had in mind. I called her and she dropped everything and drove right over to Erwin's home. The doctor had Carol assist him as he inserted a catheter and started an IV.

Both the doctor and Carol were impressed with the care Erwin had given Betty. She and the bed she was on were neat and clean. Carol remained at Betty's side for several hours. When she felt everything was stable she left Betty in Erwin's care with the idea that further decisions would be made after the doctor re-examined Betty the following morning.

Erwin called me early the next day to tell me that Betty's condition had not changed and he was ready to have her transported to the hospital. He wanted my help. I called the doctor as soon as I arrived at the house and we made all the necessary arrangements with the hospital and called an ambulance. Erwin rode in the ambulance with Betty and I followed them in my car. After Betty was admitted, Erwin and I remained at her bedside for several hours. Finally, Erwin asked me to take him home.

Betty remained hospitalized for two weeks and was then transferred to the nursing home in Castle Rock. She never regained consciousness. Erwin spent time sitting with her every day. He would call me in the evenings to keep me posted on Betty's condition. Carol prepared meals for Erwin regularly. Since they weren't fruit and nuts, we weren't sure he ate them.

The day Betty died Erwin called me. The nursing home had just called him and said Betty was near death. He asked me to drive him to the nursing home. He knew how difficult the experience would be and that was the only time he asked someone to provide him with transportation. Betty was dead when we walked into her room. Erwin looked at her and then asked me if I thought she was dead. I told him she was. He began to cry and I took him in my arms and held him. I cried too. After a short time, I asked him if he would like me to pray. "Yes", he said, he'd appreciate that. I offered a prayer and then I took him home with me.

We had a beautiful graveside service at Bear Canon Cemetery. Betty's ashes were laid in the ground that was near the old fox farm. Bud Curtis conducted the committal service using the Episcopal Book of Common Prayer. I left the cemetery with a heavy heart knowing how much Erwin was missing his dear friend.

Erwin sitting on the steps of the lookout tower.

Erwin continued to stop and visit. Each summer he and I would drive up Jarre Canon and hike to the fire lookout tower. Erwin was always the oldest person to make the hike and climb the steps to the top of the lookout. He would use an old wooden walking stick that contained numerous metal pins that commemorated hikes he had taken in Europe. He would show me a pin and then describe the hike it represented. He and I both kept our "Royal Order of the Squirrel" membership cards that were given to us by the forest ranger who worked in the lookout tower.

Erwin died after we had moved to Wisconsin so I could attend seminary. I wasn't able to attend his service. Bud Curtis conducted the graveside service and Erwin's ashes were buried next to Betty.

I'm grateful for the friendship Erwin and I shared. I'll never forget the pleasure of his company and the wonderful times we shared together. He was a friend whose memory has enriched my life.

A Marked Man

"Your impression of me is different than my impression of me. But that's OK, because your impression is impressionistic, like a Monet painting, while mine is realistic, like a Rembrandt."

Jarod Kintz, This Book is NOT FOR SALE

I was well known in Douglas County. I had lived there most of my life. My father founded the Andrews Funeral Home and served as county coroner for 35 years. I bought the funeral home from my parents and, I, too, was serving as the elected county coroner. For 45 years, the name Andrews was associated with death. People took that into account when they encountered me.

For example, one evening I drove to Parker to attend a Kiwanis meeting. I was an invited guest and my host was to meet me at the restaurant where the meeting was to occur. The restaurant had a bar upstairs and a large meeting room downstairs. I was expecting to walk in the front door and easily make my way to the meeting. Instead, I entered the front door and found myself in a dimly lit bar. As I walked in all heads turned to face me and people stopped talking. I could "feel" the silence. A patron sitting on a bar stool broke the silence with a question. "Who died?" That patron had been one of my high school classmates. I responded, "No one died, Mike, I'm looking for the Kiwanis meeting." Mike laughed and said, "Whew, don't scare us like that. The meeting's downstairs."

Another example of being a marked man did involve a death. It occurred on a weekday morning after Betty Brooks, 76, was struck by a Rio Grande freight train in Castle Rock. Mrs. Brooks lived alone in an apartment house that sat on High School Road just north of the Franktown highway. She was very deaf. Every day she would walk south along High School Road, turn west at the Franktown highway, cross the rail road tracks and continue to the post office to collect her mail. She followed that routine on the day of her death. By the time she reached the rail road tracks a northbound freight train had triggered the crossing lights, lowered the traffic gate and the engineer was blowing his horn. Without hesitating, Mrs. Brooks walked around the traffic gate and stepped directly in front of the lead engine. She died instantly.

I was called to the scene. The train was blocking the Franktown highway, the signal lights were flashing and the streets were filled with cars that couldn't move. I was at that scene for about 1½ hours taking pictures, measurements and statements. After completing the investigation, I took the body back to the funeral home.

I knew Mrs. Brooks and I knew that her daughter was a county employee. My next task was to locate that daughter and notify her of her mother's death. News of the accident traveled fast. Everyone who worked in the county administration building knew me and they knew that someone had died in that accident. As I entered the county building conversations stopped and people watched where I was going. When I walked into the office of the person I was seeking, Mrs. Brooks daughter looked up at me and said: "It was my mother wasn't it?" I said, "Yes, I'm so sorry to have to tell you."

Without any further conversation, she gathered her coat and purse and followed me out. As she left those in the office gave her their sympathy. They hadn't heard our conversation. They simply "knew" I had delivered a death message.

One more incident involved a death that occurred in Alaska. The deceased was the father of Dr. Kerry Tyler, an optometrist and a close personal friend. Kerry's father owned a logging company located on a remote island off the Alaskan coast. He used a small boat to travel to and from that island. When he failed to return one day, his wife alerted the Coast Guard and a search was launched. The search turned up pieces of a boat, but Kerry's father was not found. That evening, Kerry's mother called to notify him, but the only people home were Kerry's wife, Linda, and their three children.

Kerry was a member of the Castle Rock Town Council and that evening the entire council was having a dinner at the Old Stone Church restaurant. Linda called me, informed me of the situation and asked me to find Kerry. I was to notify him of his father's presumed death and have him call home.

I immediately went to the Old Stone Church and as soon as I entered people seemed to sense I was there on serious business. Conversations stopped and a hush came over the diners. I walked to the table where the town council was seated, made eye contact with Kerry, and he simply got up and we walked outside together. He asked me what had happened. I told him. He returned to the council table, excused himself and left for home.

These incidents, and others like them, made me aware of the effect my presence had on others. There were times my presence generated a certain fear. I wasn't someone others encountered lightly. I didn't like having that effect on others, but that was part of the role I had in that community.

It was Heart-Breaking Work

"Sometimes I wished I was a little kid again, skinned knees are easier to fix than broken hearts."

Author Unknown

For much of my life I've been asked, "How were you able to handle all that death and grief?". For years I would answer, "I don't know". As I became a more committed Christian, my answer became, "I'm only able to do that by the Grace of God."

Saying that I was able to work in the midst of death and grief does not mean that I wasn't emotionally touched. There were many instances where my heart was broken. It was emotionally hard both on me and on my family. There were times the only way I could respond was to cry. One evening as I was sitting in our living room I was overcome with tears. I had responded to 17 violent death scenes that month. Several days later I answered the knock at our door to be greeted by a couple I barely knew. They told me they had been aware of all the violent deaths I had recently handled and they simply wanted me to know they were praying for me. Wow. They have no idea how much their prayers meant to me.

Four different death investigations immediately came to mind as I wrote this.

I was called to the scene of a double homicide-suicide early one Sunday evening in the Fall of 1979. The scene was a house located in a rural area 2 ½ miles south of Castle Rock. A neighbor had spotted smoke coming from the house and called the Castle Rock Fire Department. Assuming there were people inside the house several of the first firemen to arrive at the scene put on air packs and forced entry into the front door. Smoke was so thick they had to crawl as they searched the first floor. They didn't encounter open flame, but the smoke forced them out before they could complete their search. Firemen arriving on the second truck drove to the back of the house where they found open flame in the basement. They broke some windows, shinned lights in and attempted to put out the hot spots with fire hoses. One of the firemen saw a human body lying on the floor. A paramedic made his way to the body; and a quick examination revealed the victim was dead. He had a massive head injury. A revolver was lying at his side. A sheriff's deputy at the scene was notified and I was called.

When I arrived, the house was still an active fire scene. Firemen were putting out hot spots and attempting to ventilate the smoke. A deputy sheriff informed me that two more

177

bodies had been discovered. The body of a dead woman was lying on the floor of the master bedroom; and another dead woman was lying on the floor in the bathroom attached to the master bedroom.

I first entered the basement through a garden level door. I examined the victim and it appeared the man had died of a gunshot wound to the head. His body had suffered only minor burns. The revolver was still lying by his side.

I next went upstairs. The smoke was heavy, but Dale Row, the sheriff's investigator, and I both felt we had to work quickly in case flames broke out again. We had to process and collect all the evidence we could. I first examined the woman's body lying in the bedroom. She appeared to be middle aged. She'd been shot multiple times including once in the head. It appeared that some sort of accelerant had been poured on her body and lit. I then entered the bathroom and found a young female who also had been shot multiple times, including in the head. An accelerant had been poured on her body and lit.

Dale Row and I continued to process the crime scene for the next 6 hours. Charlie Bowman, one of my deputies, assisted us at the scene. Charlie, an off-duty police officer, also was sent to interview witnesses.

Investigators from the Colorado Bureau of Investigation were called to the scene to assist. The bodies were transported to our funeral home, and arrangements for autopsies were made. Over the following two days the details of this crime became clear.

The victims were 45-year-old Charles Kelsey, his 41-year-old wife, Donna, and their 12-year-old daughter Brenna. The Kelsey's marriage was so troubled that friends at church had attempted to help. Charles firmly rejected those efforts. On the evening of the deaths, the couple had fought. Charles produced a gun and chased his wife into the bedroom where he shot and killed her. His daughter had also run into the bedroom either to try to stop the violence or she was in there with her mother attempting to hide from Charles. As her father was shooting her mother, Brenna ran into the bathroom for protection; but it was of no avail. Her father stepped into that room and killed his daughter. He then took a can of gas and poured some on his wife and daughter. He continued pouring fuel throughout the first floor. He lit the fuel and went into the basement where he lit the gas and committed suicide. The fire exploded causing extensive damage. In time the flames died down because Charles had failed to open the windows to provide oxygen. Without oxygen, the fire wasn't as devastating as it might have been.

All these details became evident as we processed the scene. I had children at home and I could imagine the panic and fear that preceded the deaths. There were times I had to wipe tears from my face as we worked. Relatives of the Kelsey's asked me to handle the funeral arrangements. I spent a lot of time with those folks and their sorrow touched me deeply.

People ask, "How can you do that". It was only with prayer and the grace of God.

Early one Friday evening in June of 1979 the Rodriguez family was traveling south on U. S. Highway 85 about 4 miles south of Blakeland, Colorado, when their car ran out of gas. Mr. Rodriguez caught a ride back to Blakeland to obtain fuel, leaving his wife, their 8-year-old son, and their 10-year-old nephew with the car. The two children got out of the vehicle and began playing near the railroad tracks. A short time later a north bound Santa Fe freight train struck both boys, killing them instantly. Officers from the Colorado State Patrol, the Douglas County Sheriff's Office, along with the Louviers Fire Department and a paramedic crew from Care Ambulance responded to the scene. I too was notified and responded immediately.

Upon my arrival, I parked behind a state patrol car. As I stepped from my vehicle both front doors and one of the back doors of the patrol unit opened and three officers exited that unit. A woman was sitting in the rear seat screaming. One of the officers told me the woman was the mother of one of the children. She had just arrived at the scene and had been told her son was dead. I stepped to the back door of the patrol car and climbed into the back seat with the woman. She was screaming and screaming and screaming. Her screams were too much for the officers. They were almost more than I could bear. I placed my arms around the woman and held her as she continued to scream.

Years of responding to critical situations like this had taught me that I could help the shocked mother by talking to her in a calm, low, soft voice. At first, she couldn't hear me; but she knew I was some sort of authority and I had important information to share with her. Slowly she gained control of herself. Finally, she grew quiet enough she could hear me. I told her who I was and how much I shared her grief. I stayed with her until some of her relatives appeared and joined her.

My next task was to crawl under that train, examine the bodies of both children, take photographs and then remove the bodies. Again, I was faced with the death of children who were near the age of my children. Tears stained my face. I wasn't alone, the police and paramedics also had a difficult time dealing with their sorrow.

People ask, "How can you do that?" It was only through prayer and the grace of God.

One Sunday afternoon a young housewife and her elementary-school-aged son sat watching TV in the den of their home in Castle Rock. Suddenly the woman suffered a massive stroke, stiffened, and fell to the floor. Her son ran to his mother's side and tried to arouse her. He yelled for help and ran to the phone to dial the police. His father entered the room as the boy was trying to call for help. He examined his wife and realized the situation was desperate. The young boy was having no luck dialing the phone so his father grabbed the phone and successfully made the call. An ambulance and several police officers responded. The young woman was unresponsive. She was transported to the Swedish Emergency Medical Center. She was dead on arrival.

The woman's husband and son followed the ambulance to the medical center in one of the police cars. They were taken to the waiting room while medical personnel were attempting to treat the woman. She did not respond to their efforts and I was called to pronounce her dead.

The husband and son were still in the waiting room when I arrived. They had not yet been informed of the death. When I entered the medical center the husband recognized me and suddenly realized his wife was dead. He asked me if that was the reason I was there. I told him it was. The man's son began to sob. Over and over again he kept saying, "I killed her. I killed her." His father held the boy and tried to assure him that his mother's death wasn't his fault.

This emotional scene was witnessed by the medical staff, the police and the ambulance crew. Some of the first-responders knew the boy was blaming himself because he had such a hard time dialing the phone. They tried to comfort and reassure the boy; but he couldn't be consoled. His poor father was not only in grief over his wife's death; but he struggled to help his son who was having a mighty battle with guilt. It was a tough, heart breaking situation that touched everyone present.

The Swedish Emergency Medical Center was the scene of yet another heart-breaking situation. I had been called to the center to pronounce a 2-year-old-child dead after he was run over by his father. The child's father had been loading wood into a trailer attached to his truck which was parked in the family's driveway. He thought his son was playing in the yard. The father got into his truck and re-positioned it. As he exited the truck he found he had backed over his little boy's head. He picked the child up, put him in the family car and rushed to the medical center. All attempts to save the child failed. I was called and responded.

After pronouncing the child dead, I was informed that the child's mother and grand-parents were enroute to be with the father who was in the waiting room. I knew the family was going to be very emotionally upset so I called Carol and asked her to come to the center and assist me. I then sat with the father until Carol arrived. Soon his wife and his parents arrived. It was so sad. The family held each other and cried. Finally, they said they all wanted to view the child. I cautioned them that the injuries were severe but they still wanted to see the little boy.

Carol and I accompanied the family into the room where the child was lying on a hospital cart. It was a disturbing sight filled with raw emotions.

Carol never responded to death scenes with me. While she had seen many dead bodies at the funeral home, she had never seen or experienced a violent death like this. It was shockingly difficult for her. That night Carol couldn't get the sight out of her mind. She had a hard time going to sleep. Every time she awoke she would again experience the horror of that death and its effects on the family.

Carol had been reading about God's ability to heal memories. According to the material she was reading, one could pray for God to heal memories with the expectation that the Lord would honor that prayer. Carol placed her trust in God and prayed that her painful memory would be healed. The next day she found that God had honored that prayer. While exercising in a yoga class she realized that she could remember everything about being with the family without experiencing the emotional pain.

People ask, "How can you do that?" It was only through prayer and the grace of God.

First responders and medical personnel pride themselves in their ability to handle heart-breaking situations. Compassion and empathy are the gifts that both enable them to be effective and the tender side of their personalities that leave them venerable to the emotions they encounter. After I returned from the death of the young mother at the medical center I was visited first by the two patrolmen, and then later, by the ambulance crew. All four said they just wanted to "stop by and talk". It turned out all of them were struggling with their emotions and I was a safe person to whom they could talk.

Within a month of that death, I received a request from the emergency room staff of the Swedish Medical Center in Englewood asking me to present a training seminar on how to respond emotionally to sudden and violent trauma situations. It was the first of many seminars I presented to fire and police departments in the surrounding area. In those presentations, I affirmed the importance of recognizing one's emotions, and the value of allowing yourself to respond appropriately. And, I shared my trust in prayer and the grace of God.

John Everett, one of my deputy coroners, was an artist and calligrapher. He designed a small plaque which contained a Biblical quote about God's peace which passes all understanding. That plaque hung in the funeral home morgue where all the coroner's autopsies were performed. Those autopsies were attended by police officers and representatives from the District Attorney's Office. Attendance was mandatory and it was considered an unpleasant task. The number of comments about the words on that plaque never failed to amaze me. God's peace does pass understanding and I found it to be the only way I could do what I did.

The Missing King Cobra
"Thinking will not overcome fear but action will."

W. Clement Stove

I will never forget the night of October 9, 1983, and neither will the sheriff and coroner of Elbert County. That was the night the St. Francis Hospital's Flight-for-Life helicopter was placed on standby alert as we carefully opened the door of a car containing two badly decomposed bodies. The dead bodies weren't the problem. The problem was the possibility the vehicle also contained a missing and highly dangerous 14-foot king cobra snake.

This story began long before that night. It began when Jerry Colver's father met, fell in love with and married a woman named Pamela. They lived together in a rustic home on a ranch in a remote section of Elbert county. Jerry, who lived in the same home, fell in love with his father's wife. He started a romance which led Pamela to divorce Jerry's father. Then she and Jerry were married. This very awkward and difficult family situation was further compounded by the fact that Jerry and Pamela continued to live in the house with Jerry's father, Pamela's ex-husband.

Obviously, Pamela liked to live on the edge. She even had a hobby that had an element of extreme danger. She had a collection of snakes that included 20 reptiles, six of which were venomous. The poisonous snakes consisted of a south African puff adder, a dusky pygmy rattlesnake, a Sonoran sidewinder, a speckled rattlesnake, a 3 ½ foot timber rattlesnake and a 14-foot king cobra. No one, and I mean no one, messed with Pamela or her snakes.

Life in the Colver home was anything but peaceful. The toxic environment contributed to unstable relationships and a careless approach to life. Things were so bad that Jerry, aged 28, convinced his wife, Pamela, aged 40, to join him in a suicide pact. They made plans, obtained Pamela's daughter's Datsun and mysteriously disappeared.

One week after their disappearance, the Elbert County Sheriff's Department received a telephone call which registered concern for the care of Pamela's snakes. The sheriff called the Denver Zoo and asked for assistance. Bill Turner, a herpetological (snake) expert responded. A search of the house was made and all the snakes except the king Cobra were found.

Bill Turner informed the sheriff that a king cobra is the largest venomous snake in the world. It has a reputation for being aggressive. The cobra's poison is "… neurotoxic … it affects the nervous system causing respiratory difficulties and ultimately, heart failure."[16]

Two weeks after their disappearance, Pamela's sister and her boyfriend drove to the ranch where they found a note which indicated Jerry and Pamela could be found "on the hill" behind the ranch. They immediately went up the hill where they found the Datsun partly hidden in the pines. The locked vehicle contained Jerry and Pamela's decomposing bodies. They returned to the ranch house and notified the sheriff.

Sheriff George Yarnell, several of his deputies, the Elbert county coroner, Mike Graeff and EMT's from the Elizabeth Fire Department responded to the scene. I was called to transport the bodies to the funeral home. Sterling Monroe, one of my deputy coroners, accompanied me to the scene. When we arrived, Mike Graeff and Sheriff Yarnell briefed us.

Both bodies were still in the front seat, the car was still locked and a hose that had been taped to the exhaust pipe was still inserted in a small rear window. The authorities feared the missing king cobra was somewhere in that car. They had not seen the snake, but they thought it might be hibernating due to the cold temperatures. Fearing the snake would awaken, crawl out from under the seat and strike, the Flight-for-Life helicopter was placed on stand-by.

Sterling was quickly convinced we could be in danger. He wasn't either willing or interested in standing anywhere near the vehicle when the door was opened. The sheriff thought Sterling was wise. He suggested that Mike and I break the window on the front passenger door since the car was locked and we had no keys. So, Mike and I took a deep breath and approached the car. Mike broke the window with his flashlight, reached in and unlocked the door. Carefully we opened it. Nothing moved. We stood still and listened. Nothing. We were so nervous we decided to walk back with the rest of the officers and simply wait for a respectable period of time.

About thirty minutes later we again approached the car and very carefully shined the flashlight under the seats. We didn't see anything suspicious, but the odor of the decomposing bodies was almost overwhelming. With no snake in sight, we took photographs and then pulled the bodies out onto the ground. They were placed in rubber crash bags, strapped onto the two stretchers and placed in the back of my Buick station wagon.

The sheriff removed the keys from the ignition and unlocked the trunk. He was careful to jump back when he opened the trunk lid. Again, nothing happened. The trunk did not contain the cobra.

If it hadn't been so spooky it would have been funny to watch the mood change as the officers realized the snake was still missing. It quickly dawned on everyone that if the snake wasn't in the car, it could be anywhere in the dark bushes and pines that surrounded us. In no time at all, the decision was made to secure the scene by placing an officer in a car and a further search would be conducted the following day when the sun was out.

---

[16] The Elbert County News, Thursday, October 13, 1983, front page.

Sterling and I drove down the hill to the ranch. I told Sterling I would have to talk with Jerry's father to obtain necessary information for the death certificates. When we arrived I asked Sterling to join me. He did so reluctantly, reminding me that we needed to be cautious because the snake could still be in the house.

Jerry's father was standing in the open door when we got out of the car. He invited us into the kitchen. As we sat down, Sterling placed the back of his chair against the back of mine so that he was sitting facing the opposite direction I was facing. That was strange, but I pretended it was normal.

Jerry's father left no doubt in my mind that he hated his son and his ex-wife turned daughter-in-law. He said he would not be liable for any of the funeral expenses. "Cremate the bastards," was his theme, "but don't look to me for any money."

After finishing our business, I stood and began walking out. Sterling stood, and, with his back to my back he followed me, backing all the way. When we got to the car I told Sterling he was acting strange. "No, I'm not," he said, "I was protecting us. Don't you realize that snake could stand 7 feet tall and still have 7 more feet of slithering power on the floor?!?!" I laughed and we drove off.

Several days later the king cobra was found. It was in the house. It had crawled into a bedroom ceiling. When it got hungry it broke through the ceiling tiles and dropped into the room where it was later discovered and captured. It was taken to the Denver Zoo to join the other snakes that had been removed from the house.

The autopsy on the two bodies confirmed they had died of carbon monoxide poisoning. They were cremated. No services were held and the county paid for all the expenses. That brought to a close one of the most unusual coroner cases I ever attended.

Death on the Fourth of July

"The most beautiful people I've known are those who have known trials, have known struggles, have known loss, and have found their way out of the depths."

Elizabeth Kubler-Ross

I've always enjoyed the Fourth of July. If possible, we'd take the day off, watch a parade, enjoy a barbecued meal and then end the day watching fireworks. July 4, 1982, we were able to do that. Carol, Doug, Eric and I watched the town parade sitting in lawn chairs on the corner of our property. The parade was long and full of interesting floats as it made its way down 4th street and south along Jerry Street. Later, Carol prepared hamburgers and I grilled them as we listened to neighborhood children discharging their illegal fire crackers. We finished that meal with large slices of watermelon and then, in the evening we watched the fireworks that the fire department shot off the top of Castle Rock. It was a great day and the whole family was in bed and asleep by 10:30 PM

The Wafai family was still awake. Said Wafai, 41, his wife, Debra Ann, 29, and their four children lived in the Black Forest Estates subdivision in rural Douglas County, northeast of Parker. They, too had been celebrating Independence Day.

Said was born and raised in Jordan. After arriving in the United States, he met, fell in love with and married Debra Ann. Their marriage produced four children: Zein, age 8; Tereq, 6; Khalid, 4; and Matthew, 6 months. Said worked for a Denver car dealership and he was considered one of Denver's most successful car salesmen.

Said remained in contact with his family in Jordan. His older brother, Badawi Wafai, 42, had come to America on a visitor's visa and he was living in an apartment in Denver. Badawi was a troubled man who suffered from depression and a mental disorder called narcissism. Badawi experienced feelings of profound inadequacy and compensated for that by coming up with super ambitious and grandiose schemes. One of his grandiose plans was to open a restaurant. He was so sure this would be successful that he had asked Said to loan him $50,000. Said refused and Badawi considered that refusal a personal rejection.

Badawi also believed Said's children should be raised in Jordan. On numerous occasions he urged Said to divorce Debra Ann and take his children back to his native country. Said's refusal to consider such a move led Badawi to threaten to kidnap his nieces and nephews.

185

To make matters worse, Badawi had developed a perverse interest in his niece, Zein. He imagined they were in love with each other and he had plans to take her to Jordan and marry her.

One can only imagine the tension all this created in the Wafai family. In fact, the tension was so great that Said had purchased Badawi a one-way ticket to Jordan and he was to fly back home on the 5th of July.

Said had invited his brother to spend the 4th in Parker with his family. It's unclear if Said wanted to give his brother the pleasure of one last visit with his American family or if he simply wanted to keep an eye on Badawi to assure he didn't do something to avoid the trip back to Jordan. Either way, on the afternoon of July 4, Said drove to Denver to pick up his brother. When he arrived, Badawi wasn't in his apartment. Said drove around the neighborhood until he found Badawi walking alone. Before returning to Parker, Badawi insisted they return to his apartment so he could obtain his jacket. The two brothers arrived home in Parker at about 4 PM and, according to Debra Ann's sister, Linda, Badawi neatly folded his coat on the couch in the living room. No one was aware that he had a .38 caliber revolver hidden in the coat.

The family spent the afternoon and evening together. They were joined by their neighbors, the Thomas Archer family. Dinner was served at 7 PM. Badawi refused to eat with the others, and so he ate alone. The rest of the evening was spent sitting in the back yard visiting and watching the children set off fireworks.

Finally, at about 10:10 PM, the Archers went home. As Linda was preparing to leave approximately ten minutes later, she found Badawi sitting alone on the couch in the living room. Knowing he was to fly home the next day, she wished him a safe journey. She then got into her car and drove back to Denver.

The exact details of what happened during the next 40 minutes will never be known. The children came into the house. Zein began watching TV. Matthew was placed in his crib. The other two children went to their rooms. An argument broke out between the adults in the living room. Then suddenly shots rang out. Zein ran into the living room and saw her uncle shooting her parents. Her brother, Tereq, joined her and they both ran screaming out the front door of their home.

The children ran next door to the Tom Archer residence. They pounded on the door and screamed that their uncle had just shot their parents. The door opened and the children ran in. Mr. Archer had the foresight to shut and lock the door. Mrs. Archer ran to the phone and called the Douglas County Sheriff's office while Mr. Archer tried to calm the children and watch the Wafai residence. Suddenly he saw Badawi Wafai, gun in hand, walking toward his home. Badawi began knocking on the door and calling for Zein and Tereq. When no one answered the door, Badawi returned to his brother's home and went inside. Mrs. Archer remained on the phone with the sheriff's dispatcher, George Couzens, Jr., keeping him informed of Badawi's movements.

All four Douglas County patrol units were dispatched to the scene as well as two off-duty deputies who lived in the area. A Parker Fire Rescue unit was also dispatched.

Deputy James Kimble was the first to arrive. Dispatch informed him that Badawi was in the Wafai home and two small children were with him. Within minutes two more deputies arrived. As the deputies rendezvoused, dispatch notified them that Badawi had telephoned the Parker Fire Department requesting medical aid for his brother and sister-in-law and he told the fire dispatcher he was willing to give himself up.

Deputies Southers and Wood, who had just arrived, entered the house. They found Said and Debra Ann lying in pools of blood on the living room floor. As deputy Southers began checking for signs of life, deputy Wood heard a small child whimpering. He followed the sound to an upstairs bedroom where he discovered Khalid, who was calling for his "mommy". Wood stooped to pick up the child to comfort him, only to hear deputy Southers holler that he'd found a pulse on one of the victims. Wood put the child down, ran to his patrol car and radioed for the Flight-for-Life helicopter to be sent to the scene.

Wood went back to the bedroom, picked Khalid up and carried him outside where another neighbor took him. Parker Fire Rescue and a Reed Ambulance arrived at the scene. Paramedics rushed inside and quickly determined that Said and Debra Ann were dead. (Southers was apparently feeling his own heart beating.)

As soon as the rest of the house was searched, Matthew was located and taken to a neighbor's house. The house was then secured and no one was allowed entry until Sheriff's investigator Dale Row and the coroner arrived.

My phone rang at 11:45 PM, waking me from a sound sleep. Deputy Couzens told me he had officers at the scene of a double homicide in Parker, that Dale Row had been notified and was enroute, and I was to respond immediately. He added the fact a suspect was in custody and was being transported to the jail in Castle Rock.

I hung up the phone and called my deputy, Ed Anderson, on the intercom. Ed also worked for me full time as a funeral director. Within seven minutes, Ed was sitting next to me as I drove to the scene. My vehicle was equipped with a six-channel police radio and as soon as I called in-service Dale Row responded telling me he had notified the Colorado Bureau of Investigation and that agency was sending an investigator.

Dale was the chief investigator for the sheriff's office. He was about 35 years-old, and single. He was a quiet, serious man who was respected for the methodical way he conducted investigations. He and I had worked hundreds of death investigations together and we worked as a team. I liked Dale and that feeling was mutual.

Dale arrived at the scene at 12:08 AM. Upon his arrival he was briefed by his fellow deputies. He then spoke with Thomas Archer, the neighbor in whose home the children had sought refuge. I arrived at 12:15 AM and was taken into the house where I examined both victims and officially pronounced them dead. The scene was photographed, sketched and each item of evidence was carefully measured and located on the sketch. Agent Mike Igoe, a C.B.I. agent, arrived at 1:30 AM. He too photographed the scene and then offered technical assistance as it was needed.

About 2 AM, Dale asked me to accompany him to the neighbor's home to interview the victim's 8-year-old daughter. That was the last thing any of us wanted to do, but it was absolutely necessary. That child was an eye witness to a capital offense and no investigation would be complete without her story.

We knocked on the neighbor's door and were invited into the dining room. The neighbor said Zein was in a bedroom, but she wasn't asleep. She disappeared and a few moments later she re-appeared with a pretty little girl. My heart was breaking for that small child as we introduced ourselves. Dale explained why we needed to talk with her, then he asked her to tell him what had happened. In response to questions, Zein said:

"I was watching TV. I heard a shot and didn't know what it was. I thought it was firecrackers. I came out and my mother and father were on the floor, my uncle was standing over them, killing them. I ran. He came looking for me. They were both lying on the floor, my mom was lying by her chair and there was a hat covered with blood, and my dad was lying on the floor. My uncle was standing by the couch shooting at them. Tareg and I ran out of the house screaming. I was worried because my baby brothers were still in the house. I knew it was going to happen. He is weird, he does dumb things. He always fights."

The actual interview took 15 minutes, but it felt like an hour. Zein cried off and on during the interview. I felt like crying too. I suspect Dale felt the same way, but we never talked about our feelings.

We returned to the crime scene and prepared to remove the bodies. Once the victims were placed in black rubber crash bags and tightly strapped to the two stretchers we were using, we were ready. We knew we were going to be photographed by at least two Denver television crews who had been at the scene for an hour. Ed and I took the front of one of the stretchers, Dale and Mike took the back and we all lifted. As we approached the front door, the powerful lights on the television camera's turned on. Ed and I squeezed through the front door and stepped onto the front porch. Dale and Mike followed through the door, and suddenly, Dale tripped and fell. He went down and the rest of us lost our balance, falling to the ground with the stretcher on top of us. Someone hollered: "Oh, no! That was awful!" The camera lights went off. One of the cameramen ran over and asked if we were alright. We were so embarrassed none of us said a word. We just quickly scrambled to our feet. Finally, I said: "If you promise not to use that film, we'll carry the body back into the house and do that all over again so you'll have some good footage." "It's a deal!" both cameramen said. So, we did it again. And thank God, that piece of film was never used.

The sheriff's department was able to locate and notify Debra Ann's sister, Linda. At 5 AM on the morning of July 5, Marvin and Patricia Klingbeil received a phone call from Linda who simply said: "Please come, I need you. Badawi had just shot Debie and Said." Pat, who had answered the phone said: "Are they OK?"

"No, they're dead!" Linda answered.

Several hours later I received a phone call from Marvin Klingbeil. He explained he was the children's grandfather, their nearest next-of-kin, and that he and his wife, Pat, were going to be in charge of the funeral arrangements. They wanted Andrews Funeral Home to conduct the services. They wanted to drive to Castle Rock and begin making those arrangements that afternoon.

Marvin and Pat had not been married long. They were kind, pleasant people with a genuine concern for Marvin's grandchildren. Social Services was quick to grant them temporary custody of all four children. They were taken to the Klingbeil residence in Denver.

The first thing Marvin and Pat asked when we met that afternoon was: "How can we help those children move through their grief in a healthy way?" We discussed all sorts of options. From the funeral home library, I gave them books describing how children grieve. We made plans for the children to view their parents after they had viewed a video designed to assist children express their grief. Finally, we made arrangements for a double funeral.

Said's mother lived somewhere in Amman, Jordan. The homicides would present her with the double shock of a dead son and another son facing homicide charges in the United States. It was my responsibility to locate and notify her of the deaths. Badawi had sold his mother's home before he came to the United States. She not only didn't have a phone; she didn't have a permanent residence. To further complicate matters, I was told there were only about 20 telephones in Amman. Using information from Said's in-laws, I was able to obtain the name and a phone number where I could reach a man who knew Said's mother. I made the phone call and spoke with a man who barely understood English. I told him what had happened and asked him to locate and notify Said's mother. Then, I gave him my phone number and we agreed on a time he would call me back. He was planning to have Said's mother at his side when that call was made.

Several days later, at the appointed time, I received the return call. Said's mother had been notified and she was listening to the conversation on a speaker phone. She would ask a question in Arabic and her friend would translate. I'd answer the question and again, the man would translate so she could understand. It was a long conversation and several times I could hear Said's mother crying. She wanted to know how the grandchildren were; who was caring for them; where Said would be buried; and where Badawi was being held. When I hung up the phone, I sat thinking how much grieving parents share in common regardless of cultural differences. I felt sorrow and sympathy for that woman.

My role as coroner had required me to arrange an autopsy. Several hours prior to the scheduled autopsy, investigators from the sheriff's department and an assistant district attorney arrived to collect evidence and clothing from each body. Then I transported both bodies to the Swedish Emergency Medical Center and assisted the nurse practitioner as she obtained X-rays. The X-rays help the pathologist locate bullets within the body. Dr. Ben Galloway, a pathologist in the Denver coroner's office, performed the autopsies in the funeral home morgue with a gallery of observers that included myself, sheriff's investigators and the assistant D.A. When all that was completed the bodies were released to be prepared for family viewing.

After the bodies had been embalmed, dressed and placed in matching caskets, Marvin and Pat brought the children to view their parents. All the adults, myself included, had tears running down our cheeks as we went through that very difficult and painful experience. The grandparents and children, along with Debra Ann's sister and her children, returned several more times prior to the funeral. It didn't get any easier, but the children seemed more willing to talk and ask questions each time they returned.

After the funeral, Pat kept in touch with me. She and Marvin were granted permanent custody of the children in September. Eight months after the slayings, Badawi was convicted of first-degree murder and given a life sentence in the Colorado State Penitentiary. Marvin suffered a heart attack and died several years later. Pat, who had married Marvin late in life, was left with the responsibility of raising those four young children alone. She is to be greatly admired for her splendid efforts. But if you were to tell her that, she would give God the credit. Her devout faith and trust in God was the source of her wisdom, patience, love and strength.

Badawi died serving time in Canon City. He had a rare genetic disease that was present in this blood. After his death, Pat called me and informed me of Badawi's death. She asked if I had kept any of Said's blood. She was afraid he might have had the same disease, and; a simple test of his blood would reveal it. If it wasn't present, the children would not have to worry about having the disease. I called Dr. Galloway. Unfortunately, there were no samples.

As the children began graduating from high school, Carol and I began receiving invitations to attend their graduations. Circumstances prevented us from attending until Matthew's graduation from Arapahoe High School in 2000. We gathered in Pat's home with a large number of family and friends, including Judge Richard Turelli, the District Court Judge who sentenced Badawi. We met and talked with each of the grown children. They are fine people. Matthew, an infant the last time I saw him, is a handsome young man who is looking forward to attending college and majoring in video production. Perhaps he'll end up being a cameraman for some major news affiliate. I'm sure he's the type who would agree not to use pictures of a clumsy crew of rural coroners and sheriff's investigators.

A Noisy Customer

"Breathe. It's just a bad day not a bad life"

Author unknown

Everything seemed to be going smoothly. The chapel was full of mourners, the family had arrived and were comfortably seated, and the minister had opened the funeral service with prayer.

This was an important service. The dead man had lived in Douglas County many years and had been very active in his church and in the community. The size of the congregation attested to his popularity. We had set up chairs in our living room to accommodate the large, over-flow crowd and those preparations proved necessary. A beautiful, comforting service would reflect well on our business.

As the soloist began singing the first hymn a loud, high pitched sound filled the air. Thinking it was an electronic feed-back emanating from our sound system, I headed for the music room. I quietly opened the cabinet that housed the amplification system and adjusted the knobs. To my horror nothing changed.

I went to the speaker in the living room to make sure the speaker connections weren't making the irritating noise. No luck. The speaker was not only working; it was clearly broadcasting the noise from the chapel.

I next went to the rear of the chapel to see if I could locate the source. As I entered through the rear doors I confirmed that the noise was coming somewhere within that room. I concluded that the only possible source was the overhead fans that were operating to reduce the heat. I switched them off. The awful sound continued and the heat in the room began to rise.

By this time everyone was aware of the noise. Instead of listening to the sermon, people were shifting in their seats and sharing disgusted glances. I couldn't have felt more uncomfortable and embarrassed but there was nothing else to do. By the time the service ended, my face was flushed and my spirits were down.

My assistant and I opened the casket for people to pass by as Carol led those who had been seated in the living room into the chapel. As the last of those folks filed in, I moved to the rear of the chapel to assist with the ushering. At this point the noise was so loud it could be heard above the organ postlude.

When I motioned for the last row to stand and join the procession past the casket, those folks stood and slowly began to move forward. To my surprise the noise began to move too. In fact, the noise seemed to be connected to Buggs Lambert, an elderly gentleman who wore large hearing aids in both ears. As he moved past me I realized his hearing aids were the source of the awful sound. Either he was so deaf he couldn't hear the noise or he assumed someone else needed to adjust their hearing aids.

After Buggs left the chapel the comforting sound of organ music filled the air and a deep sense of peace settled in. Relieved that the problem was solved, I felt my red, flushed cheeks return to their natural color.

Later at the cemetery the minister suggested we have the hearing impaired check their aids before they're allowed admission to the services. Not a bad idea.

Loosing A Finger

"God will not look you over for medals, degrees, or diplomas, but only for scars."

Anonymous

Since the early 1940's my father had sold monuments as part of the funeral home business. So when we bought the funeral home we were also buying the monument business. We sold brass and bronze markers, granite and marble monuments, and we ordered and set government military markers. These products came from several different companies. Each company provided us with a catalog and a display case with samples of granite or marble or bronze. All our customers had to do was examine the catalogs and select the type, size and shape of the material they wanted. We would help them select special fonts and specialized carvings and we could even arrange to have a picture of the deceased attached to the monument on a porcelain disk. Once all the decisions were made I would mail their order. Four to six weeks later the monument would be delivered by truck to my back yard.

I preferred using the Kollmann Monumental Works located in St. Cloud, Minnesota. They offered a wide variety of granites. Their catalog contained hundreds of different designs, and each monument could be purchased in a variety of sizes. They welcomed custom designs and they would send me a blue print of the proposed design before it was carved.

National Monument Company, located in Mississippi, was the only firm from which I could obtain marble. Their white marble monuments designed for a baby's grave were very inexpensive and that made them popular with young couples whose baby died.

The sale of a monument always included the preparation of a concrete foundation upon which the monument was set at the grave site. That prevented the stone from tipping over. Before delivery of a stone I would go to the cemetery, locate the grave and prepare the foundation. I'd have to dig a hole about ten inches deep, place a wooden frame in the hole, mix and pour concrete, and then create a smooth finish on the surface as the concrete dried. That process would take several hours. People liked to purchase monuments prior to Memorial Day. It wasn't unusual for me to have twenty to twenty-five foundations to pour in the weeks prior to that holiday.

I enjoyed preparing, pouring and finishing foundations. It was physically hard labor. I was usually alone in the cemetery and that gave me the opportunity to think and pray as I worked.

On occasion my son, Eric, would spend the day with me. We always enjoyed being together and Eric loved to explore the rural cemeteries.

When the monuments arrived, weight was always a factor that had to be taken into consideration. Small marble markers and military markers were relatively light, weighing about one hundred pounds. The granite monuments weighted considerably more. The largest granite monument I ever sold weighed one ton and it took a crane to lift it off the flat-bed 18-wheel truck that delivered it. I also sold a granite columbarium cabinet that held forty-eight urns to the Cedar Hill Cemetery Association. That cabinet stood seven feet tall and was five feet wide and twelve feet long. It weighed more than two tons. The same crane was used to lift it off the truck and onto its concrete foundation.

The monuments were commonly shipped to a freight house in Denver and the Castle Rock Transfer Company would then bring them to the funeral home. They appreciated the business even if it occasionally created problems. For example, one of their drivers placed a seven-hundred-pound monument in the back of the truck and failed to secure it with ropes. While enroute to Castle Rock he had to make a hard application of his breaks. The monument slid from the back of the truck to the front, crushing a brand new metal oven hood that was being delivered to a local restaurant.

The weight of monuments created problems for me too. Monuments weighing more than a hundred pounds required special equipment in order to move them from place to place. When I first purchased the business I found an old, light weight metal dolly and began using it to move monuments. I had an old trailer that attached to the back of our nine-passenger limousine. I'd place the ends of two 2 X 12 planks, twelve feet long, on the ground and the other end in the trailer. Then I'd pick up the monument with the dolly and pull it into the trailer. That worked well until one day when I was removing a five-hundred-pound monument from the trailer. As I was slowly descending the ramp the metal bar that held the dolly wheels began to bend under the weight. Before I reached the bottom of the ramp the wheels bent and fell off leaving the monument on the plank several feet above the ground. I was forced to drive the trailer forward until the wooden planks and the monument fell to the ground. Then I had to go to town and borrow a huge metal dolly from the local lumber yard in order to finish my work. After that experience I purchased a dolly designed to carry fifteen hundred pounds of weight. It had four large wheels, a canvas strap and brakes that were activated by levers attached to the handle bars.

Later I purchased a pickup truck and had a hydraulic lift welded near the right rear bumper. That lift enabled me to pick up heavy monuments and swing them into the truck bed with little danger of injury to myself or others. It was a wonderful tool. I lifted so many heavy monuments that the truck frame bent. The truck looked odd, moving down the highway, tilted to one side; I didn't care. One Halloween a couple of high school boys visited both the Parker Cemetery and Cedar Hill Cemetery and turned almost a hundred stones over. I drove my truck through both cemeteries and was able to lift most of those monuments back in place with my hydraulic lift. That gesture built a lot of good will for my business. I only wish I would have used my hydraulic lift the day I lost my finger.

That incident came about after I decided to use a new monument company. The new company had sent me their catalog and samples which included a beautiful pink granite. I had had people request pink granite but I'd never worked with a company that offered that color. A short time after receiving the catalog I sold a four-hundred-pound upright monument. The stone arrived encased in a wood crate and it was unloaded onto the concrete patio in the back yard of the funeral home.

Having never received a monument in a wooden crate; and, having never received a monument from that particular company, I called the funeral director who worked for me and we went right to work removing the crate. Two metal straps were wrapped around the wood. I cut the straps and then I pried off the wood on the top while Ed held the sides. Once the top was removed, I began to peel the wood from the front. As I was loosening the last board on the front the monument began to fall forward out of the crate. Without thinking, I grabbed it. My effort had absolutely no effect on that four-hundred-pound rock. It fell on my hands and my left foot.

"Ouch!" was all I said as I pulled my hand out from under the monument.

Ed's response was: "Oh my God, it's cut your finger off."

Blood began to flow. The fingers on my left hand and my left foot were throbbing with pain. I immediately realized that the end of my left little finger was lying on the ground next to one of the medal straps. The strap had ended up between the monument and my fingers. My left foot prevented the monument from falling completely flat on the concrete. If my foot hadn't been in the way that monument would have severed all four fingers on my left hand. Instead it amputated the end of one and cut the others to the bone. Three toes on my left foot were broken.

I limped to the back door of our house and yelled for Carol to bring the car keys immediately. She ran to the door, saw the blood and disappeared. In moments she was back with a wet rag and the keys. We jumped in the car and she drove to the Swedish Emergency Medical Center north of town.

A rather humorous incident occurred as we made our way to the center. A car turned in front of ours. Carol honked the horn hoping the driver would let us pass. Instead the driver took offense and slowed down. Carol again honked and I held up my hand thinking the driver would see the trouble I was in. Unfortunately, the driver thought I was giving her an obscene gesture…giving her the finger. Truth is…that was impossible. I didn't have a finger to give.

We made it to the center and then had to go to the main hospital. They tried to reattach my finger but found that would not work. To this day, I look like many monument dealers I know. I'm one finger short of a full hand.

I wonder if that will be one of the scars God will be looking for.

Death in a Car Trunk

"Nobody is impervious to misfortune."

Ferdinand Marcos

It's hard to imagine the range of emotions that swept over the driver of the 18-wheel diesel tractor-trailer as his rig slammed into the back of a 1971 Pontiac sedan during a snow storm that left I-25 ice packed. Both vehicles were north bound several miles south of Castle Rock at 7 AM on that fateful Sunday morning in the Spring of 1981. The impact sent the Pontiac careening into the burrow pit where it stopped upright with the trunk lid crushed and open. The truck driver was able to stop near the Pontiac. As he opened the door to exit his rig his eyes were drawn to the flurry of activity around the Pontiac. The car doors opened and more people than one would ever imagine possible came tumbling out. Two dazed young men crawled out of the trunk, and all of them took off running in different directions.

The truck driver walked to what he thought was an empty car only to be further shocked by the presence of a dead body lying in the open trunk. Stunned, he walked back to his truck, climbed back into the cab, and sat in silence hoping the Colorado State Patrol would arrive soon.

I was notified by the Douglas County Sheriff's Department and was enroute to the scene prior to the arrival of the first state patrol unit. Sheriff's officers at the scene kept the sheriff's radio channel alive as they worked to locate and roundup the car passengers who had fled the scene. At least five young Hispanic males had been arrested and were being detained when I pulled up next to the Pontiac. A sheriff's officer greeted me saying: "Your man is in the trunk of that Pontiac." He was right. The young man was lying in a pool of blood. He had died instantly from a crushed skull.

I assisted state patrolman Garcy Vasquez investigate the accident. After we had obtained statements, measurements and photographs, we removed the victim's body and placed it in a black rubber crash bag. A search of his clothing turned up no identification. I transported his body to the funeral home in Castle Rock.

Officers at the scene arrested a total of 10 Hispanic males and transported them to the Douglas County jail in Castle Rock. Officer Vasquez, who speaks fluent Spanish, met with the group of frightened aliens who were gathered in the 'day room' of the jail. He asked the group to identify their dead companion. Jose Luis Quiroz Francia shyly offered the name

Salvador Cabrera. Then he agreed to accompany officer Vasquez to the funeral home to identify the body and provide information to help locate and notify the dead man's family.

Jose Francia was a small man in his early thirties. His head was downcast and he was quiet when he and officer Vasquez walked into my office. Garcy was the first to speak. He said Jose spoke no English, he was a personal friend of the deceased, and he was willing to look at the body and make the identification. Jose was looking at me as Garcy spoke. I tried to visibly convey my sympathy, but there was no response. Both men then followed me to the morgue in silence.

It's painful for anyone to see a friend dead, but massive head wounds make the gruesome task even more difficult. Tears welled up in Jose's eyes as he looked at his friend. He turned to Garcy and confirmed the identity. We all stood in silence for a few moments and then we returned to the office.

We sat down and I offered Garcy and Jose coffee. Both of them welcomed the hospitality. After a few minutes, Jose began sharing information with Garcy. He said his friend was 20 years old. His parents and six brothers and sisters lived in Valle de Santiago in rural central Mexico. The village was so small there was no telephone communication. We would have to notify the Mexican police and ask them to locate and notify the family.

Jose told Garcy that the group of aliens were headed to Longmont, Colorado, where they had been promised work as laborers at the Tanaka Farm. The group met Blaz Vasquez-Valle, the driver of the car, in a bar in Juarez. Each man had paid Blaz anywhere from $100 to $300 dollars to drive them to Colorado. The group had left Juarez on Friday with three men lying in the trunk and the rest tightly packed in the front and back seats. The trip had been uncomfortable and frightening. The threat of arrest had been a topic of conversation throughout that weekend.

After Garcy left to take Jose back to the jail, I called the Mexican consulate in Denver and asked for their assistance. My request wasn't unusual in light of the large number of illegal aliens who are smuggled into Colorado annually. I would later find that smuggling rings transported 500 to 1,000 aliens a month into Denver alone, at that time.

Within several days I received a call from the consulate informing me that Salvador's parents had been notified and they asked that his body be sent to a funeral home in Juarez. The Mexican consulate wanted me to make the arrangements through a Mexican funeral home in Denver. They further assured me they would pay for any and all expenses. Once I contacted the Trevino Mortuary in Denver all the arrangements came together quickly and easily. By noon Tuesday the United States Immigration and Naturalization Service had deported Jose and the other nine aliens back to Mexico.

Several weeks later I was surprised to receive a telephone call from Juarez, Mexico. The call was from an English speaking friend of Jose, who had asked him to make the call on his behalf. Jose wanted to tell me that his friend's body had arrived and the family was grateful. He also wanted to thank me for my kindness. The call surprised me and I was emotionally moved to think that someone as culturally different as Jose would take the time and spend the money to make that call. I told Jose's friend how impressed I was by Jose's willingness to undertake the difficult task of identifying the body. With no hesitation, Jose's friend responded: "Jose is a very good worker. If you liked what he did why don't you hire him? He could be there in no time and he would even learn to speak English if that would help." I laughed and said I had all the help I needed.

Fatal Airplane Accidents

"I ran out of altitude, airspeed and ideas all at the same time." …when asked why he ejected. Attributed to Tony Lavier, Chuck Yeager, and just about every other well-known test pilot.

Douglas County is located in the center of the state with the foothills to the west and the high plains to the east. Denver is 25 miles to the north and Colorado Springs is 30 miles to the south. A number of airports are located along the front range. Small aircraft flying into and out of those airports are in almost constant flight over Douglas county. Aircraft accidents occur on a regular basis in both Douglas and Elbert counties.

I responded to and investigated multiple airplane crashes that resulted in 40 fatalities during the time I served as coroner. The vast majority of those accidents were due to pilot error and/or the weather. The weather conditions along Colorado's front range can change rapidly, leaving inexperienced pilots in trouble. So many of the accidents I responded to occurred in bad weather that all the paperwork in our investigator's kit was enclosed in plastic so that rain and snow couldn't damage our notes.

John Everitt (4ᵗʰ from L) and I(3ʳᵈ from L) at double fatal on Crowfoot Valley Road

Each airplane crash was unique. Some scenes I responded to involved a single fatal while others involved 2, 3 or more victims. Most were discovered in daylight. Each scene presented unique problems and challenges that had to be addressed and overcome.

One of the first scenes I responded to occurred after dark. It involved a small plane that flew out of Centennial Airport which is located north of Douglas County. The pilot had just filled his fuel tanks. He lifted off heading south into Douglas County with one passenger aboard. His plane was so heavy that he had a hard time gaining altitude. He cleared the hill just south of the airport; however, he failed to see a tall electric power pole. His plane hit the pole, crashed and burned. The pilot and his passenger were both killed instantly.

There were no roads near the scene. The only access was through gullies, around rocks and trees and through heavy underbrush. It took the fire units a long time to arrive at the scene. With the airplane fuel tank's full of fuel the resulting fire was intense and both bodies were badly burned.

At that point I had little experience with fatal airplane investigations and I was ill equipped to remove two hot and completely burned bodies. I didn't even have gloves that were heavy enough to protect my hands. It was not unlike a chef picking up a fully roasted piece of meat, placing it into a rubber bag and transporting it to the funeral home. Somehow, I managed. That experience led me to gather all the special equipment I would need and use later.

Another scene I responded to at night involved a large UPS cargo plane that crashed just east of Castle Rock as it was approaching Centennial Airport. The pilot and his co-pilot died in that accident. That scene was also located in an uninhabited rural field that was difficult to access. It was impossible for me to drive to the scene; I loaded my equipment on a fire truck and rode that unit to the accident site.

One of the most memorable crashes occurred during a snow storm on the night of December 7, 1982. Karen Key, 29 years old, the first woman television news helicopter pilot-reporter in the nation, and, her passenger, Larry Zane, an aviation mechanic, were both killed when the KOA-TV helicopter she was piloting crashed into a hillside near I-25 in southern Douglas County. Key was enroute to an area south of Pueblo, Colorado, where a Pioneer Airlines commuter plane was reported missing in treacherous icy weather. One helicopter crew from another Denver TV station had refused to take that trip due to the weather; another crew turned back in mid-flight. But that didn't stop Karen Key from attempting the flight.

The evening TV news carried a story that the KOA-TV helicopter was missing and presumed down. Weather conditions prevented any search until early the next morning. A TV News helicopter from Denver TV Channel 9 discovered the wreck. The Channel 9 pilot had his station contact the Douglas County Sheriff's office who in turn called me. As I was preparing to leave for the scene, the Channel 9 newsroom telephoned my office and offered to take me, my deputy coroner and our equipment to the scene. I politely declined the offer. I didn't feel real confident riding in a helicopter to go investigate a helicopter crash.

It had quit snowing but the temperature was well below freezing and the ground was covered with fresh snow. The scene was located about 300 yards west of I-25. Karen Key was not instrument certified; she was flying in a heavy snow storm and fog was present requiring her to stay low in the air. She was probably using I-25 as a directional guide when her helicopter slammed into a grove of pine trees. She and her passenger died instantly.

The resulting investigation revealed that Karen Key had been drinking alcohol at a ski resort beginning at 9:30 AM on the morning of the accident. Her blood-alcohol level was .09 at the time of the crash. It was further discovered that she had been hired by Chanel 4 in spite of the fact that she had been arrested for drunk driving during the year before her hire. And finally, it was determined that she had exaggerated her experience and she was not to navigate by instruments at night.

When she arrived at the hanger at the Jefferson County Airport prior to lifting off on that fatal flight, airplane mechanic Larry Zane offered to accompany her. His concern for her safety led to his unfortunate death.

That accident resulted in numerous television and newspaper reports. The December 27, 1982, *Time* magazine even carried an article about the accident. It was noted in that article that … "No Denver station has revamped its policy on using choppers, though Key's crash was the city's fourth accident in 2 ½ years."[17]

I recall one more incident related to this investigation. After I had returned from the crash site I received a phone call from an executive of Channel 4 News. I recognized who I was talking to as soon as he mentioned his name. He had called to obtain some appropriate information about the death of the station's helicopter news reporter. The conversation was formal and I was able to provide the information that was requested. When we were about to end the conversation, I asked the man how he was feeling. Silence followed. Then, with some emotion, he said no one had asked him that. He thanked me and then he said he hadn't taken the time to experience his emotions. He said he was sad, thanked me again and we concluded the call. After putting the phone down, I prayed for him, and for the families of both victims.

Carol and I will, for the rest of our lives, remember May 18, 1981, as our "Black Monday". We had four funerals scheduled that week with the first one occurring at 2 PM that afternoon at a church in Elbert County. For our small family-owned funeral home, that was about the limit of funerals we could handle. At 6 that morning I received a phone call from the sheriff's office informing me of a suicide at a home near Sedalia, Colorado. Since I had a lot to do to prepare for the 2 o'clock service, I called Ed Anderson, my full-time funeral director and deputy coroner, and asked him to respond and investigate the suicide. That left Carol and me to prepare for the afternoon funeral. That also meant that we would have five bodies at the funeral home after Ed returned.

We worked all morning and then, at 10:57 AM, our day turned into a nightmare. Ed had not returned from the suicide investigation; however, Carol and I had loaded all the equipment, the casket and all the flower arrangements in the hearse and pallbearer's car. One of our part-time assistants had arrived and we were preparing to leave for the funeral in Elbert County when the phone rang. It was the sheriff's office. The dispatcher informed me that deputies had been dispatched to an area east of Castle Rock to search for a possible airplane crash. I was to stand by in case they found fatalities at the scene. I told Carol she should be

---

[17] Time, December 27, 1982, pg. 59

prepared to handle the funeral if I had to respond to an airplane crash. I helped her prepare to leave as soon as Ed returned. This was a major event because Carol had never assisted at a funeral without me being present; I had never failed to direct a funeral that I had personally arranged with a family.

At 11:23 AM one of the Deputies located the wrecked aircraft in a muddy pasture four miles east of Castle Rock. He made his way to the site and found four people in the plane. They all died instantly. I was notified and I called Mark Stover, another deputy coroner, and asked him to respond to the scene with me. When we arrived at the command post it was raining lightly and the wind was blowing hard. One of the sheriff's deputies helped us load our equipment into a 4-wheel drive vehicle and we proceeded to the crash site.

The plane, a Cessna 210, appeared to have dropped out of the sky and had broken apart without skidding. That indicated that the plane stalled and then dropped almost straight down. All four-people on board died instantly and their bodies were still strapped to their seats. I was informed that the plane was enroute to the Arapahoe County Airport from Ames, Iowa. The occupants were two brothers and their parents. The pilot was 42 years old, his brother was 41 and both lived in the Denver area. Their parents were from Ames. The plane had been damaged so severely that it took us three hours to disentangle the bodies from the wreckage.

Removing one victim from crash site. I am 2nd from left.

By the time I was leaving the scene, Carol and Ed had concluded the funeral service in Elbert, enabling Carol to return to the funeral home while Ed oversaw the concluding rites at the cemetery. My first responsibility after I returned with the four bodies was to make positive identification of the victims and begin the process of notifying the next-of-kin. Once I had accomplished that, I gave Carol the names and she was going to have the Denver Police Department send an officer to notify the relatives. Before she was able to request assistance from the police department she received a phone call from a man who asked for the names of the victims. He said he thought the victims were his parents and his two brothers. He was frantic. We never gave information like that over the phone; but the man was emotionally distraught and said he believed the victims were his brothers and his parents and Carol felt she had no choice but to confirm this . It was a traumatic experience for both that man and Carol.

There was one more unusual detail to this accident. While at the scene we found that there was a dead dog in the wreckage. I decided to bring that dead animal back to the funeral home. One of the first things the victim's family asked was if we had found that dog. They were grateful we had recovered it and they made arrangements for it to be properly disposed of.

The National Transportation Safety Board (NTSB) and the Federal Aviation Administration (FAA) sent investigators to every scene. I had utmost respect for the NTSB investigators. They had the primary responsibility for the crash site investigation. I did nothing at the first two crash sites I responded to until the NTSB investigators arrived. We worked so well together that I gained their trust. They were often slow to respond to the scene. I was told I could photograph the scene and remove the bodies prior to their arrival. They made sure I had extra serology kits to collect the samples they required. They always came to the funeral home after their examination of the scene. While I had good relations with the FAA investigators, their responsibilities were such that I didn't have a lot of interaction with them.

The crash of a small plane into Dawson Butte created another memorable experience. On April 1, 1979, the Douglas County Sheriff's Office was notified that an aircraft flying from the Meadow Lake Airport in Colorado Springs to an Arapahoe County Airport was missing. The aircraft had lifted off during a snow storm. Visibility was poor due to heavy snow fall and low cloud cover. Civil Air Patrol attempts to locate the plane failed.

The airport tower at Stapleton Airfield notified the sheriff's office at 3:06 PM on April 3 that the wreckage of an aircraft had been spotted from the air in the area of Tomah Road and Highway 105, approximately 7 miles southwest of Castle Rock on the side of Dawson Butte. A wreck was spotted from the air by a pilot in a small aircraft who had been searching for the missing air plane. He notified Stapleton Tower who in turn called the sheriff's office. The first officers to respond had no way to communicate with the aircraft that had located the wreckage. The reporting pilot could only circle the site of the downed plane in an attempt to help the responding sheriff's deputies. The sheriff's officers used a 4-wheel drive vehicle to get closer to the scene but they had to abandon that unit due to the steep terrain and snow cover.

At 4:15 PM St. Anthony's Flight for Life helicopter arrived at the scene, spotted the wreck near the top of Dawson Butte and landed nearby. The flight crew, with direct radio communication with the sheriff's officers, pinpointed the site for the responding deputies. The wrecked plane, a single-engine Cessna 170A, was lying upside down about 25 feet from the top of the butte. A member of the flight crew crawled down to the wreckage and found the pilot and a passenger still strapped to their seats, dead and their bodies frozen.

The sheriff's dispatcher notified me at 3:30 PM. I called my deputy Charlie Bowman and we arrived at the sheriff's command post located in a field about half a mile from the scene at 4:40 PM. We were told that the only access to the scene would be by helicopter. Ten minutes after we arrived the St. Anthony helicopter landed at the command post. The helicopter pilot agreed to lift Charlie and me and our equipment onto Dawson Butte.

Charlie standing next to one of the recovered bodies.

When we arrived on top of the butte we had to climb down to the wreckage. The front of the plane was badly damaged and both bodies were hanging upside down, held in place by their seat belts with their legs tightly wedged in place having been smashed up under the dash by the force of the impact. The plane was lying on such a steep slope that we had to tie ropes to the plane and around nearby trees to keep the aircraft from sliding down the mountain.

The helicopter pilot had informed me that he was low on fuel and we only had a short time to recover the bodies. Charlie and I worked as fast as we could photographing the scene and recovering personal property and evidence. Then we attempted to extricate the bodies. We cut the seat belts hoping that would free the bodies. They didn't move. All attempts to pull they free failed because the legs were so tightly jammed under the dashboard.

I knew that we would have to leave the bodies in the airplane and return to the scene the next day if we couldn't quickly find a way to extricate them. If we had to return the next day we would not have the use of a helicopter and access to the scene by foot would be extremely difficult and time consuming. We were under great pressure. I silently prayed asking God to give me an insight into the problem. In answer to that prayer I spotted a tire iron. I used the tire iron to cut a hole in the side of the plane which enabled me to reach in and push the legs of both victims free. We placed the bodies in rubber crash bags, placed them in Stoke's litters (wire basket stretchers) and carried them to the helicopter. We were then flown back to the command post.

The NTSB investigation later found that the pilot should not have been flying in that heavy snowstorm. The pilot was not qualified to fly with instruments. He was probably using highway 105 as a guide to find his way to the Arapahoe airport. The visibility was so poor he did not see the butte until the last minute and he was unable to raise his aircraft fast enough to clear the top of the mountain.

I was deeply grateful for Charlie's able assistance and St. Anthony's helicopter. And I believe God answered my prayer, giving me insight into what was available to extricate those bodies.

This is only a few of the numerous airplane accidents I investigated. From a technical view point, each one presented unusual problems that often-required creative responses. I quickly learned that I had to be flexible when I responded to those scenes.

Elbert County Turboprop Crash

"It always seems impossible until it's done."

Nelson Mandela

It was a cold day, very cold. Colorado was the center of a blizzard that was dumping a huge amount of heavy, wet snow. The snow storm would continue for the next three days. The wind was whipping the snow into deep drifts. Automobile travel was so dangerous that the highways along the entire front range from Pueblo to Fort Collins and east to the Kansas border were being closed periodically.

The storm didn't arrive unexpected. The Weather Bureau had been forecasting the snow for several days. I had a funeral on the day before the storm hit and I felt fortunate that I didn't have any funerals scheduled. As the storm developed, I was working in the garage with John Everett, my full time funeral director. We worked on some small projects, took an hour off for lunch, then returned to the garage to continue our work. At 3:15 PM the extension telephone on the work bench rang. When I answered it I immediately recognized the voice on the other end. It was Mark Hamilton, an Arapahoe County Deputy Coroner. He told me that the Arapahoe County Sheriff's Department had placed his office on stand-by because a small jet was reported down south of Centennial Airport. He thought it was possible that plane had crashed in Douglas County and he suggested we prepare ourselves because the plane held ten people.

I ran into the house and got my police radio so we could listen to the patrol units that were searching for the plane. By the time I returned to the garage, Mark called again. He told me he had good news, the plane hadn't gone down in either Arapahoe or Douglas Counties. It had been located in Elbert County. My heart sank. That wasn't good news. The Elbert County coroner depended on me to assist with all the coroner cases occurring on the west side of her county. She had no equipment or experience responding to an airplane accident with multiple fatalities.

The aircraft was a four-year-old Beechcraft Super King Air. It was a twin-turboprop aircraft owned and operated by Lufkin Industries, Inc., located in Lufkin, Texas. The plane had arrived at Centennial Airport at 10:17 AM that day. The plane was fueled and, as a Lufkin employee welcomed seven male guests aboard, the pilot and co-pilot found room for their passenger's baggage and golf clubs. The guests were to be flown to Lufkin to tour the company and enjoy several days of golf.

All details of the trip had been carefully planned except one. The group of engineers and their baggage weighed too much. An investigation by the NTSB would later estimate that the baggage weighed 260 pounds, the golf clubs weighed about 250 pounds, and the guests themselves had a combined weight of almost 1,900 pounds. That weight combined with full fuel tanks and the freezing weather conditions would prove fatal.

Prior to the 2:34 PM departure, snow had to be brushed from the aircraft. Airport radar tracked the plane as it climbed through 7700 feet at a rate better than 1400 feet per minute. Unfortunately, ice began forming on the wings. Seven minutes into the flight, after reaching a maximum altitude of 12,800 feet, the climb rate diminished to zero. At 2:44 PM the pilot, B. Ray Fisher, radioed the tower at Stapleton International Airport and reported that heavy icing was forcing him to turn back. Minutes later he radioed again. Tower Operations Chief Ken Hukriede could hear the concern in the pilot's voice. He was at 11,000 feet in a gradual descent. Chief Hukriede advised Fisher to maintain whatever altitude he could. Five minutes later the pilot radioed saying he wanted to go to any airport and he was ready to declare an emergency. Controllers were preparing a course to Buckley Air National Guard Base when the tower lost radar and radio contact. It was 2:52 PM and the aircraft had crashed 14 statute miles east of Centennial Airport.

Hukriede would later be quoted saying he never detected panic in the pilot's voice. "You don't find too much panic in such situations." Hukriede said. "He just told us two or three times that he couldn't maintain his altitude. There was nothing on the tape after that."[18]

At 3:13 PM the Douglas County Sheriff's dispatch phoned the Elbert County Sheriff's dispatch and advised them that an aircraft was down, that Douglas and Arapahoe Sheriff's units were searching for the plane, and they wanted Elbert County to join the search, concentrating on the northwest portion of Elbert county.

Several minutes later a pickup truck topped the hill near the downed aircraft and the vehicle's occupants spotted the wreck. There were no flames, but smoke was pouring from the front of the plane. The two female occupants of the truck drove one mile to the Running Creek Ranch and called the sheriff. Several men returned to the site with the witnesses, arriving at about 3:30 PM. Flames were now coming from the right front of the airplane. The group approached the plane from the left side and they found the interior of the craft filled with thick black smoke and there were no obvious exits. One of the men ran to the right side of the plane which was free of smoke. He removed a broken window to see if anyone might be alive. The cockpit area was filled with fire and the witnesses were startled by a very loud popping sound. Fearing an explosion, they quickly moved away from the plane.

For the next thirty minutes they helplessly watched the aircraft burn. No emergency equipment arrived during that time and none could be seen or heard in the area. Finally, one of the witnesses returned to the Running Creek Ranch and again phoned the Elbert County Sheriff's Department.

---

[18] The Rocky Mountain News, article by Jay Pfeiffer, news staff

At 3:27 PM the Elbert dispatcher notified a deputy that an unidentified female reported an aircraft accident approximately 16 miles north of Elizabeth. If that report was accurate the accident would have been in Arapahoe County. At 3:46 the dispatcher received the second phone call. This time the witness provided clear details of the location and advised that the plane was burning and no assistance had arrived.

Two Elbert County deputies were dispatched. When they arrived they found the aircraft totally engulfed in flames and smoke. They requested that the Elizabeth Fire Department, the Elbert County Sheriff and Coroner be dispatched to the scene.

Sheriff's deputies from Arapahoe County and fire trucks from Aurora Fire Department arrived on the scene and were soon joined by the Elizabeth Fire Department. By the time the fire was extinguished the entire top of the plane had burned away.[19] The heat and smoke were so intense that no attempt was made to remove or identify the victims.

Sheriff George Yarnell and Coroner Ethel Kilgore arrived at the scene. Shortly thereafter, two federal investigators arrived, one with the NTSB and another from the FAA. The area was roped off and secured for the night.

Our phone didn't ring for hours. As time went on I began to think that Elbert County had called another agency to assist them. Then at 8:30 PM I received a phone call from the Elbert County Sheriff's dispatcher. He told me that the coroner wanted us to respond to the scene the following morning and we were to be prepared to recover ten badly burned bodies.

I called John Everett, Chuck Bowman and Bill Weir and asked them to meet me at the funeral home by 7:30 AM the next morning. The snow storm had continued to intensify that day and it continued unabated that night. I urged everyone to dress warm and be prepared to spend the day outside. I had a full set of down clothes which included a hat, coat and pants which I always wore when I responded to coroner calls on cold days.

I awoke long before dawn. The storm was still raging and though all the roads were closed, I knew that Douglas and Elbert Counties would be assigning snow plow crews to open the 27 miles of road that stretched between the funeral home and the scene. I remember lying in bed. The room was dark. I could hear the wind howling. I was scared. I knew that nothing had been done at the scene and I would carry the responsibility for the recovery of the bodies. I had no idea what the scene would be like or how complicated the recovery operation would be. The newscasts had reported that the plane was carrying petroleum engineers, most of whom were young married men with families. I felt sorrow for the families and I felt a heavy responsibility to do all I could to make positive identification of the bodies. As I quietly laid in bed, I prayed that God would protect us, that He would guide and direct our efforts.

I got up, ate and organized the equipment we would need. By the time John, Chuck and Bill arrived both hearses contained the necessary body bags, body tags and all of our camera equipment. Most airplane accidents happened in bad weather, so I had prepared a special kit that included containers to collect blood and other fluid samples, assorted forms, files and writing utensils that could be used in wet weather.

---

[19] Notes from the NTSB report and reports from the Elbert County Sheriff's Department.

It was still snowing when we began driving to the scene at 8:30 AM. The roads were snow packed and icy. An Elbert County snow plow had opened the county road between Elizabeth and the crash scene. However, the snow had continued to create drifts and we began experiencing difficulty following the road. Several miles from the scene I drove into a ditch and became hopelessly stuck. Chuck was driving the second vehicle behind mine and was able to stop without getting stuck. We decided to leave John and Bill with the stuck vehicle and Chuck and I continued on to the scene. Upon our arrival, I asked the sheriff to have a snow plow pull our car out of the ditch and again clear the road. A radio equipped plow was immediately dispatched to find our vehicle.

Sheriff Yarnell, Coroner Kilgore, Chuck and I examined the scene. I clearly remember walking to the side of the plane and looking down into the interior through the opening that was left as a result of the intense fire. The plane's interior was black except for the snow that had settled in. There didn't appear to be any bodies, just snow. The recovery operation was going to be a challenge, to say the least. George and Ethel offered some suggestions; but it was obvious they both expected me to take charge of the recovery, so I did.

I had us respond just as I would at any crime scene. We began by photographing the entire scene. An Elbert County deputy sheriff was assigned to draw a rough sketch of the plane's interior. He, Sheriff Yarnell and I then entered the plane and made our way to the cockpit. I brushed the snow away until I located the first body. A body tag containing the number one was placed on the body and photographed. The body's position was then measured and it's location and position were noted on the sketch. The body was then closely examined to determine if the seat belt was attached. A body tag containing the number one was attached to the seat that contained the body. Finally, the body was placed in a body bag which had a tag containing the number 1 attached. The area directly beneath was then carefully searched and any personal effects found were placed in the body bag next to the victim.

The same procedure was then used for the recovery of each of the other victims. Chuck Bowman kept notes on bodies 1 through 6; John Everett kept notes on bodies 7 through 10.

This tedious process took hours. During that time, it continued to snow. We were all cold and wet. There was very little conversation other than discussion of the work at hand. The longer the task continued; however, the more confident I was that we were competently processing the scene, that we were doing all we could to ultimately assure the correct identification of each body and the reconstruction of the accident scene. I became so absorbed in the recovery effort that I forgot the snow and cold.

As the ninth body was removed from the plane, Sheriff Yarnell moved to the location of the tenth body and, in a loud voice, said: "There you are! We have been looking for you all day!" His attempt at humor brought a smile to everyone's face. What he said was true. Slowly, methodically, we'd been working our way from the front of the plane to the rear, knowing that the recovery effort would only end when the last person's body had been carefully examined and removed.

Each recovered body had been moved to a staging area near the plane. When the last body was removed, all the body bags were then placed in the two hearses. The slow trip back to

Castle Rock began at 1:30 PM. A snow plow led the way from the scene, down the county road into Elizabeth. State Highway 86 was plowed and open from Elizabeth to Castle Rock. We arrived at the funeral home about 3:00 PM. We placed the bodies on the floor of the garage. The temperature in the garage was 34 degrees, just above freezing, an ideal environment to store human remains.

John, Chuck and Bill went home, mentally and physically tired. I had more work to do before I could end my day. I telephoned Dr. Ben Galloway to arrange the autopsies. Dr. Galloway, a pathologist in the Denver Coroner's office, had been expecting my call. In addition to his work for the Denver coroner, he had a private practice through which he performed autopsies for coroners located in small counties near Denver. He conducted all my forensic examinations. He'd been following the television and radio news reports of the accident and he was aware I was at the scene. He told me he'd already called Dr. Gary Wilson, a forensic dentist who worked at the University of Colorado School of Dentistry. He and a colleague were to make identification through dental examinations. We made plans to begin the examinations at 10 the following morning. Next I telephoned Sheriff Yarnell and asked him to contact each of the victim's families and request dental records. The records were to be taken to the University of Colorado School of Dentistry. He agreed to do that and assured me that he and Ethel Kilgore would be at the autopsies.

That evening I was both thankful and anxious. I was thankful that no one else had died, that I didn't have any pending funerals. And I could devote all my energy to the work at hand. I was anxious, knowing that the phone could ring at any minute and the heavy responsibility I was carrying could be further complicated by another coroner case or funeral home death.

The phone rang constantly. If it wasn't a reporter seeking some details, it was a member of a victim's family desiring information. I even received a call from a representative of Lufkin Industries. He informed me he'd made arrangements with a Lufkin funeral home to receive the Texas victims, and representatives of the funeral home would be calling me later.

I didn't get to bed as early as I had hoped, and interaction with my family was almost non-existent. My sister, Kendal, and her husband, John, were visiting. While I was at the scene, Kendal and John drove to Denver and picked up my niece, Kim, and a friend at the airport. They all returned to Castle Rock and stayed with us over night. At least that's what Carol said. I was so busy that I forgot they were visiting. At any rate, I didn't sleep well that night and I got up early to begin preparing for the autopsies. John also arrived at the funeral home early.

Together we prepared an area where two bodies could be examined at the same time. Both stations had adequate lighting, camera equipment, evidence bags of various sizes, and tables to examine and sort personal property.

By mid-morning everyone had arrived and the processing began. The bodies were so badly burned that visual identification was impossible. To everyone's surprise the portion of each body that was in contact with the aircraft seat did not burn. That meant that we were able to recover some wallets, and we could identify some of the clothing each victim wore. To his credit, Dr. Galloway was able to make tentative identifications of each body. To confirm those identifications, the dentists removed each victim's upper and lower jaws with teeth intact. Those extractions were then taken to a laboratory where they were compared to the dental charts each family had provided. Between the dental and forensic examinations, positive identifications were made on each body. Dr. Galloway also established the cause of death of each victim. Most died immediately upon impact from massive injuries.

I retained custody of the bodies for several days while the dental examinations were conducted and the identifications were confirmed. As soon as those examinations were concluded, the jaws and positive identifications were returned to me and I was finally able to begin releasing each body to the family's mortuary.

During the nine years I owned and operated the funeral home I was called to numerous air plane crashes. I investigated more than 40 airplane deaths, but this crash was the most complicated and it involved the most fatalities at one time. I felt a sense of pride in the way we responded to and handled that disaster. We received letters of appreciation from Lufkin Industries, the Lufkin Funeral Home, and many of the family members. We even received a letter of commendation from one of the forensic dentists who wrote an article about the investigation in the Journal of the Colorado Dental Association. Those letters made me feel that the many tedious hours of labor were worth it. I felt like we not only did something well; we did something that made a difference in the lives of others.

When I first received the telephone call alerting me of a possible airplane accident involving ten people I felt overwhelmed. I knew that if we were to be involved the task would be horrendous. But by the grace of God and with the help of dedicated people, we accomplished all we were called upon to do.

Grieving Guests

"Do not neglect to show hospitality to strangers, for by doing that some have entertained angels without knowing it."

Hebrews 13:2

We will never know if they were angels or not, but we did show hospitality to strangers who came to us grieving and vulnerable. Before arriving each one had experienced a life-changing emotional trauma. They walked through our door sad, emotionally injured and in shock. Their visit was filled with phone calls, sudden and unexpected tears, moments of disbelief, and even outbursts of anger and denial. Carol talked to them, listened to them, fed them, gave them emotional space and compassionate love, and prepared them a place to sleep. I offered practical suggestions, handled death related details, and offered a sympathetic ear. In short we provided our guests a safe environment where they experienced compassionate love.

A gray-haired lady in her mid-70s was the first of these strangers. She and her husband had been traveling south on I-25. Their trip was taking them from Los Angeles to Arkansas and they were near the end of the second day of travel. The woman's husband was driving their Chrysler sedan with a 25-foot travel trailer in tow. They were planning on spending the night at an RV park in Colorado Springs.

It was near 7 PM and the couple had been engaged in a pleasant conversation. Suddenly the woman's husband stopped talking and the car began drifting off the road. The woman cautioned her husband to stay in his lane of traffic, but neither he nor the car responded. As the vehicle moved off the pavement onto the shoulder, the woman grabbed the wheel. By this time her husband had slumped onto the driver's door and his foot was still depressing the accelerator. She unbuckled her seat belt and scooted to the center next to her husband. With one hand on the steering wheel, she moved her husband's legs enough that she could apply the brake with her left leg. As the car began to slow she carefully steered the vehicle off the road, stopped and put the car in park.

She shook her husband but there was no response. She got out of the car and ran to the back, frantically waving at the oncoming traffic. She was so frightened and frantic that cars had to swerve to avoid hitting her. Motorists began to stop. Some stayed at the scene while one man made a U-turn in the median and drove back to Castle Rock where he called the Colorado State Patrol. The patrol dispatcher in turn notified the Castle Rock volunteer fire department, the Sheriff's Department and Care Ambulance. Units from each agency responded, but all that emergency aid was too late. The woman's husband was dead. He had died from a massive heart attack.

I was called to the scene and arrived about 30 minutes after the first motorist had stopped to help. When I stepped from the coroner's car a deputy sheriff told me the victim was still in the driver's seat and his wife was in the rear seat of the state patrol unit. I examined the body and officially pronounced him dead. My assistant began taking photographs and interviewing witnesses while I got into the back seat of the patrol car with the victim's wife.

The woman was surprisingly composed and able to provide vital statistic information, describe the events of the day and supply me with a detailed account of her husband's medical history. Her composure indicated that she was in shock. After explaining that I would take her husband's body to the funeral home I asked the woman what plans she had.

"I don't have any plans." She said. "I don't know what to do next. I don't even know how to drive our car with that trailer attached."

"Well", I said, "why don't you come home with me? The state patrolman can drive you there and I will have one of the volunteer firemen bring your car and trailer and park them in our driveway."

She looked relieved and she accepted the offer. My assistant and I placed her husband's body in the coroner's car and we drove back to the funeral home. When we arrived, I ran into the house and told Carol that we were going to have a guest for the night. Carol's first response was: "She probably hasn't eaten, I'll warm a plate and prepare a bed."

Carol greeted our guest as she stepped out of the patrol car, took her into the house and offered her coffee. The two women talked as I showed the fireman where to park the car and trailer.

I helped my assistant carry the body into the morgue and left him in charge of those details. Then I returned to our living quarters and Carol and I began helping our guest work through all the decisions and notifications that had to be addressed.

A distant relative, a young Los Angeles dentist, was among the many relatives our guest called. He told her he would make arrangements to fly to Denver to assist in any way he could. He had no idea how far Castle Rock was from Denver, but he assumed it was close enough he didn't need a rental car. After he obtained his airplane ticket he called me with the time of his arrival in Denver and asked me to meet him at the airport. I made a note of the time and arranged for one of my part-time employees to meet the man early the next morning.

Our guest asked me to obtain airplane reservations for her and her young relative to fly back home. Then, to my surprise, she told me she had a small dog in the trailer. Since she was going to fly home she asked me to also make arrangements to have the dog sent on the same flight.

The car and trailer had to be driven back to California. I solved that problem by locating a bonded and insured company that provided drivers for cross-country transportation of vehicles. With our guest's permission, I made the necessary arrangements.

The woman asked that her husband be embalmed and dressed in clothing she would provide from the trailer. She wanted me to arrange for his body to be flown to California. She then selected a casket while my assistant was embalming. I notified the California funeral home and obtained reservations to ship the body by plane the next morning.

While I was working on all these details, Carol was providing food, comfort and companionship to our guest. That was complicated by the fact our two young children needed attention and love, too. Carol's time was divided and busy.

The woman decided she would sleep in her trailer. When it appeared we had done all we could, she retired for the night. We left the back door unlocked and the light on so she could use our bathroom as needed.

The next morning was busy. After breakfast, our guest viewed her husband's casketed body then my assistant drove the remains to the airport. I sent a car to pick up the dentist and bring him back to Castle Rock. Carol prepared lunch for our two guests and I drove them, and the dog, to the airport in Denver. While our guests were checking in I took the dog to the freight office and completed its travel arrangements.

That whirlwind of activity occurred in less than 24 hours. While much of what we did was "task oriented," the most important connection we made was emotional in nature. That lady was able to share her grief in the safe confines of our home. She was fed and given compassionate love and support. We know she appreciated all that because we received a lovely thank you letter several weeks later. That event, however, was so unusual that we thought we would never again have to face a similar experience. We were wrong.

Within a year we had more grieving guests. Three young men traveled to Colorado to celebrate their graduation from high school. Their adventure was to culminate with an all-day climb up the steep rock face of a mountain north of Woodland Park in remote Douglas County. Shortly after their technical climb began one of the young men fell to his death. It would be hours before the other two climbers could descend, confirm the death and then make their way to a phone to call for help. It took more time for a rescue unit and sheriff's deputies to respond and verify the death. By the time I was notified, drove through Colorado Springs and then west to Woodland Park and north on the Rampart Range Road to the scene it was late afternoon.

I met the two shocked and grieving rock climbers at the command post near the scene of the death. Both boys were visibly upset but helpful and cooperative. They wanted to accompany me to the scene to recover the body. As we made our way to the base of the rock face, they provided me with all the information I needed. After examining the body and processing the scene, those young climbers helped carry their friend back to the command post.

While we were slowly making our way down the mountain trail I asked the boys where they were planning to stay that night. They had no plans. Since I needed to be able to talk with them as I notified the relatives of the victim, I invited them to follow me home where they could eat and spend the night. They were grateful for the opportunity. They were hungry, tired and wanted access to a telephone. I had the sheriff's dispatcher notify Carol that I was enroute home with several over-night guests.

These guests were less demanding that our first one. Their greatest need was the telephone. They spent lots of time talking to friends and family. Carol fed them and both of us gave them space and privacy. They seemed to gain strength and comfort from each other. After breakfast the following morning, they left for home. We never heard from them again.

Our third experience was more intense and sad. It started with a 3 AM phone call from the Colorado State Patrol dispatcher who informed me of a fatal car crash on Lincoln Parkway north of Parker. When I arrived I pronounced the driver of a small sports car dead. The woman appeared to be in her early 40's and she was nicely dressed. I later learned that she was a cocktail waitress who was on her way home at the end of her shift. I also later determined that she had cocaine in her system. She had driven her car too fast and it rolled over as she was trying to navigate a curve. She was thrown from the car and died instantly. Her driver's license listed a Parker address.

After completing my investigation at the scene I drove the woman's body back to Castle Rock and telephoned one of my deputy coroner's, Pastor Ron Beckman, a Lutheran pastor who lived in Parker. I asked him to accompany me as I notified the woman's family.

I met Ron at about 4:45 AM and we drove to the address listed on the dead woman's license. The house was a small white wood frame house. Other than one lamp in the living room, the house was dark. We stepped onto the front porch and rang the bell. We were surprised when a sleepy 12-year-old-girl opened the door. I asked her if her father was home. She said she and her mother lived alone, and her mother hadn't arrived home from work. I explained who I was, and then, with a lump in my throat, I told her that her mother was dead. She didn't know how to react or what to say. Her eyes filled with tears.

We all stepped into the house and sat down in silence. After some time, I asked her if her parents were divorced. "Yes," she said, and she didn't know where to find her father. The only relatives she knew to contact were her grandparents who lived in California. She went to a desk and located an address book. As soon as she found their phone number, I called their home. A man answered, I identified myself and asked his name. He was the girl's grandfather. Again, with a lump in my throat, I gave him the sad news his daughter was dead. He wanted the details, and as I was describing them he stopped me and asked about his granddaughter. I told him I was with her. He asked to talk with her and I gave her the phone. She cried as she talked. Ron and I wiped tears from our eyes as we listened. When I got the phone again, I offered to take the child home with me. Her grandfather was grateful and my offer was accepted.

The girl placed some clothes, a hairbrush and the address book in a small bag while I telephoned Carol to prepare her for yet another grieving guest. The trip home was quiet and it felt like it took forever.

Carol met us at the door. She took the girl's bag and led her into the kitchen where she had prepared some breakfast and a glass of milk. Carol had a lot on her mind. She needed to develop rapport with the girl. When our boys woke for school she would have to explain the girl's presence and prepare them to meet her. I left Carol and the girl to get acquainted.

The girl was used to fending for herself and she settled in quickly. After the boys left for school, she took a nap. Her grandparents caught the first flight out of California, arrived at Stapleton Airport around noon, rented a car and drove to Castle Rock. They had a tear filled reunion with their granddaughter and then viewed their daughter's body. It was an emotional afternoon. They got a room in a local motel and returned later that evening to make arrangements for their daughter's body to be shipped to California.

We received a case of fresh-picked California grapefruit each Christmas for the next two years. Both times the gift was accompanied with a note of thanks and gratitude from the young girl's grandparents. I've often wondered who raised her and how she is doing today.

The last grieving guests to arrive at our home were the youngest and they suffered the greatest. The tragedy that preceded their arrival occurred on a warm Sunday afternoon.

The sheriff's dispatcher notified me of a serious fatal auto accident five miles north of Castle Rock in the southbound lanes of I-25. "The quickest way to get there," he said, "is to take the exit ramp at the Silver Heights, cross over I-25 and then proceed north in the southbound lanes of traffic." He told me not to worry about going north in the southbound lanes because nothing was moving south. He also told me there were "at least" two dead bodies at the scene and several ambulances had been dispatched to transport the injured.

I was on my way within minutes. The dispatcher was correct, there were no vehicles traveling south on I-25. About a mile north of the Silver Heights exit I could see the flashing lights on the ambulances, fire trucks and police cars. As I approached the scene I could see three badly damaged vehicles, two were in the southbound traffic lanes and the third was on the west shoulder. Two motionless bodies were lying in pools of blood on the highway. Police and rescue personnel were frantically working on an injured victim. As I stepped from my car a sheriff's deputy ran up and said: "That dead man is the father of two little boys who are sitting with some witnesses on the grass over there!" I looked in the direction he was pointing and saw two small, frightened children sitting between some people who appeared to be of Middle Eastern descent.

"How do you know the dead man is their father?" I asked.

"They told me." The deputy said. "They were going to Colorado Springs to pick up their mother. Their father stopped to help those foreigners change a flat tire. A drunk lost control of his car and plowed into them. Those kids saw their dad killed. We need to get those children out of here."

"Can you drive them to the funeral home?" I asked.

"Yes." He said.

"Then do that." I said. I returned to my vehicle and radioed the dispatcher. I informed him that several children of a victim were being transported to the funeral home and then I asked that my wife be notified so she could prepare for their arrival.

I returned to the scene and began my investigation that would keep me at the scene for over an hour. I discovered that a family from India had rented a car in Denver. While traveling toward Colorado Springs a tire on the car blew out. They pulled to the right shoulder. Being unfamiliar with American cars, they didn't know how to change the tire; so, they all got out and sat down on the small hill next to the highway. A man with two boys, ages 5 and 8, stopped to help. He too was enroute to Colorado Springs. He was going to pick up his wife who was attending a church retreat. He had his children get out of his car and sit next to the Indian family while he and several of the Indian men began changing the tire. An intoxicated man driving south on I-25 drifted onto the shoulder of the road and struck the two vehicles killing one of the Indian men and the boys' father. A second Indian male was severely injured. He was transported to a Denver hospital where he died several hours later.

The deputy transported those little boys to the funeral home, and Carol again had her hands full. She knew few details other than the fact the children witnessed their father's death. The children were in shock and could offer little more than their names and their parent's names. They didn't know their home address and they didn't know where their mother was attending a retreat. The only thing Carol could do was to stay with them and provide them with a loving and caring presence.

When I arrived at the funeral home with the two bodies, a state patrolman and I searched the father's belongings for information to help us locate the children's mother. A police officer was sent to the address on the man's driver's license, but no one was home. We did locate a business card of the pastor of St. Philips Methodist Church in Denver in the man's wallet. I called the church and got an answering machine. I then called information and obtained the minister's home phone number. When I telephoned that number the pastor answered. He knew the family, and he knew where the children's mother was attending the retreat. The state patrol dispatcher sent an officer to the retreat. The mother was located and notified. Some women at the retreat drove her to the funeral home to reunite her with her children.

All that took hours. While I was dealing with the Indian family, the police and numerous calls from the press, Carol remained with the children. At one point the oldest child asked Carol if his father was dead. Carol told him the truth. It was such a sad and difficult time. Our children were home and they, too, had to be given attention.

When this incident was over we never again heard from that family. What tremendous grief that mother had to deal with. We have never forgotten the experience or those fragile lives. Little angels, that's what those boys were, little angels who needed love and care.

While each of these experiences were unique they probably reflect the care given to countless people by small town funeral directors and their families. Rural communities seldom have a formal system to respond to emergencies that leave individuals alone and vulnerable due to a sudden death. Carol and I responded to these situations because we saw the need and knew we could help. When they occurred, there was no time to prepare, only to act. We believed we were providing our community with a Christian ministry and, with God's help, that's what we did.

It Didn't Always Run Smoothly

When it gets difficult is often right before you succeed"

Chris Garrett

The funeral home was ultimately a very successful venture for Carol and me. During the nine-years we owned the business, we tripled the volume of funerals and quadrupled the value of the business. While that sounds impressive, we could never have done that without help.

When we negotiated the purchase of the business my parents wanted to retain ownership and have me manage the business as their employee. We refused to even consider that possibility. My father would not have been open to my style of management, and I would resist operating the business as he had done in the past. Our personalities would have clashed. The business and our relationships would have suffered.

After a long discussion, my parents agreed to sell the business and attached property. Carol and I used our small savings account and the money I had invested in my police pension plan as a down payment. The terms of the sale stipulated that I was to manage my parents' four apartment buildings and the other rental properties they owned in Castle Rock in addition to making monthly payments of $1,000 until the business was paid in full. The sale included the business, the property the business sat on, a small rental house next-door to the funeral home, a hearse and limousine (both of which were 18 years old!) and a 10-year-old station wagon. The funeral home included our living quarters and a small apartment.

The vehicles we purchased were so old they were in constant need of repair. Every two weeks I had to attach an old trailer to the station wagon, drive to the rear of each of the apartments to collect the trash, and drive to the city dump where I deposited the trash. One day as I was returning from the dump smoke began to rise from under the dashboard. The car was on fire. I thought I could make it back to the funeral home, but I was mistaken. The smoke got so thick I had to pull over to the curb and stop the car. Fortunately, a state patrolman happened by. He ran to my car with a fire extinguisher and put out the fire. The car was a total loss. Carol and I made the best of the situation by claiming it was our first cremation.

The station wagon had to be replaced. We couldn't afford a new car so we purchased a used station wagon. That the was first of 10 used cars we bought and traded during the time we owned the business.

The funeral home was located in a building that was 100 years old. It was originally built as a dairy creamery by the Carlson-Frink Dairy. The plumbing was ancient. The pipes would leak and the drains would clog. Ken Noe, our go-to plumber, saved us time after time. He would respond day or night, weekends and holidays. He showed us what excellent customer service looked like.

There was only two bathrooms in the building (not including the upstairs apartment). One was on the ground floor in our living quarters, another upstairs in the living quarters by the 3 bedrooms there. The main floor bathroom was our family bathroom. But we had to share it with people who made funeral arrangements, as well as the public attending funerals.

The business included pre-need funeral accounts. People would pre-pay their funerals and the money was deposited in a bank account to be used at the time of the payee's death. When we audited that account, we found that it was short thousands of dollars and it became our responsibility to restore it to full value.

I was not a licensed funeral director and embalmer. When I was 18 years old my dad had me obtain an apprentice license. I retained that license when I was in college and later on the police department. The license required me to practice under the direction of a licensed funeral director. Terry Payne, a young funeral director, who was living in the funeral home apartment, was willing to work for us and his presence provided the license under which I could function.

Cemetery monument sales was another business that went with the purchase of the funeral home. I could sell granite and marble monuments and brass markers to families using catalogs. After a sale, the monument was engraved and shipped to me and I would transport the monument to the cemetery plot and set it on a concrete slab that I had to prepare.

The business averaged about 50 funerals a year. We also arranged a few cremations annually. Income from those funerals and the sale of the monuments was simply not enough to pay our one employee's salary, meet our expenses, provide us with an income and pay my folks a $1,000 a month. By the end of the second year we began to fall behind on our mortgage payments. As we struggled making timely payments, Dad told me that he had expected that would happen. He told me to be patient. He believed that the financial situation would improve as we increased the business. We were so grateful for his patience and understanding. But that didn't lessen the stress we felt as our income continued to fail to meet our needs.

I entered college when I was 18. I worked part-time for my parents (weekends and summers) until Carol and I married at the age 22. I was 33 when we bought the business. I had been gone from the area long enough it was important that I become involved in the community. I needed to meet people and enable them to know me. I joined the Lions Club and the Optimist Club. I ran for and was elected county coroner, we were actively involved in our church, I became a member of the Friends of the Library, and I helped establish a county-wide hospice organization. I was selected to serve on the Castle Rock Planning Commission; and I was asked to assist in the selection of a new police chief. Carol was active in the church, took the major responsibility for the boys, kept the business books and assisted at the funeral home. The business and coroner's responsibilities required me to be on-call 7 days a week, 24 hours-a-day. We were so busy we had only one five-day vacation in the 9 years we owned the business. We worked our butts off.

I felt it was important to have a funeral director's license. I asked Terry Payne if he would loan me all of the books he used when he attended mortuary school. I studied those books and then contacted the Colorado Mortuary Science Board and asked if I could take their examination to be licensed. I was given permission. I took the test, passed and was licensed.

All those efforts did help us build the volume of our business. But the additional business still didn't cover our expenses. We continued to fall behind in mortgage payments. I would give Carol money to buy groceries and other small expenses; but there were never enough funds to provide a steady salary. That was a particularly difficult adjustment for us because prior to the purchase of the funeral home both of us had a steady income from our employers.

My father told me that he had always set aside 10% of any funds he collected. He would use that money for the purchase of new equipment or to cover unexpected expenses. We thought that was a good idea and we put that into practice.

Prayer was a part of life for Carol and me. We both prayed daily and often numerous times throughout the day. Our financial situation was front and center in many of those prayers.

The situation became acute during the fourth year we owned the business. I remember being so desperate one day that, while jogging on the CCC Camp road, I came to the conclusion that I would have to tell Terry Payne we could no longer afford to pay him, giving him notice to find other employment. I told Carol my plan when I returned home and we spent the rest of that day talking about the future. That night someone died and we were called to handle the funeral. Someone else died the next day and we continued to get more and more business over the next few weeks. I didn't have to let Terry go. But we still weren't making enough money to cover our expenses.

I had been purchasing caskets from the Law and Sons Casket Company, which was located in Denver. John Trout, an ex-FBI agent and salesman for the Batesville Casket Company, contacted me and asked if I would begin using some caskets from his company. I liked their selection of caskets and I liked working with John, so I began purchasing caskets from Batesville. John would stop at my office at least once a month to show me new casket designs and offer help displaying his units. He came to know the prices I placed on the caskets we had in our display room. He told me our prices were entirely too low.

John later called me to ask if he could bring one of Batesville's financial advisors to the funeral home to examine our books and offer suggestions about our finances. At first I resisted. I told him I would have to talk with Carol and I'd give him my response after we discussed the matter. We did give consideration to John's offer and decided we had nothing to lose. I called John and made arrangements to meet with the financial advisor.

Carol and I both brought talents to our business. We believed in the services we provided, we were compassionate and we viewed our efforts as a Christian ministry to grieving people. But neither one of us had ever taken a course in business management. We didn't have the management or financial skills we needed to successfully operate the funeral home. We needed more than good intentions to make a fair profit which would cover our expenses.

The advisor asked us to produce all of our financial records. Armed with our expenses, income and future plans, he sat in our living room for hours working over all the information. When he was finished, we were given a detailed document that carefully outlined his suggestions to change our pricing schedule. He urged us to study it and to implement the plan as soon as possible. We did both.

John had been telling me we were underpricing our services and merchandise. We were shocked to find that he was correct. The detailed information given to us by the financial advisor clearly demonstrated why we weren't making a profit.

The plan made sense. It provided us with the tools we needed to determine the cost of the services we offered and provided suggested casket costs so we could make a reasonable profit. With that information, we prepared a document which itemized our services. I would present the itemized list to families when they were making funeral arrangements. The list gave families the opportunity to pick and choose what services they wanted us to perform; whatever they choose provided us with the funds to cover our expenses and realize a profit.

That financial advice changed our income from losses to a positive income. From that point on we began to catch up on the mortgage payments, establish a contingency fund for future expenses, pay our salary, purchase new equipment and perform some minor remodeling of the funeral home. Over the next few years all our automotive equipment was brought up to date. We had a public rest room built in the funeral home and we furnished the chapel with attractive individual upholstered chairs. We could arrange the chairs in a number of different ways which made the chapel more functional.

I had hired John Everett, a college educated funeral director. He was a wonderful addition to our staff. He worked well with families, was very active in the community, and he had lots of innovative ideas. He and I decided we wanted to compete in the National Funeral Director's Pursuit of Excellence Program. Competing funeral homes were dedicated to the establishment of new programs to assist grieving people. Some of the ideas we implemented included a traveling grief library. We built a book case and filled it with books about death, dying and grief. We took the book case to different churches each month. Interested people could check out any of the books and then return them by using an attached mailer that was pre-paid. Carol organized a grief therapy program called THEOS, which stood for They Help Each Other Spiritually. Several pastors offered to mentor the group. Membership in the group was open to anyone struggling with grief. Carol and I began teaching classes on death and dying. We provided the class to schools, church groups and service clubs. One of the county judges who oversaw DUI cases asked us to present our class to recovering alcoholics who had to attend weekly meetings as a result of their conviction in court. We were surprised at how well the class was received. Those alcoholics were in grief over the loss of their lifestyle. We had people attend the classes who were in grief over the loss of a job or grief following a divorce. We found that people grieve over the loss of anything they value.

Needless to say, we and our staff were busy. We became so well known that the second time I ran for county coroner I received more votes than anyone else running for political office in Douglas County. That included state and national races.

By the time we sold our business we were financially solid and the business had a good reputation. The people who purchased the funeral home asked us to finance the proposition. We did. Interest rates prevalent at that time were so high that the loan we financed was at 11.5% interest! The monthly payments from the sale of the business enabled us to pay for my seminary education and cover all of our expenses. Unlike many of my classmates, we didn't have to obtain a student loan when we moved to Wisconsin.

We believe God inspired us to buy the funeral home. He answered our prayers providing us with the people, ideas and resources we needed. We will forever be thankful to my parents who were patient and willing to see us through tough times. And I don't believe all this could have happened without Carol's commitment and participation. When we got married she never imagined she would live and work in a funeral home. She made so many sacrifices on behalf of the business, and was a constant source of love and support. What a wonderful blessing to go through this experience with my best friend.

Called – Again

"Before I can tell my life what I want to do with it, I must listen to my life telling me who I am."

Parker Palmer

Called again! You might think I wasn't listening, but I was. After experiencing the Annual Christian Renewal Conference and the Renewal Weekend at Christ Church my life changed radically. I resigned from the police department, Carol and I purchased the funeral home, and we dedicated our lives to a Christian ministry focused on people who were in grief.

One of the first things we did after moving to Castle Rock was to join Christ Episcopal Church. I grew up in that congregation. The church contained members who had known me all my life as well as a large number of people who had joined after I left home. The rector, our parish priest, was Fr. Don White, a dynamic spiritual leader whose style of ministry had attracted many new members.

The next nine years were intense. I was on call 24 hours a day, 7 days a week. We would occasionally take a day off and we did take one 5-day vacation during the 9 years we owned the funeral home. The work was trauma and crisis centered. My coroner responsibilities required me to respond to all deaths, to examine the deceased and pronounce death, to locate and notify the next-of-kin, to order and attend all autopsies, and certify each death. I personally responded to about 125 coroner calls a year. Those calls ranged from traffic accidents to airplane crashes, homicides, and suicides, as well as natural deaths. Those calls were often heart rending and they demanded a compassionate response.

I always prayed as I responded to a coroner call. I would pray for the victim, the victim's friends and family, for the emergency responders, and for myself. I would silently pray as I notified the next-of-kin that someone they loved was dead. I would try to visualize God's presence and draw from that peace and strength.

When we first moved to Castle Rock the funeral home was handling about 50 funerals a year. That number quadrupled over the next 9 years. Because we lived in a rural county and the funeral home had been in my family for 45 years, we knew most of the families we served. My contact with those families was close and personal. I would spend a lot of time with each family from the time the death occurred until after the funeral. I would follow up with families after the funeral and was always available when people wanted to talk about their struggle with grief.

Again, God was the source of my help. I would pray for families who choose our funeral home from the first time we were notified of the death until, and sometimes long after, the funeral. Those prayers made a real difference in me, the situations I encountered and the problems I faced. And I believe they made a difference in the lives of the people we served. The Lord was my constant companion.

Carol and I felt that we had a responsibility as owners of a funeral home to provide educational programs to the community that centered on death and grief. We prepared a teaching focused on the stages of grief. Fr. Don White asked us to make the first presentation at a weekend retreat at Christ Church. Two days prior to making the presentation, my mother died. We chose to continue with the teaching. The Colorado Episcopal bishop was also making a presentation that weekend and he attended our workshop. It was a difficult experience in light of our grief, the fact it was our first time offering the class and the presence of our bishop.

Our teaching was well received and, as a result, we began receiving invitations to teach at churches and retreats throughout the state. One of our presentations included a workshop at the national Episcopal Church Women's Triennial which met in Denver. It wasn't long before we were asked to offer death and grief classes in junior high and high schools. All of our teaching had a spiritual component that left no doubt we believed one's relationship with God made a marked difference in the grief process.

I began receiving invitations to offer presentations to emergency room staffs, rescue units, fire departments and police departments focused on assisting survivors at the scene of traumatic deaths and on techniques of making death notifications.

Throughout the time we were in Castle Rock, Carol and I were very active in our parish. I was a eucharistic minister and a lay reader serving at the altar almost every Sunday. I was responsible for the acolyte program, I taught junior high Sunday School and I was enrolled in a two-year Bethel Bible Study instructors course. I taught an adult confirmation class and I served one two-year term on the vestry. (The vestry is the church board.)

The Colorado Episcopal bishop invited Carol to become a member of the Diocesan Examining Chaplains, a group of people who were charged with the responsibility of orally examining people who were in the ordination process.

Two years after we purchased the funeral home, Fr. Don White and I attended the Anglican Fellowship of Prayer Conference in Denver. After that conference, we decided we wanted to pray together once a week. We began the following Monday morning and we continued that practice for the next 7 years. At some point Fr. Don asked me if I had ever considered ordination. I told him about my failed experience when I started college. He listened and then suggested I pray about the possibility. I respected his suggestion, after all, he was chairman of the Diocesan Commission on Ministry, a commission that examined calls to ordination.

Fr. Don wasn't the only person who urged me to consider the possibility I had a call to ordained ministry. Two other pastors, The Rev. Bill Weir, a Presbyterian minister, and Pastor Ron Beckman, a Lutheran minister were both deputy county coroners. I would call upon them to assist at death scenes and to accompany me when I made death notifications. At different times, under different circumstances, both of those pastors told me I should consider ordination.

Carol and I talked and talked about ordination. At first she didn'y believe I was called to ordination and she really didn't support the idea. Then, one Sunday after she returned from an Examining Chaplains meeting, she said she did feel I had received a call. She had participated in the examination of a young man, the son of a retired bishop, who felt called to diaconal ordination. Having heard that man's description of his call left her convinced I had been called by God.

A short time later I began the process. I knew it would take years to accomplish. I had been listening to what my life (and others) were telling me about who I was; and finally, I decided I could tell my life what God wanted to do with it.

So Much to Consider

We all make choices, but in the end our choices make us."

Ken Levine

I was accepted as a postulant for holy orders in February of 1983. My first responsibility was to carefully examine my vocation to ministry in the church. Was I being called to be a priest or a deacon?

From the beginning, I believed God was calling me to be a priest. If that was the path I was going to follow several factors had to be resolved first. If those factors weren't resolved I would have to seek ordination to the diaconate. Then, later, after the problems were resolved, I could attend seminary and seek ordination to the priesthood.

The problems centered on my family. First, our oldest son was having a very hard time adjusting to school. Ordination to the priesthood would require me to obtain a master's degree which could only be obtained by attending a seminary out of state. Carol and I felt that Doug would have a difficult time adjusting to a move and to a new school. We didn't want to put him through that.

The second problem involved my father. If we sold the funeral home, which he bought in 1938, he would be very upset. He wanted it to remain in the family. He held the first option to purchase; I was afraid he would exercise that option. At 74 years of age, his purchase of the business would be a disaster.

There is a marked difference in the ministry of priests and deacons. Deacons assist bishops and priests in the proclamation of the gospel and administration of the sacraments; but, they are not authorized to celebrate Mass or perform marriages and they cannot pronounce the church's blessing or declare pardon in the name of God.

In the Diocese of Colorado, a person in training to be a deacon receives their education by attending the Bishop's Diaconal Training Program. It is a two-year program that meets on weekends enabling attendees to remain employed in their secular jobs and live at home with their families. Most are employed in jobs that involve caring for others such as nurses, counselors, teachers and professionals working in non-profit service organizations. Their secular work serves as a model of Christian care in the world.

My secular work fit the diaconal ministry. The fact I would not have to sell the funeral home and we would not have to move from Castle Rock was not only appealing, it was an answer to the problems we faced. But, unfortunately, that was not the ministry I believed God was calling me to.

Fr. Don had accepted a call to serve a congregation in Greeley, Colorado; and, Fr. Ed Rouffey was called to serve Christ Church in Castle Rock. Fr. Ed was a wonderful support. He had assigned me to lead a Morning Prayer service every Monday. He had me prepare and preach a brief sermon at those services and then he would critique me. One Monday in May the assigned gospel was Luke 14: 24-35. The lesson was about the cost of discipleship. I was really struck by verse 26 which reads: "If anyone comes to me and does not love less his father and mother, wife and children, brothers and sisters, even his own life, he cannot be a disciple of mine." Oh boy, that appeared to reflect on my situation. Fr. Ed and I spent time discussing the implications of that passage.

Then, at the May meeting of the Bishop's Examining Chaplains, Carol learned that diaconal training might change. It would involve a 4-year study called Education for Ministry. That meant that diaconal training would take an additional 2 years. I had hoped that within 4 years the problems with my son and father would be resolved. Doug would have graduated from high school, and hopefully my father would be more open to my call. It wouldn't make sense to spend 4 years in EFM training and then 3 more years in a seminary.

In late June I made a business trip to Springfield, Colorado, by myself. I took some tapes of talks given by Fr. Terry Fullam. As I was listening to those tapes, a statement he made touched my heart. He said: "The peace of God lies in the path that God wants you to walk and nowhere else." I had felt a spiritual tension ever since I was accepted as a postulant in February. I kept trying to find a way to respond to my call by remaining at the funeral home. Yet, I knew that was not where God was calling me. I did not feel peace because I was only willing to give a partial response to God's call. I was not walking in his path.

In my daily Bible study, I had come across yet another passage that spoke to this situation. It was Luke 9: H57-60, where Jesus responds to three people who wanted to follow Him. He tells them the cost of following Him. One person told Jesus he wanted to go and bury his father first, and Jesus responded saying the man should "leave the dead to bury the dead." Being a mortician that intrigued me so I went to Barclay's commentary to better understand the passage. The commentary said that in all probability the man's father was not dead and the man was telling Jesus that he would follow the Lord after the death of his father. Oh, I didn't want to hear that!!! Jesus' reply to the man was "leave the dead to bury the dead; you must go and announce the Kingdom of God."

In late June, Fr. Ed and I had a discussion about the fall program at Christ Church. He asked me if I would teach a Bible study course that involved a 2-year commitment. I told him I couldn't get involved in a 2-year commitment because I might be participating in the EFM program. We discussed other options. Finally, Fr. Ed said I should sell my business and go to seminary. He said it was his belief I was called to be a priest and until I made the appropriate response I would never find peace. I left that meeting and went home. Carol and I spent the rest of that day talking, praying and reflecting on all the events of the past months. Our discussion concluded with a commitment to sell our business and do all we could to attend seminary.

When one is accepted as a postulant for holy orders they are given a long list of tasks that have to be completed prior to attending seminary. When I got my list I immediately began focusing on one task at a time until it was complete, then I would move to the next task. For example, I had to be personally interviewed by the Commission on Ministry and the bishop. I had to undergo a physical examination and submit the results to the Bishop's Office. I had to successfully complete a Bible content examination. I even had to have a psychiatric examination and the psychiatrist had to certify that I was mentally fit to attend seminary.

A funny thing happened when I went to the psychiatric examination. I had arranged to meet with Dr. Nelson Rangell, a physician who had once practiced in Castle Rock. He had moved to Denver and purchased a house that my grandparents had once lived in. It was a beautiful house and Dr. Rangell used it as his office. When I arrived for the appointment I was ushered into his office, which, years earlier, was my grandparent's bedroom. After greeting the doctor, I said my grandparent's bedroom looked wonderful. Dr. Rangell did not know the house had belonged to them, so when I said that he gave me the strangest look. I quickly filled him in on the past ownership of the house. The examination went well after that.

We invited my father to spend the weekend with us to discuss the funeral home sale. It was a pleasant experience. He took the news well. He had no intention of exercising his option. He expressed his best wishes when he learned we would move to Wisconsin to attend seminary. He told me he thought I would make a good priest. He always carried a shirt pocket full of funny stories and jokes. He offered to share his jokes and stories with me with the hope they would make my sermons more interesting. He also made it clear that he would never call me "Father".

One doesn't just list a funeral home for sale with the local realtor. The funeral industry had a large number of traveling salesmen who personally visited each funeral home in their assigned area. They were a valuable asset because they knew who was selling and who was interested in buying. They were the source of some leads. We also contacted several large funeral homes in Denver asking if they were interested in expanding to Castle Rock.

The forensic pathologist who performed autopsies for the coroner's office was our best source of help. While conducting an autopsy, I told him we were going to sell our business. Several days later Loys Caldwell, the owner of a funeral home in Idaho Springs, Colorado, called me. Dr. Galloway had informed him we were interested in selling, and he, his wife and another funeral director were interested in buying. After many weeks of negotiation, the sale was completed.

Accounting and legal research are among Carol's many talents. She spent hours and hours working with our attorney preparing for the sale. She read the contracts, negotiated the terms and oversaw the closing. I didn't have to do anything except say: "Yes, Carol, that sounds great!"

When the Rev. Elmer Moeller, pastor of Zion Lutheran Church, heard I was going to attend seminary, he came to my office. He had been a seminary professor at Concordia Lutheran

Seminary prior to accepting a call to serve at Zion. He and I had worked together numerous times when members of his congregation experienced a family death. He wanted me to know that he supported my call. Further, being a Missouri Synod Lutheran, he believed his church had the most faithful doctrine and he urged me to consider joining the Lutheran Church and attending his old seminary. I was honored by his visit.

After the sale was completed, we contacted the Douglas County News and informed them of the sale. They ran a wonderful article announcing the sale to the public. The new owners arranged an open house for members of the public to meet them and to say good-bye to us. We were surprised and pleased with the response. Almost every minister, priest and clergy member in both counties, along with many of the families we had served, attended. We also received many kind letters.

I was still the elected coroner of Douglas County. I made an appointment with the county commissioners and offered my resignation. I recommended Mark Stover, one of my deputy coroners, be appointed to fill my term of office. He was selected, he accepted the appointment and went on to serve the county for many years.

There were so many things to accomplish before we could leave. We had to sell, give away and store nearly 50 years of family possessions. We had to locate a home in Oconomowoc, Wisconsin, which was near Nashotah House Seminary. We had to make a visit to the seminary before I was accepted. The bishop had to approve the choice. We had to arrange for Doug and Eric to attend school. The list of things went on and on. It wasn't until the late summer of 1984 that we actually made the move.

We made the choice to move and attend seminary. Now that choice was about to make us!

The Episcopal Priesthood

Nashotah House Theological Seminary

"Life is either a daring adventure or nothing at all"

Helen Keller

I was 41 years old when I entered Nashotah House Theological Seminary. I enrolled in a three-year master's degree program. The experience was a daring adventure that was both frightening and empowering. I was an average student in high school. I was accepted but I almost flunked out of CU at the end of my first year of study. It wasn't until the second year at CU that I discovered that I had to almost memorize the class notes I took in order to make the grades I needed to stay in school. I did that and it enabled me to remain on the Dean's Honor Roll from then on until I graduated.

I didn't like academic studies. If the material I had to master wasn't clear and logical, I would quickly find myself confused. (In later years, I've come to believe that I'm mildly dyslexic.) I entered seminary with a fear that I might have taken on a task that was more than I was equipped to handle. I had sold the business that provided my family with an income and entered an academic program that could be my undoing.

There was another factor that raised the level of my concern. All Episcopal seminary students must successfully complete 5 days of written examinations before they qualify for their degree. Following that, the Colorado diocese then requires each Colorado student to successfully pass 3 days of oral examinations conducted by the examining chaplains. Prior to entering Nashotah House, Bishop Frey had appointed Carol to the team of diocesan examining chaplains. Carol would return from those examinations with stories about the difficulty of the examinations and other stories of students who failed. Those who failed were denied ordination. They were required to take additional studies and retake the oral examinations before they would be considered for ordination. Eight days of written and oral examinations loomed large in my mind.

The positive side of my experience outweighed those concerns. I found a lot to value and enjoy in seminary. To begin with, Nashotah House is a Benedictine community. That means student life is centered on Benedictine Monastic Rules requiring a life centered in prayer, work and study.

Every day began and ended with communal prayer. Before breakfast and classes, the faculty, staff and students gathered in the school chapel for Mass. Then the entire community went to the refectory for breakfast. Each morning was filled with classes. The community again gathered for communal lunch followed by time for study. Each day ended with sung Evening Prayer at 5 pm. That was a routine that had been followed at Nashotah House for more than 150 years. Prayer was a focus of our communal life.

Once each week students were required to spend an afternoon working for the community. Students sweep the grounds, clean the facilities, assist with farm labor, work in the refectory, assist in the library, and many other tasks. I had taken up the hobby of designing and constructing stained glass windows when we owned the funeral home. With that experience I was assigned to repair the many old leaded glass windows on campus.

The third leg of the Benedictine stool was study. Nashotah House is a fully credited graduate school that focuses on academic preparation for pastoral ministry. The academic program is rigorous. Our classes centered on church history, pastoral, sacramental and systematic theology, church music, Hebrew, Greek, Old and New Testament, and homiletics (preaching). At least half of every school day was spent in class and the rest of the time was devoted to study and research.

The school is located on a large piece of land that accommodates the campus, an active farm, student and faculty housing, and a cemetery. All the married student housing was full when I was accepted so Carol and I and our children lived about 10 miles from the seminary in the town of Oconomowoc. Four other students and their families lived near us. I car pooled with those four students every day. We formed close bonds and we enjoyed our shared experiences.

I jogged five days a week. One of the students who car pooled with me was also a runner. At noon every weekday he and I would change into running gear and run for five miles on the roads that circled the campus. We ran in rain, snow, ice and even on nice days. Running was a wonderful way to relax after hours in the classroom. We believe the total miles we ran during the three years we were in seminary would be equal to running from one end of the United States to the other.

Our son, Eric, attended junior high school and Doug attended senior high school in Oconomowoc. They quickly adjusted to their new school and easily made new friends.

All social activities centered on the seminary. There were regular community gatherings, celebrations, and special programs. Carol, the boys and I spent most of our free time on campus.

The seminary was going through a search process to hire a new dean. Carol was hired to be the secretary to the search committee. When that work was completed, she was transferred to the development office as a secretary; later she became the seminary's receptionist. She was very active in a group called the Women of Nashotah. During our last year on campus, Carol was elected president of that group.

During the summer after the first year of study, all first-year students were required to participate in a 13-week program called Clinical Pastoral Education. Credited CPE programs are found in hospitals, nursing homes, and prisons. They include an academic element and a practical element. Half of each day the students function as chaplains and the other half is spent either evaluating the chaplain experience or specialized education. I was accepted in the CPE program at the Woods Veterans Hospital in Milwaukee.

During the second semester of the second year of study students were required to complete a 7-week intern assignment at an Episcopal Church. My internship program was at Church of the Redeemer in Houston, Texas. I lived with the rector's family and assisted at the 500-member church. My mentor was a Nashotah graduate with 25 years of experience. I taught classes, preached, and was assigned some pastoral duties. One unusual aspect of that experience involved my evening meals. Every night for 7-weeks I was invited to have dinner with different families who attended the church. I enjoyed many delicious meals, heard all the church gossip, and came to personally know many of the church members.

Seminarians were expected to be active in Episcopal congregations near the seminary. My family attended Zion Episcopal Church in Oconomowoc. During the second year of studies I was hired by the Masonic Nursing Home in Dousman, Wisconsin, to function as a chaplain. The home had two facilities, an assisted living unit and a nursing home. I conducted worship services and preached every Sunday in the nursing home, I visited patients who were hospitalized, and I officiated at funerals. I loved being a chaplain. The organist for the Sunday worship was in her 90s and she was so spry that she would drive to the assisted living unit and pick up a car load of residents for worship each Sunday. I got to personally know many of the residents. One couple I fondly remember were in their late 90's and had been married 75 years. I had such a close relationship with the residents that a bus load of them showed up at my graduation ceremony.

Most of the residents were not from the immediate area. All of them were Protestants. Very few were Episcopalians, so the Sunday worship service was not liturgical. A number of residents asked me to arrange a communion service on Easter Sunday. Since I wasn't ordained I asked one of the seminary clergy to conduct the Mass. Everything went well until after the service. One of the residents, a Baptist, confronted me saying: "Was that wine you served us?" "Yes," I said. "Well that is the first time in my entire life that liquor has ever passed through my lips!" It wasn't until I explained that we believe that the wine had become the sacred blood of our Lord Jesus Christ that she calmed down. I was careful to warn everyone the next year that the communion service included wine.

The seminary hosted numerous distinguished guests including the Archbishop of Canterbury. Bishop Runcie was the head of the Anglican Communion, a world-wide church that includes 70 million members. I had the opportunity to meet him and to serve as arch deacon at the mass that was held to commemorate his visit. When Carol was about to be introduced to Archbishop Runcie, I excitedly called her on the phone to tell her I had just met the prelate. Unfortunately, the archbishop left her office while she was talking to me. She missed the chance to meet him and she has never let me forget it!

Another memorable visitor was the Rev. Reginald Fuller, a British New Testament scholar and highly respected author. He had recently retired. He and his wife Illsa spent a semester at Nashotah while he offered special instruction. Carol and I were invited to a meal at their apartment. We dined on English fare which included microwaved cauliflower and a trifle dessert.

Nashotah House had a close relationship with a nearby Roman Catholic seminary. Professors from both schools would exchange teaching assignments which expanded our educational opportunities. We also shared some worship experiences, though we never shared Holy Eucharist.

Seabury Episcopal Seminary, located in Chicago, was considered our athletic rival. Each fall students from the two schools would gather to compete in a football game. One year it would occur at Nashotah and the next year at Seabury. It was called the Lavabo Bowl. (A lavabo bowl is a dish a priest washes his hands in during Mass.) The game was always fun. Since Nashotah is considered the most traditional and conservative seminary in the Episcopal Church, the students drew on that reputation. We used incense to cleanse the field and the football before the game, we splashed holy water on the goal posts and we chanted our school song at half time. What fun. But we always lost. Each game was followed with Evening Prayer and a meal in the refectory.

On Halloween, the children on campus were encouraged to dress up as a church saint. One year our son Eric decided he wanted to dress up as Samuel Isaac Joseph Schereschewsky. Samuel was a bishop in China from 1877 to 1884. He was paralyzed and yet translated the Book of Common Prayer using one finger and a typewriter. Eric had to explain who he was at every house he visited!

The last half of the last year of study grew more and more intense. All of the students, especially me, were dreading the General Ordination Examinations. They were a culmination of all the studies we had undertaken. I kept wondering how much I would be able to recall, and how well I would integrate the material I had encountered. During the week before the 5-day ordeal we were told what academic material we could bring to the examination, where the exams were to be held, and details on the use of personal computers.

The following week from 9 am to noon and then from 1 pm to 4 we sat at our computers responding to written questions. It was grueling. I went home each night exhausted. I had a hard time sleeping because I was so anxious about what I'd encounter the next day. It was a tremendous relief when the tests were over.

Our written answers were sent to a team of academic readers and they combed over our responses. About 3 weeks later the results were mailed back to Nashotah House. You can't begin to imagine the tension as students opened the letters. One of my classmates failed. Others did well. I passed, to my astonishment.

Now I faced three days of oral exams in Colorado. I flew to Colorado Springs and drove to a retreat center. I was one of three seminarians taking the orals. We were assigned a room to sleep in then introduced to the examiners and those taking the exams. We ate dinner together and the exams began that evening. Each student was examined alone by a group of three examining chaplains. We were examined in the morning, the afternoon and the evening. We had to prepare and present a sermon. One of the examiners was particularly focused on Holy Scripture. He would recite a passage and ask us to identify where in the Bible the passage came from. Other examiners were posing questions about church history, liturgy, and theology. Some examiners would present a theoretical situation and ask for my response.

Bishop Frey sat in on one session. He asked me to comment on the Star Wars program. That was a political question that was of concern because clergy from many denominations were demonstrating against it at the Rocky Flats Nuclear Plant near Boulder. I didn't expect a question like that and for the life of me I couldn't recall what he was talking about. I said I didn't know anything about Star Wars. He was disappointed in my answer and he told me so. Well, that was tough to hear. The tension within me increased.

I was to preach just before lunch on the last day. I was to be examined by one of the teams just prior to preaching. As that team sat down to examine me, tears began to form in my eyes. One of the team members asked me if I was OK. "No", I said. I was then asked what the problem was. I told them that I thought the process we were subjected to was wrong. As tears dripped off my cheeks, I told them the process was anything but pastoral. They listened politely, apologized, and encouraged me. What a difficult situation to endure just before I preached.

At the end of that day the results of the oral exams were announced. I passed. The other two students failed. I was so relieved for myself and I felt so bad for the two who didn't pass. I wondered what my high school principal, who had written that I would never be more than an average college student, would have thought. It didn't matter. I was headed toward ordination.

Bishop William Frey and I con-celebrating Mass at my ordination. The ordination was at Saint Ann's Roman Catholic Church in Grand Lake, Colorado. The altar covering was designed by my sister, Kendal Abbott and it included patches from Colorado churches.

Thoughts from the Court of the Gentiles

"Doubt your doubts before you doubt your beliefs"

Chace Crawford

Worship is serious business at Nashotah House Theological Seminary. Twice a day, every day, students, faculty, staff and visitors gather in the Chapel of Saint Mary the Virgin to worship God. Every day for more than one hundred and fifty years, the community has begun each day with celebration of Holy Eucharist and has brought each weekday to a close with a 5 pm service of Evensong.

Worship is so important that faculty and students vest for every service. Many arrive early, vest in a cassock and surplus, kneel at the pre dieu in front of their chapel seat, and offer private prayers. Some pray the Rosary, others pray spontaneously, and still others use the Book of Common Prayer for their private devotions. Using a wide variety of prayer forms, at least a third of the community can be found at their seats, vested and in prayer 10 minutes before a service is scheduled to begin.

Music is an indispensable part of worship. Nashotah emphasized Anglo-Catholic worship including sung Eucharist. Students are considered members of the choir. When I attended the seminary, choir practice was held at least once a week and as much as three times a week during Lent in preparation for Holy Week and the Easter Vigil. If practice makes perfect, then you can be sure the chapel music was done well. And, if the music wasn't performed to the choirmaster's satisfaction, he would schedule extra choir practices at times that were inconvenient to all.

Chapel seating was determined by two factors. First, each class was assigned to sit together in specific areas. And second, students were assigned according to their voice range. All second and third year students were assigned seats in the two rows on each side of the chapel facing each other. Seniors sat in the seats closest to the center aisle and the juniors sat behind them. First year students sat in assigned seats located behind the rood screen, directly behind the faculty, near the rear of the chapel. The rood screen was a beautiful carved wood partition that separated the chancel from the nave. It created the impression that the first year students were not yet fully incorporated into the community. Seating for the first year students was so far removed from the altar that it was called "the Court of the Gentiles!"

New students were required to audition before Chuck Thompson, the organist and choirmaster. He would then assign each student to a seat according to the voice range they sang. The tenors sat in one section; the bases, altos and baritones were grouped together in another section. I sat and sang with the tenors.

One of the most difficult moments of my early seminary training occurred when I stood before the choirmaster and belted out a hymn so he could evaluate my musical ability and determine the range of my voice. I was asked to choose the hymn I'd sing. Since I couldn't read music at that point, I chose something I knew from memory, "Amazing Grace". As I sang, I kept monitoring Mr. Thompson's facial expressions. When he didn't wince or screw up his mouth after the first verse, I decided I was doing all right. I sang the rest of the hymn with increasing gusto. When I finished, he told me I'd sit with the tenors; then he urged me to sing quietly when I did sing.

When I first entered seminary I felt very uncomfortable with these arrangements. In the first place I didn't think I sang well. I preferred attending the early Sunday service in my home parish because music was never sung at that service. When I attended the later service, I was so unsure of my musical abilities that I'd only hum the tune of the hymn being sung. I considered hymn singing an interruption. To me, it was effeminate for a man to sing unless, of course, he happened to be Johnny Cash or Hank Snow or Willie Nelson.

Vesting twice a day was another thing that didn't sit well with me. A cassock and surplus look like a fancy dress. I felt like a sissy putting on those ornate flowing garments. Combine that with singing and I began to question not only my masculinity, but also my call to the priesthood.

The level of my discomfort seemed to peak one hot afternoon in September as I stood in the Court of the Gentiles singing a hymn during Evensong. There I was, standing in the middle of a bunch of men, all of whom were wearing feminine appearing apparel; trying my best to read the music and sing a hymn I'd never heard before. And all the while I was keeping the volume of my voice down and trying to worship God. None of it felt right.

When we sat down to listen to the lector read the assigned lessons, my mind began to wander. I thought: "This isn't me! I'm not an effeminate sissy. Hell no! I've seen things and done things others in this congregation could never fathom." Then a particularly tough incident came to mind.

Late one night about a year before I sold the mortuary to attend seminary, a couple of cowboys were involved in a traffic accident just north of Castle Rock on Interstate 25. Their day had begun in Florence, Colorado, where they loaded an 18-wheel cattle truck with Brahma bulls. Then they transported the huge animals to a stock market in Cheyenne, Wyoming. They weren't able to begin their trip back home until well after dark. They were approaching Castle Rock at about 2 am. The tire marks at the scene told the story. As the driver dozed off, the truck drifted off the road, along the shoulder, and smashed into a concrete pillar that supported the Santa Fe railroad overpass. The impact was so great that the truck engine was rammed into the driver's compartment. The driver's door flew open, broke off and was found several car lengths in front of the wreckage.

The first person to happen on the scene found the truck driver sitting behind the crumpled steering wheel, severely injured. The State Patrol, Douglas County Sheriff's Office, Castle Rock Fire Department, and Care Ambulance all responded to the scene. As the driver was receiving medical attention, a state patrolman was able to pry open the exterior door of the truck's sleeper compartment. There he discovered the second man lying in the bed, dead.

The fatally injured cowboy was co-owner of the trucking company. He and his brothers had a large fleet of trucks and they hauled cattle all over the western United States. Handling and transporting cattle is a hard, dirty and difficult job. It was a profession the dead cowboy was built to handle. He stood six feet four inches tall and he weighed well over 350 pounds.

One of his brothers told me that his brother was so big that he'd step into a loading shoot and single handedly shove bulls into his truck.

As soon as the state patrolman discovered the fatality, he had his dispatcher request my presence at the scene. I was awakened by the phone call, dressed and responded. The ambulance had left by the time I arrived, but thank goodness, the fire department's rescue unit was still on the scene.

I was told I would find the deceased lying in the sleeping compartment. One of the firemen had placed a small step ladder against the truck and I climbed it. The beam of my flashlight revealed the dead cowboy's head and upper torso. I'd never seen someone so large lying in such an inaccessible place. When I uttered the words: "Oh my God!" several firemen laughed. I turned to the firemen gathered at the foot of my ladder and asked if anyone had any idea how we could go about extricating that poor man. Don Ditmar, a volunteer fireman and a private contractor who built fireplace chimneys, said he'd be glad to go to his shop and pick up his scaffolding. I told him that was a great idea. He jumped into one of the fire trucks and disappeared.

A half an hour later Don was back and erecting the scaffold. Once it was in place, half a dozen firemen assisted me as we pried and pulled and tugged that dead body out of the sleeping compartment, onto the wooden platform on top of the scaffold. Then it took as least a dozen rescuers to lift the body off the platform, onto the stretcher and into the back of the coroner's car. To my relief, the firemen said they would follow me to the coroner's office and help me unload the body.

My mind drifted back to the present moment, as the preacher droned on in the Chapel of Saint Mary the Virgin. I sat thinking: God has been with me through many difficult situations. With His help I've been able to maintain an appropriate attitude so that unpleasant tasks could be accomplished to His honor and glory. "Surely", I thought, "if the Lord has really called me to the priesthood, then He can help me develop a positive attitude toward music and vestments."

And I was correct. He did and I did. If you don't believe me, come to Mass some Sunday and worship as I celebrate. I'll be wearing the most beautiful vestments including an alb with lace inserts near the hem and a brocade or satin chasuble; and I'll be singing the service music on key and with confidence. Oh yes, the volume will be soft and controlled.

CPE

"If you have been in the vicinity of the sacred – ever brushed against the Holy – you retain it more in your bones than in your head; and if you haven't, no description of the experience will ever be satisfactory."

Daniel Taylor

I completed a basic Clinical Pastoral Education unit when I was attending seminary. It was a required course offered at various hospitals throughout the United States. The unit I enrolled in was conducted at the Veteran's Hospital in Milwaukee. That hospital served veterans living in the Chicago and Milwaukee area; and it was so large that it accommodated 10,000 patient visits each day. The chaplain staff included 12 full time chaplains, 6 CPE student chaplains and our CPE supervisor who was also a full-time chaplain.

CPE students were assigned to hospital floors where they served as chaplains for half a day. The other half day was spent in intense group sessions where the student's work was critically evaluated or in-service training sessions were presented. I was assigned to two floors. One floor was dedicated to cardiology and the other floor was the oncology unit. The students were also required to work one 24-hour shift every two weeks. When we were on 24-hour rotation we stayed in the hospital sleeping in a tiny room filled with telephone switching cables. We carried a pager and were expected to respond to all calls between the hours of 5 pm and 8 am the following morning.

The Wood National Cemetery was located on the hospital grounds and it served as the Veteran's Cemetery for both Milwaukee and Chicago. Anywhere from 5 to 10 funeral services were conducted in the cemetery chapel daily. The VA hospital chaplains had the responsibility of conducting funerals for the veterans whose bodies were buried in the cemetery.

Everyone in my CPE group knew that I had owned a funeral home so it was natural that I was the first person in our group to be assigned to conduct a funeral. The funeral was scheduled at mid-morning. That afternoon when I returned to my group my classmates wanted to hear about my experience. I described all the details including the location of the service, interaction with the family and the organist and the honor guard, and then I described the graveside service.

When I finished, my supervisor said: "OK John, that was your first real funeral service as a member of the clergy. Tell us what was really going on in your mind as you conducted the service." I laughed and said, "I kept thinking I needed to hand out the folders and organize the pall bearers and push the casket." Everyone thought that was funny.

One event that stood out in my mind occurred on the oncology floor. It began for me when I found a red sign posted on the closed door of one of the rooms. The sign prohibited anyone from entering the room unless authorized. Further, anyone entering was required to wear a face mask, rubber gloves, shoe covers and be fully gowned. Obviously, anyone entering that room was exposing themselves to some sort of possible contamination. I was curious so I went to the charge nurse and asked about the situation. She told me the patient was a young male who was infected with HIV. She told me I could visit the patient if I took all the precautions.

At that time, very little was known about HIV. Until more research was done to determine how HIV was transmitted from one person to another, every precaution was taken to protect hospital staff. At that time, HIV was a fatal disease. I did gown up, enter the room and visit that young man. I remember the patient was very frightened. He was polite but he did not want visits from the hospital chaplain. I honored his wishes. I told him to notify the nursing staff if he changed his mind and I would be glad to return.

I really learned a lot from that CPE unit and I felt comfortable in the hospital setting. In fact, the experience was so positive that I considered taking an advanced CPE unit after graduation from seminary. That didn't happens then. Instead I entered parochial ministry and worked in missions and parishes in Colorado.

Eleven years later, from November 1998 until September 1999, I had the opportunity to enroll in advanced CPE training at Swedish Hospital in Englewood, Colorado, to obtain certification as a hospital chaplain. That was a wonderful experience.

My supervisor was The Rev. William Pounds, an Episcopal priest. Other students in the program included a Lutheran pastor, a Methodist minister, the bishop of an Eastern Orthodox Church, a Baptist minister, a Jewish lay woman and a Roman Catholic layman. The advanced training included more time working on our assigned floors than I experienced in basic training. We also had intense bi-weekly group sessions that focused on our skills and patient-staff interaction.

Swedish hospital is one of the major trauma centers in the Denver metropolitan area. The hospital emergency room handles approximately 60,000 patient visits a year. A helicopter ambulance system, based at the hospital, responds to trauma scenes anywhere within a 300-mile radius of Denver. Private ambulances, municipal and county fire rescue units from surrounding communities transport the ill and injured to Swedish twenty-four hours a day.

I worked 40 hours a week with my days off scheduled in the middle of the week. My primary assignment was the neonatal intensive care unit and the labor and delivery deck. Every weekend I was the only chaplain on staff and I responded to all calls. Twice a month I was assigned to the night shift during which I would respond to all emergencies within the hospital. When there were no emergencies, chaplains could sleep in a room located next to the emergency department, next to the helicopter pad.

I really enjoyed the neonatal intensive care unit. The NICU cared for new-born infants with all sorts of problems such as premature birth, birth defects, infection, and surgical problems. Many of the babies were so small they would fit in the palm of your hand. All the babies were cared for in incubators, some had to be assisted with breathing tubes and feeding tubes. The staff included 24-hour neonatologists and surgeons, NICU nurses, a social case worker and a chaplain.

Many of the babies born premature remained in the NICU for weeks. Some remained for months. They were not released until they were healthy and had gained enough weight to sustain their health. I visited and prayed for each baby every day. Parents and grandparents were often present and that offered me the opportunity to establish a personal relationship with the families.

It was not unusual for babies to be born so premature or to be so ill that they died in the NICU. Often the baby had undergone intense care and the baby's death would impact the entire unit. It was my responsibility to be a pastoral support to the baby, it's family and the staff. My previous experience as a coroner and funeral director did provide me with training and knowledge about grief; but nothing ever prepared me for my own broken heart and empathic feelings that I encountered at each death.

Many times throughout my life I have been present when people died. I have always considered those times as sacred--holy experiences. I believe I've known and felt the presence of God's Holy Spirit as people have gone through the dying process and I was privileged to be at their side. One death experience in the NICU that remains in my heart and soul to this day illustrates this.

One of the tiny babies had been in the NICU for a number of weeks. The child's health had failed to improve. She experienced the loss of what little weight she had, her system rejected the medicine she was prescribed, and her skin even reflected abnormal color. One morning it became apparent the child was about to die. Her parents and grandparents had spent the night at the hospital. I knew them as a result of the many visits I'd had through the time the child was in the NICU. They had a strong Christian faith and they welcomed what support I could offer. I joined them at the child's incubator. I laid a hand on the little girl and we prayed. Then, for the next hour and a half we stood in silent prayer as life was leaving that dear child's body. I have never been so aware of God's spiritual presence as I was during that time. I believe God's Holy Spirit surrounded that tiny child, her family, the NICU staff and me, ministering to our sorrow, filling us with comfort and preparing us for the death. That was such a powerful spiritual experience that, to this day, when I visualize God's presence and love I do so by recalling that little girl's death.

Not all children admitted to the NICU have family love and support. An example of this occurred when a young woman was transported by ambulance to the hospital with severe abdominal pain. She was admitted and, much to her surprise, she was found to be pregnant with twins and was in pre-mature labor. She delivered two babies who were immediately taken to the NICU. She informed the social worker she did not want the children and relinquished custody.

Those two tiny children remained in the NICU for many weeks. The staff gave each of them a name; and took great care to hold them and to shower them with love and attention. I was able to hold them and feed them during some of my time on the unit. Through the efforts of the case worker a young couple was able to begin the task of adopting those two children. They began making extended daily visits as they went through the adoption process. It was a beautiful ending to a sad situation.

Throughout the time I worked at Swedish I discovered that each medical unit had its own personality. The staff in the emergency room had a different approach to their work and interacted with each other in ways that were different from the staff on the oncology floor; the staff in the cardiac unit tended to have a different personality than the staff on the pediatric floor. Those differences influenced staff acceptance of and interaction with the chaplain. I found that I was readily accepted by the emergency room and intensive care units. The staff in those units appreciated the skills of a chaplain who often encountered and ministered not only to the patient but also to the patient's family. Frightened trauma patients and their families value the support and reassurance a chaplain can offer.

I found working on the labor and delivery deck the most difficult assignment in the hospital. The staff was focused on the mother-to-be and the delivery process. They were protective of the mother, who often had adequate support from her family. Many had a relationship with their own clergy.

The labor and delivery deck is all about new life. The one event that was most stressful was the death or stillbirth of a child. That was the event where the services of the hospital chaplain were welcome. In time, the experience and skill I had helped me gain acceptance on that floor.

When a stillbirth was pending or a baby died my presence was requested. I would spend time with the parents helping and guiding them in their grief. The parents would often want to see and spend time with the child's body. At times that was very difficult because the baby had not been fully formed. When viewing occurred I was always a pastoral presence. I would help the parents plan for the burial or cremation of their child; and I was often asked to conduct a memorial service for the parents and their family.

It wasn't unusual for parents to ask me to baptize their dead baby. That is not done in the Episcopal Church. I did it anyway. I never felt that I should offer theological education at the time of a death; my responsibility was to offer support, comfort and love. Those parents needed to know that God had welcomed their child with open arms.

I encountered one rather unusual experience. A young lady was admitted to the labor and delivery deck carrying twins. Her doctor had discovered that one of the twins was alive and the other was dead. She was admitted so that labor could be induced to deliver the dead infant and it was hoped the labor could be stopped and the living twin could remain in the mother's womb until it was mature enough to be safely delivered. I met numerous times with that mother and her husband prior to the delivery of the dead infant. They were Christians and they really valued our relationship. As the time drew near for the delivery of the dead twin, the mother asked me to be present with her as that delivery was going on. I told her I would have to discuss that with my supervisor. Fr. Pounds advised against that; but urged me to consult with the nursing staff. I did and it was agreed that I would sit just outside the delivery room during the process. The parents understood and were delighted I would be near and in prayer as the delivery was occurring. The process was successful. The dead infant was delivered, the living twin was not delivered, and the mother remained healthy throughout.

I baptized the dead twin, performed a memorial service for the parents, and remained a supporting pastoral presence for the family. I was again a prayerful presence just outside the delivery room weeks later when the living twin was delivered. She was a beautiful healthy baby and I had the privilege of baptizing her.

Every weekend my duties expanded to include the emergency room and the intensive care unit. Again, my past life experiences had prepared me for the trauma I encountered. I was called to all core-0s(an acute life threatening emergency) and it was my responsibility to care for the families or friends of the patient. When a patient died family members or friends were escorted to a room located near the emergency unit that was marked Family Room.

It was the chaplain's responsibility to respond to the family room and either assist or directly inform the family that their loved one had died. All chaplains dread the trip to the family room.

Now to me a family room is a wonderful place for a family to gather and share quality time together. Carol and I have a TV in our family room. We can sit on a couch or in one of several large comfortable Lazy Boy recliners. If we want to listen to music we can turn on the CD player and listen to the speakers that provide high quality sound. If we want to take a nap, we can lie back in a Lazy Boy recliner and snooze in absolute quiet. The kitchen is next to the family room so we only have to walk several steps to grab a snack.

Since there is nothing more inviting or pleasant than a family room, you can imagine my surprise and disappointment the first time I stepped into Swedish hospital's family room. It's not much bigger than a closet. It has no TV, no CD player, not even a radio. There are three chairs and one-two person couch. Family room my eye.

To make matters worse, the activities carried on in the family room have nothing to do with fun or pleasure. People are taken to that room to be told that the one they love has just died. We usually don't tell them until the door is shut because they scream and cry and carry on. If you are in that room when that happens, it simply breaks your heart as you watch and listen to the sorrow and pain.

I felt the name on that room should be changed to: "Emotional Trauma Room". And I think that a large sign with red letters on a white background should be attached to the door. That sign should read: "Warning, enter at your own risk. Once inside your heart will break, your hopes and dreams will be lost, and your life will change forever." With those new signs the hospital would no longer fear a lawsuit for violation of the Truth in Labeling Act of 1967.

After delivering the terrible news and engaging and interacting with the emotional trauma, we chaplains would do the best we could to be a source of strength and comfort. The family usually wanted to see and spend time with the dead relative. We would arrange that and be present as it occurred. At the appropriate time we would discuss organ donation and assist the family if they needed help selecting a funeral home.

There were as many deaths in the intensive care unit as there were in the emergency room. The difference being the patient had been hospitalized for a longer period of time and often the death was expected. That did not make the trauma any easier for the family, it only meant they were more expectant.

The hospital intercom announced all emergencies. If a patient was experiencing a life threatening event the hospital operator would announce "core-0" over the intercom, giving the room number. Doctors, nurses, a team from the pharmacy and the chaplain would race to that room. If a child was abducted the operator would announce "Code Pink" and give the general area involved. The exterior hospital doors were locked, all staff would respond to the general area, and a frantic search would follow. If a patient became violent and combative the operator would announce "Paul Bunyan" and give the room number where the incident was unfolding. Again, all available staff would respond to that emergency.

I never passed up the opportunity to respond to the "Paul Bunyan" calls. It's surprising how calming the presence of a priest dressed in clericals can be. People are somehow embarrassed to behave badly in front of the clergy and on more than one occasion a violent encounter simply dissolved when I entered.

One memorable Paul Bunyan experience occurred in the intensive care unit. The patient was a large man who was being treated for alcohol poisoning. He had been transported to the hospital in an unconscious state, had been treated for several days and had finally awakened. In his confused state of mind, he decided he was leaving. When the nurse tried to stop him he became physically violent. The situation quickly accelerated, the nursing staff notified the operator and the code Paul Bunyan was activated.

I was in a distant location in the hospital so it took me a few minutes to arrive at the scene. When I walked into the Intensive Care Unit there must have been 8 or 9 doctors and nurses in the patient's room. The patient was sitting on the side of his bed with all sorts of tubes attached to his arms and body, he was angry and yelling threats at everyone. He stopped talking when I entered the room. In a quiet voice, I asked him what had happened. Somehow, he seemed to see me as his friend. He said he wanted to leave and he was being held against his will. I said "Let's talk about that and see what we can do." As we talked one of the nurses stepped behind the patient. Without the patient's knowledge, the nurse inserted a hypodermic needle into one of the tubes leading to the man's arm and injected a dose of narcotics. Within a minute the man stopped talking, closed his eyes and fell back on his bed asleep. The ugly situation was contained.

My time wasn't always spent responding to emergencies. In fact, most of my time was spent simply going from room to room, encountering patients and being a Christian presence. Most patients were hospitalized for a few days and many had visits from their own clergy.

Some patients welcomed a visit from the hospital chaplain and there were others that definitely weren't open to a visit. It would be hard to be a chaplain if you couldn't tolerate rejection.

Patients on the rehab floor were long term residents and they usually welcomed a visit from the chaplain. One of those patients really touched my heart. The man was about 55 years old. He was a wealthy man who owned a large tractor-trailer dealership in the Midwest. He had the misfortune of walking on a patch of ice near his home. He slipped, fell and broke his neck. The fall totally paralyzed him from his neck down. He was fed through tubes. The only way he could communicate was to blink his eyes. He could whisper, but only barely.

It was really hard to communicate with him. At first I tried to establish a relationship by talking to his wife in his presence; but I felt it was important to talk directly to him. Since he couldn't form facial expressions it was hard to know what his reaction was to anything I said. With help from his wife I gradually became comfortable talking with him.

He and his wife were Roman Catholics. The Roman Catholic priest whose parish was close to the hospital was so overworked that he seldom made visits. Lay people from the Catholic church would bring Holy Communion on Sunday morning, but that was the only contact the paralyzed man had with the church.

At one point I offered to celebrate Mass for the couple. They were delighted. Over the following six months I regularly visited the man and his wife and I'd celebrate communion with them each Sunday.

The man had a hobby of collecting antique cars. I was told he painted all of his cars a bright red. As his physical condition improved he was told he could be given a mobile wheel chair that could be moved and operated by the use of a tube into which he could blow. He was thrilled. He ordered the chair and his wife make provisions for the chair to be painted red.

He was still in rehab when I completed my training. The last time I visited him his wife gave me a thank-you card in an envelope. When I got home and opened the card I found a lovely note and a large personal check. Hospital regulations prevented us from accepting money so I went to my supervisor and asked for direction. Fr. Pounds told me to accept the money. I did.

Working as a hospital chaplain had a lot in common with life on the street as a policeman. Each day was unique. Each incident had its own problems and solutions. There were many opportunities to help and care for others. The big difference was I could do all that as a Christian. I could and did offer prayers. Over and over again I saw God provide in ways that were unexpected. I am so grateful for that experience. It was one of the most Holy, spirit-filled times I spent as a priest in God's church.

Tippy Canoe

"Everyone must believe in something. I believe I'll go canoeing,"

Henry David Thoreau

They say "Minnesota is the land of lakes." Well, so is Wisconsin. We lived in Oconomowoc, Wisconsin, and it felt like we were surrounded by water. Lake Oconomowoc was located several blocks to the east of our condo, and Fowler Lake was several blocks to the west. The seminary was only five miles from our home. That drive took us past numerous lakes. Upper Nashotah Lake was located next to the seminary and it fed into Lower Nashotah Lake. Two more lakes were connected to the Nashotah Lakes by waterways large enough they could be traversed by motorboats. There were numerous other lakes nearby and they left us feeling like we were living on islands surrounded by water.

With all that water it was only natural we'd buy a boat. Well it wasn't exactly a boat. It was actually a canoe, an aluminum canoe just large enough for two adults and a case of beer, or three adults with little or nothing to drink.

Eric and I loved that canoe. In fact, we spent the better part of one entire summer sitting in it. Some days we'd fish. Other days we'd paddle slowly and voyeuristically peer into the back yards of homes that were located near the water. There were times we'd find and explore passageways that connected one lake to another. We particularly enjoyed exploring Fowler Lake because it's shoreline included a pier containing small businesses, the grounds of the parish we attended (Zion Episcopal Church), a cemetery and a waterway that connected to Lac La Belle. As we paddled the scenery was constantly changing. Carol once joined us to explore the waterway that led to Lac La Belle. She wanted to see the exposed docks and backyards of the beautiful homes that were accessible only by water.

Carol worked for the seminary as the receptionist and telephone operator. Her office was located in the main administration building which was on a small hill just above Upper Nashotah Lake. On more than one occasion, Eric and I would pick up a bucket of Kentucky Fried Chicken, a tub of coleslaw and a six-pack of Old Milwaukee Beer. Then, after work, Carol would change into a tee shirt and shorts, climb down the hill, and hop into the canoe. With three people and food on board, the canoe would settle deep into the water. Slowly and carefully, with the water level within several inches of the top of the canoe, we'd paddle across Upper Nashotah Lake and find a secluded picnic site. What fun.

Needless to say, Wisconsin summers are hot and humid. Consequently, the lake water is comfortably warm. If the fishing was slow or the heat was more than we could take, Eric and I would simply roll out of the canoe and take a swim. You could never do THAT in Colorado!!

The lakes contain all sorts of fish. We were aware of crappie, sun perch, small and large mouth bass, walleyes and northern pikes. We were eluded by everything but the perch and small mouth bass. We didn't mind though because we enjoyed catching whatever attached itself to our hook. We used night crawlers for bait, and red and white plastic bobbers to alert us to a "bite". We'd float past the boat docks throwing our bait into the shade near the boats and, nine times out of ten, we'd get a bite. Most of the fish we caught were too small to keep so we'd throw them back, re-bate the hook and try again. We could fill an entire day with this mindless activity.

Often, Eric and I would paddle across Upper Nashotah Lake into Lower Nashotah through the waterway into Upper Nemahbin Lake. Upper Nemahbin was not only larger than the two Nashotah Lakes, it seemed to have more fish. We'd spend the morning paddling and fishing. Close to noon we would make our way across Upper Nemahbin to a crummy bar on the far side of the lake. It had a dock where we could tie up the canoe. We would go inside and order a greasy hamburger. Then, while we ate, we quietly listened to the other patrons talk about the fish that got away or the best bait for the current fishing conditions. On our way out, I'd pay the bartender for the meal and buy a Styrofoam cup filled with long, fresh night crawlers. It wasn't unusual for the bartender to bring his customers a cup of night crawlers in one hand and have someone's plate of hamburgers in the other. As I write this I'm sad to say that I can't remember ever seeing the bartender wash his hands. Perhaps that was the secret of the unique taste of the food served in that establishment.

Carol, Eric and I will never forget another special outing with our canoe. And, it's safe to say that our experience will never again be duplicated. We had packed our lunch, placed the canoe on top of our Dodge van, and drove to the Horicon Marsh. The marsh is a beautiful federal wildlife refuge known as the roosting site for migrating Canada geese. In the fall, during the migration season, a hundred thousand geese stop at the marsh as they make their way from the north to warmer climates in the south. Our visit occurred when the marsh was full of ducks, fish and small song birds.

We parked the car, carried the canoe to the water, helped Carol stow the food and then we all climbed in. Almost immediately we were rewarded by the sight of huge bass and slow moving walleyes. We were amazed at the large number of beautifully colored loons and the haunting melody of scores of song birds. Having never seen a marsh up close and personal, we were fascinated by the wide variety of vegetation and underwater plants there were visible in the crystal clear water.

We found a shaded spot where we enjoyed our picnic while we watched nature at its best. None of us spoke a word. We just quietly ate and marveled at the sights and sounds. It was an awesome experience.

As we paddled back to the car we realized that we hadn't seen one other person in the marsh. Why, we wondered, weren't others on the water enjoying this very special place? That puzzle was solved as we ended the journey. As Eric and I were pulling the canoe out of the water, Carol spotted a sign next to our van. Somehow, in our excitement to get started, we had failed to read the sign which stated in no uncertain terms NO ONE was to enter the marsh under penalty of the law! We had spent hours exploring the restricted waters of a federal wildlife refuge, and thank God, we were never discovered. That was truly a canoe trip to remember.

When we moved back to Colorado, we took the canoe with us. I recall one afternoon Eric and I were able to catch lots of fish. They were Colorado trout, no less. We had taken the canoe onto Grand Lake and we were fishing near the east shore. An older man appeared on the patio deck of his vacation home and he yelled at us: "Salmon eggs, fifty feet out, on the bottom!" I though the man was drunk so I told Eric to ignore him. Again, the man yelled: "Salmon eggs, fifty feet out, on the bottom!" Now I was sure he was drunk. I told Eric we would humor him by shaking our heads and fishing in the general vicinity he was directing us to. But that approach did not help. The man yelled at us a third time: "Didn't you hear me? I said, salmon eggs, fifty feet out, on the bottom!" Now we had no choice. I asked him to point out the exact spot and I asked Eric to get the salmon eggs out of the tackle box. When we were positioned just right … fifty feet from the man's deck … and we attached led sinkers and salmon eggs to the line, unbelievably we immediately began to get strikes. With genuine delight we both caught our limit of large, beautiful Colorado trout!

When we were done we drifted over to the dock and struck up a conversation with the man. It turned out he was about to close his house for the season. He had been feeding the fish all summer with salmon eggs, on the bottom, so that he was assured good fishing when the mood struck. He could see we weren't having any luck and he simply wanted to share his secret spot with a couple of "good looking guys." We thanked him for his thoughtfulness and generosity.

The final story I will share was painfully embarrassing. It occurred on a Sunday late in the fall of the last year I attended seminary. Eric and I had been spending time on Upper Nashotah Lake and, rather than take the canoe home after each use, we had chained it to a tree on the seminary grounds. On the day in question, I had Carol drop me off on the seminary grounds and then drive across the lake to a spot we could easily take the canoe out of the water and place it on the roof of our Toyota before I attended Evensong at St. Mary's Chapel.

Carol dropped me off on the hill above the lake. I had the key to the padlock and one paddle. I climbed down the hill and unlocked the canoe. Then I drug it to the old wooden dock which contained a half dozen people who were busy fishing. I placed the canoe into the water at the far end of the dock, placed the paddle in, and then carefully slid into the seat. As I began to settle into position a cramp developed in my stomach muscles. The cramp reminded me of the extra effort I'd put into my exercise program that morning. It had been days since I had worked out and I wanted to make up for lost time, so I had done twice as many sit ups as normal.

Steadily the cramp got worse and I realized I needed to straighten out to relieve the sharp pain. The only way to straighten out was to stand up. As I stood up, the canoe began to tip over. I didn't want to upset the canoe so I quickly sat down, only to have that cramp immediately return with unbearable pain. I stood up again. This time the canoe rolled even more than the first time. At the same moment I realized the canoe was going to tip over, I spotted six pairs of eyes watching my silly moves in disbelief. I remember flashing an embarrassed smile as I hit the water. I also remember trying to quickly think of something clever to say as soon as I surfaced. Nothing better than "Damn" came to mind. So I said "Damn" to the unlucky fishermen who were aware that any fish within 50 yards were seeking better feeding grounds.

The cold water cured my cramp but it did nothing for my pride. I was able to pull the canoe back on to the dock, drain the water from inside, and slip it back into the lake under the watchful eyes of those unlucky fishermen. The rest of the trip across the lake was uneventful.

When Carol saw me and I told her the story, she laughed so hard that she had a difficult time helping me lift the canoe to the car roof. She kept giggling as we drove to the chapel.

Attendance was required at Evensong, so we drove back onto the seminary campus. I went straight to the vesting room and put on my cassock and surplus. That hid my wet clothes. I thought I could keep the event secret until I realized water was still dripping off my clothes onto the floor leaving small puddles wherever I stood. To make matters worse, the water in my shoes made me squeak as I entered the solemn procession to the altar. Everyone was looking my direction, wondering what had happened and why. By the time the service was over, my seat was wet and my wet clothes had soaked the backside of my vestments. It was not pretty.

I'm so glad we bought that canoe. It provided us with hours of pleasure, took us on many adventures, and occasionally put us in touch with the humility that is so important to a balanced character.

Exorcism

"They came to the other side of the sea, to the country of the Gerasenes. And when he had stepped out of the boat, immediately a man came out of the tombs with an unclean spirit. When he saw Jesus from a distance, he ran and bowed down before him, and he shouted at the top of his voice: 'What have you to do with me, Jesus, Son of the Most High God? I adjure you by God, do not torment me.' For Jesus had said to him: 'Come out of the man you unclean spirit.' Then Jesus asked him: 'What is your name?' He replied: 'My mane is Legion; for we are many.' Now there on the hillside a great herd of swine was feeding; and the unclean spirit begged him, 'Send us into the swine; let us enter them.' So Jesus gave them permission. And the unclean spirits came out and entered the swine; and the herd, numbering about two thousand, rushed down the steep bank into the sea and were drowned in the sea."

Mark 5: 1, 2, 6-12

Seminary was an academic experience. There was no time given to practical matters. A person was expected to learn how to keep parish records, organize marriage instruction, provide spiritual direction, and conduct vestry meetings AFTER they were ordained and working in a congregation. Ideally a person began their career as a curate and they gained their practical knowledge from an experienced rector. Not me. The first congregations I was called to serve were two rural mountain churches and no one mentored me. My bishop believed that my previous careers provided me with all the practical knowledge necessary to grapple with the challenges I'd encounter. Well, he was wrong. For example, nothing at the police department or the funeral home prepared me to conduct the exorcism of a cowboy's bunk house. Let me lay the groundwork.

The two mission churches I was called to serve were Saint John the Baptist Episcopal Church in Granby and Trinity Episcopal Church located 30 miles west in the small community of Kremmling. Both congregations contained working-class people: teachers, shop owners, ranchers and retirees. Among the parishioners in Granby was a faithful couple who owned and operated a guest ranch half way between Granby and Kremmling. During the first year of my ministry, several months prior to the beginning of the summer tourist season, that couple brought a young woman to Sunday Mass. Judy (not her real name) was introduced to me as the "new head wrangler." The "head wrangler" of a dude ranch is responsible for the care of all the horses, the organization and oversight of the summer horseback riding program and the hiring and supervision of all the other wranglers. Judy had a responsible position.

In spite of the fact that Judy was a Southern Baptist, she began faithfully attending our Sunday Eucharist. Each Sunday after the service she would pleasantly engage me in conversation. Judy grew up in Georgia. Her accent and mannerisms reminded me more of a Southern belle than a Western wrangler. In fact, I assumed her Southern background was the reason she wore long sleeve western shirts, no matter how high the temperature rose.

One day soon after the tourist season got underway, I received a phone call from the owner of the dude ranch. In a concerned tone he told me that his wife was at the bunk house with Judy. "Something's the matter," he said, "and I can't tell you over the phone. We're on a party line, you know." Then he asked me if I could come immediately and meet with his wife and the head wrangler.

"Sure", I said, "I'll be there as quick as I can." I grabbed my briefcase, jumped in the car and sped down Highway 40. I had no idea which building was the bunk house but that presented no problem. As I pulled into the guest ranch the owner's wife and Judy stepped out onto the porch of a white frame building. I parked and the owner's wife beckoned me to follow her and Judy into the house. After brief greetings we each took a chair at the kitchen table.

"What's the matter?" I asked.

"Judy tell Fr. John what's happened." Was the response.

Judy didn't tell me anything. Instead she began with a question. "Are you a Christian?"

"Of course I am," I said, "You've heard my sermons. You have a good idea of my beliefs. What has happened?"

Tears formed in Judy's eyes. "I'm scared," she said, "but I'm going to trust you." Then she began to share an incredible story. She said she had multiple personalities. She'd spent the past year in a mental hospital in Georgia undergoing treatment for dissociative disorder. The treatment had enabled her to progress to the point her psychiatrist felt she could obtain a full time job and continue treatment on an out-patient basis.

Since childhood she had dreamed of living in the Rocky Mountains. So she subscribed to the Denver Post, answered a help wanted ad and obtained the job at the dude ranch. Her Georgia psychiatrist helped her locate a Denver psychiatrist who accepted her as her patient. She admitted that she had not told the owners of the dude ranch about her past.

Early on the morning I was called Judy told the owners that she was sure the bunk house was possessed by evil spirits. Cowboys don't take well to that sort of information, and since the issue involved matters spiritual, I was called almost immediately. The information Judy was sharing with me was all new to the owner's wife. I have to admit that, as I listened to Judy, I felt as uncomfortable as the owner's wife. In fact, we both looked like Tim Russert as we leaned toward Judy, on the edge of our seats, with our ears wide open.

"Judy, why do you think there are evil spirits here in the bunk house?" I asked.

That question brought more disturbing information. Judy said that her adoptive parents had just left after having spent five days visiting her. Judy had little memory of her natural mother. She was adopted when she was three years old. From the time of her adoption until she was grown her adoptive parents had physically and psychologically abused her. She didn't describe the physical abuse but she talked about some of the psychological issues. Her parents were active in a religious cult that worshipped Satan. Judy had been forced to observe and participate in the cult rituals. Those rituals were so disturbing that the only way Judy could cope was to take on different personalities.

Judy insisted that she had not invited her adoptive parents to visit the ranch. Their presence had been an unwelcome surprise. They stayed in the bunk house with Judy and during their visit her parents performed a cultic worship service and even burned a Bible. Judy was convinced that service and their conduct encouraged evil spirits to enter and take up residence in the house. To make matters worse, she said she could smell the evil. I couldn't smell anything but the hair on the back of my neck wanted to stand up.

That morning, after her parents left, Judy went to the owner and told him she was moving out of the bunk house. When he asked why, she upset that cowboy with her tale of evil spirits.

Judy got real quiet, looked me in the eye and asked if I believed her.

My solemn and serious reply was simply, "Yes, I believe you." And that was the truth.

Nothing in seminary had prepared me for this. If I had asked Fr. Jim Griffis, my advisor and my professor of systematic theology about exorcism he would have assigned me to research the topic and prepare a paper. The only thing I could recall about exorcism was a brief note in the Book of Occasional Services that advised anyone needing such a service to consult with their bishop. Well, my bishop was on a mission out of state and not immediately available. If anything was going to happen I had to do it. As Judy talked, I silently prayed, asking God for direction and guidance.

Judy rolled up the sleeves of her western shirt. Both arms were filled with scars that marked her attempts at suicide or efforts she'd made to punish herself with a knife.

"I often feel better after I've cut myself." She said. "But I stopped cutting while I was in the hospital in Georgia."

"Judy", I said, "do you feel suicidal now?"

"No, but I feel frightened and very sick to my stomach. Please help." She said.

Feeling about the same I said: "I will. I'm going to call on God to cleanse this place and protect us."

"How" Judy asked.

I told her I was going to begin by anointing her with holy oil … oil that our bishop had blessed. Then I was going to pray for Judy's safety and peace of mind.

"Anoint me" she said.

I dug into my pocket for my oil stock, twisted the cap off and began anointing Judy. I marked her forehead with oil in the sign of the cross then I placed the sign of the cross in oil on both of her palms. She was shaking as I did this. The owner's wife was stone silent and as pale as a white sheet.

I invited both women to close their eyes and I prayed aloud. It was a fervent prayer that began by rebuking the presence of Satan and claiming the protection of God's Holy Spirit. Then I asked God to grant each of us His peace and to fill that bunk house with His Holy Presence.

At the end of that prayer I stood, went to the cupboard and found a large sauce pan. I filled it with water and blessed it. I explained I was going to take the holy water from room to room and sprinkle it as I offered more prayers. "Good!" Judy said. "Wonderful!" the owner's wife chimed in. Then we began moving methodically from room to room as I splashed holy water and prayed aloud. It was an emotional and moving experience.

When I finished all the rooms, Judy asked me to do the same to her car because her parents had used it to tour the ranch. We went to the car and I sprinkled it inside and out as I offered prayer.

Judy was so relieved she was crying with joy. She told the owner's wife she couldn't smell evil any longer. She said there was no need to move out of the bunk house. We all hugged and I drove off.

In the quiet of my car I discovered I was spiritually drained. I felt as if I had done battle. Remembering the admonition to notify my bishop, I vowed to call Dub Wolfrum, the diocesan suffragan bishop, as soon as I got home. I hoped I hadn't overstepped my authority.

Dub answered his phone on the first ring. I quickly moved the conversation to the events at the guest ranch. Dub listened quietly until I had finished. Then he said: "John, I have never been involved in a situation like that in my life. God bless you. That must have been very stressful. I think you handled the situation well. God bless you." Dub didn't know it but his words brought tears to my eyes and I cried after I hung up.

Next I called my friend, Fr. Ed Morgan, who was rector of the Episcopal Church in Estes Park. He was a trained pastoral counselor and I wanted his opinion. He listened and then said he was unqualified to give me an opinion. He urged me to call Bethesda Psychiatric Hospital in Denver and consult with their staff because they had experience working with spiritual cults.

I contacted the hospital and talked with the man who was considered the local expert in the occult. He listened to the story. Then he affirmed all I had done. He said that it was important that I had used holy oil and holy water, that I had offered strong directive prayers, and that I had affirmed Judy. He said he would send me written material I would find helpful.

After I hung up I again reflected on the event. My response had developed as I prayed. God had given me the guidance I needed and then he provided the spiritual power to effectively address the evil. Wow. Amazing. I prayerfully thanked the Lord. There was no way a seminary could ever teach the lessons I learned that day.

Two weeks later the owner of the dude ranch told me that Judy had resigned and entered a Denver psychiatric hospital to undergo full-time treatment for dissociative disorder. A week after that I received a phone call from Judy's psychiatrist. She told me that Judy's birth mother died when Judy was 2 years old. She was too young to remember the funeral. Both Judy and her psychiatrist felt Judy would benefit from participation in a memorial service that honored her mother's life. I was told that Judy trusted me and she wanted me to prepare and conduct a memorial service at the hospital. I consented to do that.

The day before that service Judy's psychiatrist called to tell me what to expect. She said Judy had a number of identifiable personalities (18, if I remember correctly), but she commonly displayed only four. When I asked which personality I'd encounter, the psychiatrist suggested I simply ask Judy who she is. I was told not to be surprised if Judy's personality changed as a result of the emotions she would experience during the memorial service. Some of Judy's personalities were male and the psychiatrist said they could be violent. The service could begin with Judy believing she was a 35-year-old bartender and ended with her responding as a 5-year-old girl.

Judy and her psychiatrist met me in the hospital lobby. I felt odd asking Judy who she was. "Why, I'm April!" she said without thinking. April, according to the psychiatrist, was a 16-year-old girl. I hid my surprise. Judy appeared and sounded like the wrangler I knew in Grand County.

The memorial service was held on the hospital grounds. A number of patients from Judy's unit, several nurses and doctors attended. I offered prayer, read several passages from Holy Scripture and then Judy planted a small evergreen tree in honor of her mother. At the conclusion of the service Judy thanked me and I couldn't discern any change in her personality. I left, never to encounter Judy again.

Like the passage from Mark's gospel, Judy had a "legion" of personalities. Unlike the passage, the secular approach to health appeared aimed at integrating the personalities rather than exorcizing them. When I last saw Judy integration hadn't yet begun.

What an experience! I admit that after this encounter I felt like I was a different person.

Our Son in the United States Marine Corps

"There are two gifts we should give our children. One is roots, the other is wings."

Author Unknown

Shortly after Doug entered high school he began talking about joining the Marine Corps. We urged him to consider going to college instead. Even after he was told we'd finance his college education he never showed any interest. He read books about the military. He and his friend Derrick spent hours and hours talking about being soldiers. He obtained recruitment literature and spent a lot of time perusing the material and gazing at the pictures.

During the middle of his senior year in high school we invited two military recruiters to our home to talk to Doug in our presence. They both arrived the same day, one in the morning and the other in the afternoon. The U. S. Army recruiter was the first to arrive. He was dressed in formal military attire, he was full of facts and information and we thought he was very impressive. He stressed the fact that after serving in the army one became eligible for free college tuition. Doug listened politely.

The Marine Corps recruiter arrived about an hour after the army recruiter had left. He was less formally dressed; in fact, he came dressed in camouflage. He looked the part. He talked about how difficult boot camp would be. He emphasized the fact that no matter what a marine was assigned to do, he was always expected to revert to the role of an infantryman if circumstances demanded it. And he kept saying the marines would make a man of Doug. Carol and I asked him if Doug would receive college tuition after he served in the Marines. "No", he said, "But the marines would make Doug a man!" Doug heard that.

After the marine left we asked Doug what he thought. Without hesitation he said he wanted to join the marines and become a man.

Doug made arrangements with the marine recruiter to enlist prior to graduation. He wanted to be trained in explosive ordinance disposal. He wanted to be a bomb technician like his dad had been on the police department. His recruiter assured him he would receive that training. His application was submitted and his background investigation began. He had to submit to a physical examination administered by a marine physician. Doug is six feet 9 inches tall. During the physical the doctor told Doug he could not be accepted because he was three inches taller than the maximum allowed. Without hesitation, Doug slouched down and asked the doctor to measure him again. The doctor laughed and said that wasn't necessary. He listed Doug's height as six feet six inches and Doug passed his medical.

He was accepted and notified of the date and location of his pending enlistment. On the appointed day Carol and I accompanied Doug to a marine recruitment center in downtown Milwaukee. There were other recruits waiting when we arrived. Doug and the others were told to stand at attention, raise their right hand and they were sworn in. The ceremony took all of 5 minutes. Now all Doug had to do was to successfully graduate from high school.

Doug's grades were poor. He did not like school and he wasn't interested in applying himself to raise the grades. But two weeks prior to graduation he was told he was failing in two classes and unless he raised his grades he would not graduate. If he failed to graduate his enlistment would be void. We were astonished to witness Doug's response. He worked day and night for the following two weeks, he coordinated his efforts with his teachers and even sought help from other classmates. He demonstrated academic skills never before seen, and it worked. I believe that one of the happiest days in Doug's young life occurred the day he was told he would receive a high school diploma.

It was now certain he would go to boot camp. That was not what we wanted to happen. But the experience Carol and I endured when we informed my parents that I had joined the Boulder Police Department was foremost in our mind. We were deeply hurt by their response. They were disappointed in me and they never missed an opportunity to remind us of that fact. We believed our responsibility as parents was to support and encourage Doug as he pursued his dreams. As such, we did all we could to help Doug prepare for a career in the military.

A short time after graduation Doug was officially notified of the date and time he was to report to the O'Hare Airport in Chicago. His notification included an airplane ticket to San Diego where he would enter boot camp. Doug was thrilled. We were happy for him but deep inside Carol and I were sad. Doug was not only leaving home; he was joining the military where he had little control over his life or safety.

The recruiter picked Doug up and drove him to the airport along with a number of other recruits. We followed in our car and were allowed to wait in the boarding area until the recruits boarded their flight.

Doug has never been an emotionally demonstrative person. He never felt comfortable acknowledging our presence when he was in public. When Carol once visited his high school, Doug spotted her and passed her on the opposite side of the hall without acknowledging her presence. With that history it wasn't surprising that Doug entered the boarding area without saying a word, found a seat and sat with his back to us. The boarding area was full of young recruits all waiting to fly to boot camp. Carol and I and one other couple were the only parents there to see our sons off. We had a long wait. As time went on, some of the young recruits came over to talk to us. They knew we were anxious parents, they too were anxious and we were a source of comfort for them. When it came time for the recruits to board the plane, Doug stood up, turned toward us, nodded and boarded the plane. We left the boarding area with tears in our eyes.

Boot camp was long and difficult. Doug was required to write home periodically and he did. His letters were brief. They primarily informed us he was alive and looking forward to having the experience end.

Boot camp graduation is an important event. The great accomplishment of successfully completing that tough training is celebrated in an impressive ceremony at the marine base in San Diego. Carol, Eric and I, along with my sister, Cindy and her husband John flew to California to attend the graduation. About 600 recruits formed the class that was honored. The ceremony began with the 600 marching in formation. Doug, who stood at least a head above all 600, marched with the United States Flag at the very front point of the formation. We couldn't have been more proud of his accomplishment.

All the graduates were given leave at the end of the ceremony. When we found Doug all of us hugged him and shook his hand. His first words were: "Let's eat. I want a Big Mac." So the first order of business was to locate the closest McDonalds. Unbelievably, Doug ordered and ate five Big Mac's. While he was consuming the Mac's and fries, he kept commenting on the vast amount of color he was seeing. He explained that he had lived in a world of brown throughout his training and it was exciting to see so many other colors.

Later we all took a tour of the bay area on a tourist boat. Before the trip began, a photographer had gathered each family as they entered the boat and took their picture. During the excursion the boat captain announced that anyone who wanted a copy of their family portrait could buy them at the end of the trip. Several young ladies kept talking to Doug as we traveled across the bay. When we docked, they followed us

Doug's first formal US Marine photo

to the vender selling the family pictures. We bought one of the pictures and each of those girls also bought our picture. They wanted to remember Doug.

Doug is strikingly tall. He obtained his height every early in his life. When he was in junior high school he was taller than everyone including the entire staff of the school. He was self-conscience of his height and he usually walked with his head tilted down. He would sit so that his head was at the level of those around him. Boot camp brought an end to that behavior. Doug stood tall. He took pride in his height. He was no longer self-conscience. You could say…the marines were making a man of Doug.

After taking leave Doug was sent to munitions training. He was disappointed that he wasn't selected for explosives ordinance disposal; however, he enjoyed learning to identify, handle and store munitions. He later put his training to good use when he deployed aboard a helicopter attach ship, the USS Tarawa.

The longer Doug was enlisted the more frequently he communicated with us. He was sent all over the world and he would call us collect from the most unusual ports of call. We received calls from ports in Africa, Asia, the South Pacific, Thailand, and the Middle East. When he wrote his letters were always short and always ended with his love. We were so grateful whenever and however he communicated.

The United States has a long history of humanitarian relief. So it was not unusual for our military to respond to Somalia to help provide food to a starving nation in August of 1992. U. S. troops were quickly drawn into inter-clan power conflicts and by October of 1993 dozens of our soldiers were killed in fierce street fighting in the capital city of Mogadishu.[20]

Doug was among the marines sent to Mogadishu. At that time, he had been promoted to the rank of sergeant. His primary assignment was the supervision of a platoon of marines at a check point in Mogadishu. His platoon would stop all vehicles entering their assigned zone and search them for weapons. He was housed in an abandoned hotel where the walls were so thin that he had to line his bed with sandbags to prevent stray bullets from hitting him.

Doug has always had a soft heart for small children. He told me that one day a male child he thought was about 5 years old came to his check point and engaged Doug playfully. Doug picked him up and put him on one his shoulders. It was a positive experience. That night clan members shot the child in the legs to make an example of him and to discourage other children from engaging the United States military. Doug was devastated when he learned what happened. It broke his heart.

Doug was in several fire fights before his unit ended their assignment and returned to the States. Neither Doug nor any of his men were injured.

It took very little time after our homeland was attacked on 9/11 for war to be declared against Iraq. Doug was among those sent to fight in that war. The night before he was scheduled to depart he called us at 2:30 am. He said he was on base, sitting on the ground talking to us from a pay phone. He was drunk. He said he wanted to talk to his dad. When I said "Hi", he said he wanted to know what my God would think of him if he killed people during the war. I sat straight up in bed and we engaged in a spiritual conversation that I hoped would be helpful to Doug as he struggled with his faith, his responsibilities and God. It was so sensitive that I have tears recalling that conversation.

Doug deployed and it was many days before we heard from him again. At one point prior to the commencement of battle, Doug called. He told us his unit was sleeping on the street and everyone was tense anticipating the fight to come.

The day action began I was driving from our home in Grand Lake to teach a class at church in Granby. I heard the news accounts of the bombing as I drove. I prayed as my eyes filled

---

[20] The United States Army in Somalia 1992 – 1994, CMH Pub 70-81-1

with tears. One fear I had was that Doug would be an easy target due to his height. When I got to the church I called Carol who was working at the bank. She came to church after work.

Having a child in the military during war time connects you with other parents with children in harm's way. Grand County has a small population which contained a very large number of people who were in the military. All the churches quickly formed prayer chains for those in the military and their families. Then the churches shared those lists with other churches. If you had a family member in the war most people knew it. It was amazing how that knowledge unified the community and produced a genuine concern for those affected.

After the fighting began the only communication we had with Doug was by letter. His communication was primarily about his needs. At one point he said he hadn't had a shower in a month. He wrote that he smelled worse than a camel and he asked us to mail him a clean set of underwear every day. We began doing that. Carol's co-workers also began sending underwear care packages daily. In another letter he wrote that he had become friends with the Roman Catholic priest's assistant. He said he thought that all the soldiers were getting religious and so many were attending Mass that the priest was running out of communion wafers. He asked me to send him a supply and he would pass that to the priest. He also wrote that one of his men had received bad news from home and he supplied the man's name and asked us to pray for the situation. Doug didn't realize it, but his actions demonstrated his quiet faith as well as his compassion for others.

Doug survived the war and was finally given leave. The plane he rode on made a fuel landing in an airfield in one of the eastern states. Again, about 2 am we received a phone call from Doug. He was excited, relieved and happy. He said when the soldiers got off the plane to stretch their legs they were met by a large contingent of civilians who wanted to thank the soldiers for their service and welcome them home. Doug had feared that he would be treated like the Viet Nam vets were treated when they returned from combat. Again Doug revealed something about himself we had never known. We were proud of our son and thankful for God's protection.

The military provided our son with many varied experiences. He trained for and was responsible for the oversight of artillery batteries, he served as a recruiter in Massachusetts, and he helped re-write training manuals at a high altitude training facility in California. He traveled worldwide. We kept hoping he would be assigned to a desirable location we would enjoy visiting. Unfortunately, all of his travel took him to third world countries, none of which we would ever chose to visit.

While working as a recruiter in Boston, Doug met his future wife. After a brief courtship they announced their engagement. Carol and I, Eric and his wife Liz, my sister Cindy and her husband John traveled east for the wedding and I had the privilege of assisting in the service at Hanscom Air Force base.

Doug's last overseas assignment took him to Iraq during the second war. Doug was embedded in the Iraqi Army as an advisor to upper-level enlisted officers. He was the only American soldier serving in that Iraqi Army unit. It was a tough and dangerous assignment that lasted one year. He and his wife Sherry had two small children at this point and his absence was very difficult for them.

Doug's last promotion was to the rank of master sergeant. There was only one rank higher he would have been eligible to receive; but he chose to retire instead. Carol, Eric and I, along with my sister Cindy and her husband John went to Camp Lejeune in North Carolina for his retirement ceremony where he was honored for his 23 years of service.

We are so proud of Doug's accomplishments. He made the right choice to enter the military. We made the right choice to encourage and support him. There is no doubt the marines made a good man of our son.

The Dewey Family

"The greatest gift of life is friendship, and I have received it."

Hubert H. Humphrey

Maundy Thursday, the day before Good Friday, is an important feast day on the church calendar. On Maundy Thursday Christians all over the world celebrate the establishment of Holy Communion by our Lord Jesus Christ. The story of Jesus' washing the disciples' feet is often chosen as the Gospel reading. After that Gospel is read and the sermon is preached, the celebrant invites the congregation to participate in a foot washing service. The celebrant begins this part of the ceremony by washing another person's feet, then the celebrant's feet are washed and the other members of the congregation then follow in like fashion.

When I was rector of Saint Gabriel the Archangel Episcopal Church, Carol was working in the bishop's office. During the morning of Maundy Thursday, the Denver Post religion editor telephoned the bishop's office to ask the name of an Episcopal Church that would allow a photographer to take pictures of the foot washing. Without hesitation, Carol suggested Saint Gabriel's. When I was informed of this exchange, minutes before the service was to begin, I realized it was too late to protest.

As I entered the sanctuary to begin the service I quickly identified the photographer. She was wearing jeans and she must have had five cameras hanging from her neck. She had absolutely no desire to be "decent and in order" as she fulfilled her assignment. Just as soon as the foot washing began, the photographer approached the altar rail as if it were a crime scene rather than a sacred ground. She must have taken thirty pictures with her various cameras. My eyes blurred from all the flashes.

Finally, there were only a few people left who wanted to participate in the foot washing. Among them were Francis Dewey and her friend Marianna Cook. Those two young friends had chosen to wash each other's feet. It was a wonderful idea that presented a major problem. They were both so young and so small that when they were sitting in the chair the adults used their feet were dangling in the air rather than soaking in the pan full of water. As I watched the girls get positioned to wash feet I kept thinking someone would need to help them. Suddenly it occurred to me that it was me who would have to assist. I knelt beside the girls and asked if I could help. My offer was warmly received, and the three of us became absorbed in the task at hand. I was so absorbed that I forgot the Denver Post photographer.

The following morning, I opened the Denver Post and found a beautiful picture of Frannie, Marianna and myself. My son was so moved by the picture that he went to the Denver Post and purchased a copy which he presented to me as a gift. That picture, along with the newspaper photo and a copy of the Gospel reading, hangs in our house as a reminder of that service. What took place that Maundy Thursday may not have been "decent and in order", but I'm so grateful it happened. It's just one of the many wonderful memories I have of the Dewey family.

When I was called to serve as Saint Gabriel's rector, the congregation was small in numbers and we had only one family with small children … the Dewey's. Most of the congregation were in their 60's or older. Those folks were so delighted to have young children in the congregation that they treated Thomas, John and Francis like grandchildren. That wasn't a bad position in which to be.

Several years after I was called, Cindy Dewey was elected to serve on the vestry. She was an excellent member who spoke her mind with clarity and challenged the other members to deepen the congregation's commitment to outreach and programs for the children. I have vivid memories of Cindy's participation in the vestry retreat we held at Saint Malo Retreat Center. She talked about her experiences living in a cabin near the retreat center prior to her marriage. She and another vestry member took a strong position in opposition to any effort to introduce visitors at the Sunday services. It wasn't that they were opposed to being friendly, rather it had to do with the value they placed on personal privacy. I was glad they were so outspoken because they reflected the personality common to many in that congregation.

The Dewey faithfully attended Sunday services and were often present at special services and gatherings. I have fond memories of Cindy and the children attending the Stations of the Cross service we held for the children during Lent. I believe that Thomas performed his first acolyte duty by leading the procession with the cross during one of those services.

John was too small to be a regular acolyte while I was at Saint Gabriel's. But we did call upon him to serve as a "boat boy" for solemn high Masses. Boat boys hold the incense container, called a boat, from which the priest takes incense to stoke the incense fire. We had to have the altar guild hem up the boat boy's cassock so that John would walk without tripping. Once those alterations were complete, John looked great in his cassock and cotta. He and his brother occasionally served at the same service. On those special occasions, Thomas didn't hesitate to give his brother the benefit of his past experience and insight. John was an excellent boat boy. To this day I don't know whether that was due to the unsolicited suggestions from his brother or his natural ability.

Cindy worked with my wife at the diocesan center. Her job was librarian in the resource section. There were times when her responsibilities as mother came into conflict with her responsibilities at work. When that happened, it was not unheard of for one or more of her children to accompany her to work. What a beautiful example that set for others.

I enjoyed the time I spent with Greg. We often shared time at coffee hours and enjoyed conversation at church dinners. But the best time occurred when we met for lunch. I'd meet Greg at a restaurant near Denver University where Greg was chairman of the chemistry and physics department. We'd eat lunch at Cucina Leone in the Bonnie Brae area. We'd usually meet to discuss church business. We'd order lunch, quickly address church matters and then enjoy each other's company. I always left those luncheons looking forward to the next opportunity to share time with Greg.

Thomas and I developed a very special relationship. We really began to interact when Thomas became an acolyte. And I must say that Thomas was one of my favorite acolytes. He was eager and well prepared. He took that responsibility seriously. He always tried to do the very best he could. I admired that.

It wasn't unusual for Thomas to drop by the vesting room prior to Sunday Eucharist to see if his services were needed. Whether he was needed or not, Thomas would visit. He always had something interesting to share. If he was scheduled to serve, he would vest and then he'd stand near me and we'd talk. Our conversations covered topics from events in Sunday School to the latest family crisis to the Gospel lesson assigned that day. Those were heavy topics for a young boy who was in middle-school.

When I resigned from Saint Gabriel's the congregation was invited to a brunch held in my honor at the Marriott Hotel in the Denver Tech Center. Close to 250 people attended that brunch. After we finished our meal, people were invited to go to the microphone and say a good word for me. Many people said wonderful things. Then, without hesitation, Thomas stepped forward and he said some of the nicest things that were said about me that day. I'll never forget that. Thomas was the youngest person to speak. What he said, he said well. His words brought tears to my eyes. God bless Thomas.

Thomas didn't forget me after I left. He called me at home regularly to tell me I was missed. He'd call me from his home or from the church. If he was calling from the church he'd usually call on Sunday evening during youth group. One memorable call came during a very special service at Saint Gabriel's. Thomas was serving as an acolyte at that service. When he called I realized the service was still in progress. I asked Thomas what he was doing. He said he didn't like the sermon, so he left the service, found a phone and was calling to let me know how much he missed me. He couldn't have given me a higher compliment.

I thank God for the Dewey family and for all the wonderful times we shared. They were just one of the many great families that I shared my life with at Saint Gabriel's. May God richly bless each one of them.

How God Answers Prayer

"If you want the rainbow, you gotta put up with the rain."

Dolly Parton

Knowing that I once owned a business and had worked in an administrative position on the Boulder Police Department, it was natural that the bishop would ask me to serve on the committee that handled the financial matters for our diocese. You see, most clergy have no idea how budgets work or how finances are managed; and furthermore, they aren't interested. In fact, I wouldn't be surprised if a third of them never learned their multiplication tables; and, fewer than that are able to read a simple budget sheet. Since clergy are so numerically challenged they usually leave the congregation's number crunching to their vestry and their personal finances to their spouse. That being the case, my first diocesan committee assignment after ordination was the budget and finance committee.

The committee work was routine, predictable and boring. However, one day all that changed. The stress of that day made my stomach churn and, eventually, it led me to discover a rather irritating way that God answers prayer. Before I reveal the details I want to describe the committee and the events that led to prayer.

All but one member of the committee were men. The only female member of the committee was an accountant who showed up for about half of the scheduled meetings. She was so quiet that it was hard to tell if she felt out of her element because we were involved with not-for-profit accounting or the fact she was the only woman on the committee.

One of the men was built like a stout hard-working cowboy. He was in his mid-60's with gray hair and thick eye brows. He spoke in a low coarse voice. Everything he said came out in a slow measured pace. His manner left one feeling he was someone who needed to be taken seriously. He worked for a large corporation and volunteered regularly at the Saint Francis Center, a homeless shelter in lower downtown Denver. I liked Ken but I was never sure of his feelings toward me.

Another member was a very successful CPA. His ability to analyze figures and solve financial problems were a great asset to the committee.

The committee chairman was an old family friend, Charlie Kirk. He grew up in Castle Rock and he dated my sister, Cindy, all through high school and college. I never knew why they didn't marry, but it's a damn shame they didn't. We both liked each other and had many common friends. When Charlie's mother died I officiated at her funeral. Charlie was a banker and he owned a part-time business appraising ranch properties.

There were several other lay people who served on the committee. They were good folks who were open, helpful and interested in sharing their talents so the diocese could make the best use of its funds.

One other member of the committee was a priest who had a lot of financial experience. He was a powerful and effective public speaker who had strong opinions about things financial. He did not hesitate to express those opinions. If he took a position on a matter it was doubtful he would change his mind. Those who were bold enough to challenge him often left the battle with their tail between their legs.

That priest seldom said more than "Hello" to me and I avoided sitting next to him.

On the day in question, the entire committee had gathered in the diocesan center for a full day of budget hearings. The diocesan budget for the coming year was expected to have less funds than it had had for years, and the director of each department had been summoned to appear and present their budget request. Fifteen minutes had been set aside for each director. During that brief time, the director was introduced, they described their department, their budget request and answered question from the budget committee members.

The tension was etched into everyone's face that day. The tasks of questioning each director and then deciding where to cut budgets was unpleasant. None of the directors appreciated the need to appear before our committee; and, even more, they bristled at the prospect of having their work and budgets evaluated.

After the first director appeared and presented his budget, the first person to ask questions was the opinionated priest. He asked questions as if the director was a defendant on trial. The resulting exchange was loud, defensive and angry. That hearing ended with that priest unilaterally declaring his intention to support a significant budget cut in that particular program. His anger and determination were so strong that no one on the committee responded.

The next director walked into the hearing and was met with silence. Budget committee members were looking at their papers as they tried to digest what had just occurred. Finally, Charlie Kirk greeted the director and invited her to present her budget. As she concluded her prepared remarks, the opinioned priest again began an aggressive verbal assault. He questioned all sorts of details, demanding answers only to cut the person off before she could respond. It was ugly.

As the morning wore on, that priest seemed to gain confidence in his approach. The committee members didn't seem to know how to respond to him. Program directors were being insulted. The tension was so great that it was difficult to concentrate on the budget requests. And so, I began to pray. "Lord", I prayed, "stop this man from hurting others and undermining the work of this committee. Make it apparent to him that his behavior is not Christian. Give this committee courage to establish a balanced and sensitive approach to its work."

As I continued to pray nothing happened. It was as if the Lord hadn't heard me or He didn't care what was happening in His Church. Then suddenly a thought came into my mind.

"John, I will answer your prayer by using you. You tell him to stop."

"No Lord." I silently responded. "I'm a poor communicator and an ineffective debater. He will verbally make me look like a fool."

That caused all sorts of thoughts to begin rolling in my head. Thoughts like:

"The Lord is speaking to you, John. Trust and respond."

"This is just me debating with myself. No it isn't. Trust and respond."

"This is scary. Yes, it is, but that IS the way God works. Trust and respond."

So, I did. As soon as that particular hearing ended, Charlie suggested the committee take a fifteen-minute break. I spoke up and said I wanted to address the committee before we took that break. Everyone looked at me as I began addressing that priest.

I looked him square in the eyes and said, "I'm asking you to stop treating the people who are presenting their budgets with such contempt. Your approach is demeaning and it is undermining the work of this committee. You've been so harsh and demanding that some of the women have left in tears. If this doesn't stop, I will excuse myself from the rest of the hearings."

Well, you could hear a pin drop. I doubt that anyone was breathing. I know I wasn't as I waited for "…the other shoe to drop." But it didn't. That priest simply said: "You're right. I'm wrong. I'll go apologize to those who have already appeared."

The committee took its break. He did exactly what he said he would do. Several committee members came to me and thanked me for taking that step. I told them…it wasn't me…it was the Lord working through me. And that is the truth.

From that point on, I have been very careful about what I pray. I recognize that God does use me and I need to be sensitive to that possibility when I pray.

Is That You, Captain?

"People only see what they are prepared to see."

Ralph Waldo Emerson

Jerry Winterrowd was consecrated the 9th bishop of the Episcopal Diocese of Colorado on a Saturday afternoon at the First Church of the Nazarene in Denver, Colorado. That site was chosen because it could accommodate more people than Saint John's Episcopal Cathedral. Following the service, a reception was held at a large hotel in the Denver Tech Center. Carol and I, along with nearly two thousand people, attended both events. I, like almost all the clergy, was wearing a black suit and a clerical shirt and collar.

When we arrived at the hotel for the reception it took some time before we were able to find a parking space. We parked and joined the throng of people as they made their way to the crowded lobby. We knew many of the guests and we traded comments and conversation with others as we slowly walked past the registration desk and moved toward the ballroom that was decorated for the reception.

Suddenly I found myself face to face with an old acquaintance, Doug Dorsey. Doug had been a patrolman on the Boulder Police Department for many years. Though I hadn't seen him since I resigned from the department, I immediately recognized him. He was nicely dressed in a sport coat and tie. He had a serious demeanor as he greeted me. Rather, I should say, as he whispered in my ear: "Is that you, Captain?"

"Yes it is." I said. "And that is you, isn't it, Doug?" "Yes", he said, "I'm the house detective. Are you working undercover?"

"No, Doug." I responded. "I am a priest and I'm attending my bishop's reception."

Doug laughed. And then, without whispering he said: "You're kidding, I thought you had bought your parent's funeral home and when I saw you in that priest's outfit I figured you'd gone back into law enforcement and you were working undercover."

Now it was my turn to laugh. I recounted my journey form the funeral home to seminary and ordination. Doug told me he no longer worked for the Boulder Police. He worked for the hotel chain as a detective.

The conversation ended. Carol and I made our way into the ballroom, and I haven't seen Doug since that unusual encounter. Life if full of surprises, isn't it?

Equality

"Virtue can only flourish among equals"

Mary Wollstonecraft

All my life I have held the belief that men and women were equal. I've felt that there was nothing a man did that a woman couldn't also do. My wife is and always has been my equal and the same holds true for other women. That conviction placed me at odds with others at several points in my careers.

I joined the police department at a time when there were no female officers. During the first 8 years I worked for the department, all commissioned police officers on the University Police, the Boulder Police and the Boulder Sheriff's Departments were male. When I went to the F.B.I. Academy in Quantico, Virginia, in 1973, Chief Donald Vendel asked me to visit the police department in Washington, D.C., and inquire about their experience using women as uniformed police officers. I interviewed a deputy chief of that department who gave me very positive evaluations of the women that agency had who were working as police officers on the street. The only qualification he made was that there were times a small woman would need assistance when she arrested a large male who resisted. But then, he said, their department had some small male officers who would find themselves in the same situation.

I returned from the F.B.I. Academy and made the recommendation that our department consider hiring women. That recommendation was accepted. The Boulder Police Department slowly and carefully began implementing that change. I was privileged to help train some of those first women officers.

The Episcopal Church restricted women from being ordained to the priesthood prior to the mid-20th century. It wasn't until 1976 that the church's General Convention amended canon law to permit the ordination of women. That act wasn't immediately embraced by many of the dioceses. When I attended Nashotah House Seminary in 1984, there were many bishops still opposed to women's ordination. The Nashotah House Board of Trustees would not allow women to serve at the altar and many of the trustees belonged to organizations that actively worked to undermine women's ordination. It was politically unpopular for a student to express their support for the ordination of women.

It wasn't until 1989 that the first woman, Barbara Harris, was consecrated a bishop in the Episcopal Church. I remember talking to Colorado Bishop Dub Wolfrum shortly after that consecration. He expressed disappointment and a fear that there would be a negative backlash as a result of her consecration. I have to say that I wasn't disappointed, but I felt it would take a long time for the church to accept the change.

While serving Trinity Episcopal Church in Kremmling in 1989, one of the members of that congregation expressed a desire to be considered as a possible Canon 9 priest. Canon 9 allowed a person in an isolated rural congregation to be ordained after they received instruction within their diocese. They did not have to attend a seminary; but, they could only serve in their local congregation. As the bishop's committee explored that possibility I suggested we invite a Canon 9 priest to address Trinity's congregation. That way everyone in the congregation could learn first-hand what was involved and could ask questions about the process. The suggestion was enthusiastically accepted. I contacted Janet Rollins, a Canon 9 priest who served the Episcopal Churches in Trinidad, Colorado, and Raton, New Mexico. She accepted my invitation to come to Trinity Church, celebrate Mass and speak to the congregation. She was the first woman priest to function in the Grand County Missions. She was warmly received and her presentation was most helpful. I felt positive about facilitating the services of a woman priest for the first time in that setting.

I was called to serve the Saint Gabriel congregation within a year after their previous rector had left the Episcopal Church and joined the Polish Catholic Church. He formed a new congregation and half of the Saint Gabriel's congregation followed him into his new denomination. His radical move was in direct response to his opposition to the ordination of women in the Episcopal Church. Needless to say, the ordination of women was a hot topic at Saint Gabriel's.

Harry and Kay Kountze were active members in the congregation. They were very popular and highly respected. Harry's family had founded the Colorado National Bank and he worked at that bank until he retired. I liked Harry and Kay. He would show up in the sacristy prior to a service just to talk with me. He often had some funny story to share. His daughter had gone to seminary and was an ordained priest in a distant diocese. One day he came to my office and informed me that his daughter would be visiting Kay and him. He asked me if I would be open to allowing her to preach at a Sunday service. I told him I would be delighted to have her preach and to concelebrate the Mass with me. He gave me her phone number. I called her and we made plans for that to happen.

Neither Harry, Kay nor I told anyone of those plans. I was a bit nervous as the day approached. After all that had occurred when the previous rector left, I had no idea how Harry's daughter would be received. On the appointed Sunday, she and I processed into the church. A sense of tension filled the air. Members of the congregation looked at us and then at each other. It didn't feel comfortable. When the service reached the time when Harry's daughter was to preach, I stepped to the pulpit and introduced Harry's daughter. There was an audible collective sigh of relief. She preached a wonderful sermon. She was warmly received as she passed the peace and everyone wanted to shake her hand after the service.

Harry was congratulated for having such a talented child. Again, I felt positive about enabling a woman to be accepted as an equal.

The Canon to the Ordinary, an assistant to our bishop, contacted me several months later and asked me if I would be open to hiring a young woman to serve our congregation. She was scheduled to graduate from seminary and needed a position. I told him I would be open to the possibility and I would ask the vestry for their permission. Our vestry considered the idea and then voted to hire her. After graduation, Catherine Tran was hired. She was ordained a deacon and later a priest and she served Saint Gabriel's as my assistant until I resigned several years later. Again, I felt I had enabled a woman to serve in a place that years earlier she could never have even been considered. I believe we are all equal in God's eyes.

If You've Had a Heart Attack – I May Not Be Your Man

"There are three things that are real – God, human folly and laughter. The first two are beyond comprehension. So, we must do what we can with the third."

John F. Kennedy

I'd just finished making a pastoral visit to a patient at Porter's Hospital and was walking toward my car when I heard a woman's voice call: "Fr. John! Fr. John!" It was Judy Stromberg, one of my Saint Gabriel parishioners. She had just gotten out of her car when she spotted me.

"Fr. John," she said, "my husband's had a heart attack. My two sons are with him in the cardiac care unit. Would you please come pray for him?"

Judy's husband was a Methodist and, to my knowledge, he had never attended Saint Gabriel's. I had never had the opportunity to meet the man. Judy was a faithful Anglican who valued the sacrament of unction (healing). I told her I would be glad to pray for her husband; and, if he was willing, I'd anoint him with holy oil. Judy was delighted, so I grabbed my holy oil and began following her to her husband's room.

As we made our way, Judy said this wasn't her husband's first heart attack. He'd had several minor attacks and this episode was no different. She thought he would probably have by-pass surgery in the near future. For the moment, however, he was resting comfortably and his vitals were being closely monitored.

When we arrived at his room we found him sitting on the edge of his bed dressed in pajamas. He had all sorts of wires attached to his arms and chest. A TV screen mounted on the wall behind his bed was alive with numbers and lines which revealed his blood pressure, heart rate, oxygen saturation, and other information. Both of his sons were seated in chairs near the bed.

Judy introduced me and told her family she'd asked me to pray for Jim. As I shook hands with the men they each offered excuses for not having ever been to Saint Gabriel's. Years of experience hearing such excuses enable me to quickly put everyone at ease.

I asked Jim how he was feeling. He said he wasn't in pain. The only symptom he now had was shortness of breath and fatigue. He was quick to accept my offer to pray for his healing. I explained that prayers for healing in the Anglican tradition included the Sacrament of Unction. That meant that as I prayed I'd place my hands on his head and then end the prayer by dipping my thumb in holy oil and use it to make the sign of a small cross on his forehead. Jim was open and receptive.

I stepped to his side. His bed tray was to my right and partly between us. Since the only item on the bed tray was a glass filled with ice water, I thought that would be a good spot to place the small container that held the holy oil.

With my eyes closed, I began the prayers. I asked God to give the doctors and nurses wisdom and skill, to fill Jim with peace and to comfort his family. Then I prayed for God's healing. As that prayer drew to a close, I placed my right thumb into the holy oil, closed my eyes and drew my right hand toward Jim. As my hand left the holy oil, it hit the glass of ice water knocking it right into Jim's lap. Jim's response was instantaneous. He yelled, jumped to his feet and almost knocked me over.

I opened my eyes and, to my horror, I say Jim standing with his pajama bottoms soaked … a shocked look on his face … and ice water all over the bed and floor. The cardiac monitor was going crazy. Both of Jim's sons had jumped up from their chairs and Judy was running to her husband's side.

What could I say? "Be not afraid." Or maybe, "God works in strange ways." Or maybe, "It may surprise you, but this is all part of the sacrament."

Instead of all that, I apologized and made a hasty but dignified exit. As I stepped into the hall, I encountered several nurses who were undoubtedly responding to the erratic information Jim's monitor was transmitting. I smiled. They passed. And I made a bee line for the nearest exit.

I returned to the scene the next day and was greatly relieved to find Jim alive. Standing inside his room, I timidly said hello and asked if I could enter. I promised I wouldn't come anywhere near his bed. Jim laughed and assured me that his Methodist training had taught him the importance of forgiveness. He was quick to add that he now felt he'd experienced an Anglican form of baptism.

Funny Things Happen on the Way to Mass

"Imagination was given to us to compensate for what we are not, a sense of humor was provided to console us for what we are."

Mack McGinnis

Funny things happen when we least expect them and I never expect humor in the midst of Mass. That would be akin to encountering a concert violinist dressed in bib overalls. When it happens, it catches us by surprise and it leaves a memory that's hard to shake. This is a potpourri of the unforgettable events I've encountered during Mass.

My family and I attended Christ's Episcopal Church in Castle Rock before I left for seminary. I'd grown up in that parish and most of the parishioners were life-long friends and acquaintances. Jo Marr had been attending that parish for years before I was born. Every Sunday Jo arrived early and sat in the same pew. In fact, legend had it that Jo never sat in any other pew.

A young paramedic who worked for Care Ambulance began attending services on a regular basis. Being a newcomer, he wasn't familiar with congregational traditions. He often arrived late and would sit wherever he could find a seat. One Sunday he had the misfortune of sitting in Jo's pew. Jo arrived late that particular day and she squeezed between Mark's knees and the next pew, knelt and said her prayers. She never spoke to Mark, but Mark would later recall that she appeared troubled or upset.

At the appropriate time, Mark moved to the altar rail to receive Holy Communion, leaving his long-sleeve, white cotton sweater in the pew. After the last prayer, Mark stood for the blessing, grabbed his sweater and started to the back of the church. Sensing that something was amiss, he examined his sweater only to find that the arms had been tied in knots. He hesitated and looked back at Jo. She was kneeling in prayer. A confession no doubt.

I will never forget the first time I experienced the Maundy Thursday foot washing service. It occurred shortly after the Episcopal Church issued the 1976 Book of Common Prayer. Fr. Don White was rector of Christ's Church and he had invited the congregation to participate in the foot washing service, which was a new addition to the prayer book. No one knew what to expect; during the service Fr. Don explained that he would be washing the feet of each parishioner to commemorate the Lord's washing of the disciple's feet. He then placed a chair in the middle aisle, produced a large bowl full of warm water and invited people forward.

I was sitting in the back pew. As Fr. Don was describing the service I noticed one of the older female members wiggling and wiggling. I couldn't image what she was doing. As I moved forward to have my feet washed I realized what brought on all the wiggling. That elderly parishioner had come to the service unprepared. She was wearing panty hose. She had to remove the hose before she could have her feet washed. She ended up ahead of me in line, but her panty hose were still in her pew.

I was always on a tight schedule on Sunday mornings in Grand County. I would celebrate Mass at St. John's in Granby at 8:30. That service would end about 9:30, giving me 60 minutes to greet the parishioners, remove my vestments, drive 27 miles to Kremmling, vest and begin Mass there at 10:30. I would usually arrive 10 minutes before the second service, compare notes with the organist, acolytes and altar guild, and then vest just in time to announce the first hymn.

One Sunday I arrived in Kremmling to find that the lady assigned to altar guild duty had forgotten to set out the communion vessels. Not having the time to do it myself, I asked Mona Blandford if she could do the honors. Mona hadn't served on altar guild for years but she was willing and I was grateful. As I was pulling on my alb, Mona appeared in the vesting room and asked where she could find the communion bread. "Mona," I said, "it's in the freezer. Place one small loaf in the microwave and defrost it, then place it on the silver paten on the altar." Like the trooper she was, she said: "OK", and disappeared.

The service ran smoothly. All the communion vessels were accounted for and in the appropriate place. The scheduled lay reader even read the correct lessons that were appointed for that Sunday. Everything was moving so smoothly I was relaxed and at peace as I began the Eucharistic Prayer. I blessed the bread and the wine, elevated those elements, and led the congregation in the Lord's Prayer. Then, as the liturgy requires, I lifted the small loaf of bread, announced that the "Lord's Passover has been sacrificed for us", and then I attempted to break the loaf of bread. I attempted, but I didn't succeed. The loaf was as solid as a rock … a granite rock. I applied pressure again and again and nothing happened. More pressure and still nothing. Discretely I placed the loaf against the corner of the marble alter and pushed. The altar moved, but the loaf remained the same.

Women in the congregation began to sense that there was a problem at the altar. Several of them smiled. I smiled back as my mind was racing to both find a solution to the problem and a reason for it. I was at a loss for the reason, but I did remember I had consecrated communion hosts in the tabernacle. I placed the consecrated stone aside and communed the congregation from the reserved sacrament.

At the end of the service, as people were filing out of the chapel, Mona made a confession. "I've never used a microwave oven, Fr. John. When you told me to defrost it I placed it in the oven, turned it to high and ran it for 5 minutes. Nancy Abbott just told me that makes bread as hard as a rock. I'm sorry."

I forgave her. My next problem was to find a way to dispose of a loaf of consecrated concrete. I buried it in the church yard the following Tuesday.

One Sunday as I was at the altar celebrating Mass in Granby, a two-year-old boy wandered away from his mother, strolled down the side aisle and walked behind the altar to watch me. I smiled when I noticed him and he smiled back. So, I picked him up and held him in my arm as I continued the celebration. You can imagine the look on his mother's face when she saw him concelebrating the Mass with me. She was mortified. I smiled and winked at her, continued the service and returned her son as I began distributing communion. It was truly a wonderful experience for both him and me.

Years later, while celebrating Mass at Saint Gabriel's in Cherry Hills Village, I had a humorous encounter with a man who was very hard of hearing. Nick was serving as my acolyte at the early service. It was the first time he'd served in years and so he was a little rusty. In fact, he was so rusty I had to keep telling him what to do next.

As I began preparing the altar for Mass, Nick stood facing me waiting for directions. Each time I'd prompt him, he'd respond quickly and efficiently. Finally, it was time for him to hand me the bread. "Bread box", I said. "OK" he responded. Then he turned and stared at the credence table. Turning back to me, he said, "I don't see any red box." I laughed as I said, "Bread box...bread...bread." Nick realized his error and began chuckling. After that service I suggested Nick consider hearing aids. He didn't laugh at that.

Mable "T" was an elderly, gray-haired widow who was not only hard of hearing, she was senile! She didn't attend church regularly, but when she did we could always depend on something unusual happening. One Sunday I approached her was she was kneeling at the altar rail to receive communion. As I placed the bread in her hands she said, "I need to see you." "OK" I whispered and began to move to the next person. "I need to see you soon." She said. I stopped and returned to her side. "Would tomorrow be soon enough?" I asked. "What time?" she said. "Nine o'clock", I said and returned to the task of distributing Holy Communion.

Nine o'clock sharp the following morning Mable walked into the church office. She walked past my secretary announcing in a loud voice that she had an appointment. She entered my office, sat in the chair next to my desk and produced a hearing aid. "I can't get the damn batteries in. Teach me what to do." "Sure", I said, thinking that wasn't something they taught in seminary.

Thirty minutes of instruction accomplished nothing. Mable couldn't distinguish the top from the bottom of the battery. She was too clumsy to open the tiny door to the battery case. And once the battery was in place, she kept trying to place her hearing aids in the wrong ear. The poor lady left my office frustrated, and I spent the rest of the day talking to myself. Needless to say, it was weeks before Mable attended another Mass.

The chairs the acolytes sat on at Saint Gabriel's had a woven wicker seat. One of the young acolytes got into the nervous habit of picking at the wicker during the sermon. He would pick and pick and pick. At the end of a service the floor beneath his seat would be covered with tiny pieces of wicker. I thought it was funny and I'd sneak a peek at Greg when I was preaching. The altar guild didn't think it was funny. It irritated some of the members so much that some would try to determine which chair Greg would be sitting in so they could rotate chairs and thereby spread the damage among all the chairs.

In 1997, Saint Gabriel's parish family celebrated the completion of an extensive remodeling project. A new organ was installed in the loft at the rear of the church and 16 speakers were placed in the ceiling above the chancel. To soften the appearance of the speakers, a parishioner designed and built a beautiful new altar. The altar was made of heavy dark wood and was physically smaller than the altar it replaced. The altar guild made new linens and frontal hangings. And the old brass communion candleholders were replaced with two large round candles that sat on either side of the altar. Each candle had three wicks which produced a dramatic effect.

One Sunday as I was celebrating communion I began to notice that one of the wicks on the communion candle positioned to my right was producing a strange flicker. Refusing to allow that to distract me, I focused on the words of the Mass. Suddenly I noticed a tan liquid pouring from the candle onto the new altar linen. Hot wax was flowing from the side of the candle. I stopped saying the Mass and stared in disbelief as the wax continued to flow from the side of the candle. Catherine Tran, my associate, quickly blew out the remaining two wicks as I moved the communion vessels to the far side of the altar. Members of the congregation sensed something was amiss, but they couldn't see the flood we were trying to stem.

I finished the consecration and began distributing the elements. Almost everyone who came to the altar rail to receive Holy Communion stood on their tip toes before they knelt so they could see what had happened. The response of the men was different than the women. The men chuckled at the sight. The women, many of whom belonged to the altar guild, responded with a horrified look and a silent gasp.

Another candle incident occurred during a funeral. Two candelabras each containing six candles sat on a ledge behind the altar. They were all new candles and they were all lit at the same time just before the service began. As the service progressed, one of the candles began burning differently than the others. The flame was higher and brighter and black smoke began curling upward. The heat from the flame began steadily melting the candle. The congregation began focusing on the candle as it got shorter and shorter. No one at the altar was aware of the drama unfolding behind them, but the altar guild was. Finally, one of the guild members stepped behind the altar and snuffed the candle out. The clergy were left wondering what happened as the congregation let out a collective sigh of relief.

I'm sure God has a wonderful sense of humor and He, too, probably chuckles as these funny incidents occur during Mass.

Cor-0

"I finally figured out that not every crisis can be managed. As much as we want to keep ourselves safe, we can't protect ourselves from everything. If we want to embrace life, we also have to embrace chaos."

Susan Elizabeth Phillips

One Sunday morning during the time I was enrolled in the CPE program at Swedish Hospital, I heard the hospital-wide emergency signal system activated. The loud pinging bell rang three times and the operator announced "Cor-0, pod A … Cor-0, pod A" over the public-address system. A Cor-0 was an alarm activated when a patient stopped breathing and was in a full cardiac arrest. Before the over-head announcement was completed, I felt my pager vibrate, alerting me to call the operator. That call confirmed I was to respond to the Cor in pod A.

As I walked into the pod I immediately knew which room contained the Cor. The second room from the entry leading to pod B was full of physicians, nurses and support staff. An intern was standing on a stool on the far side of the patient's bed administering CPR. A nurse was standing next to him operating an ambo-bag that was firmly sealed over the patient's mouth and nose. Those two people appeared oblivious to others as they carefully coordinated their efforts to maintain a ratio of 15 chest compressions to 2 assisted breaths. The hospital's supervising nurse was near the entrance to the room making a written record of each action taken, the time it was taken and by whom it was taken. A technician from cardiac care was standing by with the defibrillator, a pharmacist was present with an emergency supply of drugs, and the emergency department trauma team were coordinating efforts with the critical care team.

To the uninitiated, the scene looked like mass confusion. But that wasn't the case at all. Each person present was working under a strict chain of command. And everyone had a specific task to perform. That highly skilled team was providing the very best care one could ever expect to receive under those circumstances.

I walked to the room and caught the eye of the nurse supervisor. She recognized me and recorded my presence. I knew she was a Christian and her facial expression indicated she was glad I had arrived. I stood out of everyone's way just inside the entry where I could observe the equipment used to monitor the patient's physical responses. It was apparent that the man was still in a full arrest. He was not breathing on his own and his heart was only responding to the compressions applied by the intern.

The man's clothing had been completely removed. He had grey hair and I estimated his age to be mid 70's. He was over-weight and each compression made his entire body quiver. Tubes and wires were attached to his wrist, arms, chest and head. With absolutely no response after 7 minutes of CPR, numerous injections of powerful drugs, and at least one administration of electrical defibrillation, I thought the patient's chance of survival was slim at best. I was praying silently for the patient, the staff and the patient's family.

I did not know the patient. So I went to the critical care charge nurse and asked if the patient's family had been notified. She told me she'd just gotten off the phone with the man's wife. She and her 32-year-old son were at the family home in Conifer, Colorado. They were going to drive directly to the hospital and notify the rest of their family by cell phone as they drove. The trip would take nearly 45 minutes. I suspected the situation would be resolved by the time they arrived because Cor's normally didn't take more than 30 to 40 minutes. Within that time the patient either would respond and be stabilized or they would be pronounced dead.

Since the family's emotional and spiritual needs would be my responsibility, I asked the charge nurse what she knew about them. She said the patient was a retired businessman in his early 70's. He and his wife appeared to be very close. They had a number of grown children and grandchildren and many of them had been at the patient's bedside or in the waiting room throughout the previous night. She said she thought the family was Italian and the rosary beads hanging on the patient's bulletin board indicated they were probably Roman Catholic. She concluded our brief conversation by saying she thought the man would eventually respond to the Cor Team's efforts because his arrest had been discovered almost immediately and he was in fairly good health. So much for my inexperienced evaluation, I thought.

I moved to a position near the center of the pod where a nurse was monitoring the patient's heart rate on a machine. A record of the heart rate was steadily printing on paper that was feeding out of the machine. The nurse was hand rolling the paper as it steadily moved forward. Knowing I could observe all the action from that point, I offered to relieve the nurse. I could roll paper, pray and be available all at the same time. The nurse was grateful for my offer. As soon as she handed me the roll, the charge nurse had her go to the central supply for more medical equipment needed by the Cor team.

For what seemed an eternity, I quietly stood, rolling the paper and praying. At times like that I would make myself aware of God's spiritual presence and then I'd open myself to His strength and peace. I felt a deep peace in the midst of that trauma. In that state, I asked God to protect the family as they drove to the hospital; I prayed for the patient's recovery; and I asked God to give the wisdom, compassion and skill I'd need when the family arrived.

As time passed, I kept watching for the family to enter the pod through the main entry. I was in a position between that door and the patient's room and, once they arrived, it would be easy for me to encounter them before they saw all the activity associated with the Cor.

Suddenly, out of the corner of my eye, I saw two figures run into the pod through the door leading to the next pod. They ran into the patient's room, shoving their way through the medical staff, and finally stopped at the head of the patient's bed. Both of them were yelling.

The older woman was yelling: "Don't die! Don't die, Paul! You can't die and leave me alone!" The young man was screaming: "Come on Dad, you can make it! Don't give up! Cooperate with them, Dad"

My first thought was: The family has arrived! My next thought was: My God, I've got to get them out of that man's room. I dropped the paper recording the heart rate and ran into the room. I moved so quickly that none of the medical staff had the time to do more than fix a disgusted look on their faces as their minds were trying to adjust to the added confusion of frantic family members.

I pushed past a nurse, squeezed behind the patient's bed and firmly grasped the young man's arm. He instantly stopped yelling and looked at me. My black clergy shirt provided instant identification. With my eyes locked on his, I issued a command. "We must leave this room immediately. Our presence is a threat to your father's life, come with me!" I voiced that command with such authority that all conversation in that room stopped, and I felt every eye directed at me. Without hesitation, I drew the young man toward me and began moving out of the room. The patient's wife quietly followed us.

As we left the room, the charge nurse took my arm and said, "Take them to the adjoining patient's room. We will move the bed, close the curtain, and shut the sliding glass door to give you privacy." As we walked into the room, I told those frantic people that I was the hospital chaplain and I asked them to both be seated so we could pray for Paul and the team who were caring for him. They sat and we prayed.

My heart was beating so fast I could feel it. I felt I had really accomplished an important feat, but I also realized my work was just beginning. During the prayer, I began putting a plan together. Once the prayer ended, I told them I would have the charge nurse brief them on Paul's condition. I stepped to the door, nodded to the charge nurse and she entered the room. Without any prompting, she gave a detailed description of Paul's condition.

As she was talking I saw more family members walking into the pod through the main entrance. I thought "this is more like it," as I intercepted them. This group consisted of another son and a daughter, her husband and adolescent daughter. With firm authority I told them to follow me, and we went straight into the room where Paul's wife was quizzing the charge nurse. It was an emotional reunion. Everyone began crying and hugging each other. The level of conversation was high because everyone was talking at once.

I backed out of the room and stepped into Paul's room. The senior physician present had just made the decision to stop all efforts. The team had been working for 1½ hours without any response. It was apparent Paul was dead. I shut my eyes and made myself aware of God's Spirit present in that room. I silently asked for God to receive Paul's spirit. When I opened my eyes, I went to the physician who was in charge and asked him to talk to Paul's family. He nodded and we walked into the next room.

As we entered the room went silent. The physician introduced himself and said he was sorry, their efforts weren't successful, Paul was dead. Paul's wife screamed. One son began to sob. And the rest of the family gathered around their mother and grandmother. Within a few minutes the family was composed enough that the physician was able to share his thoughts about Paul's last two hours of life. When he finished no one had any questions, so he excused himself.

The oldest son asked me if I had performed "last rites". "No", I said, "but if you would like to join me at Paul's bedside I'll do that now." The entire family followed me back into Paul's room. They gathered around Paul's bed and we all held hands. Using the Book of Common Prayer, I offered Prayers at The Time of Death. I ended the service by anointing Paul's head.

I remained with that family for several hours helping them select and notify a mortuary. I also explained organ donation options and completed all the formal paperwork after they declined participation in that program. By the time the family was ready to leave the hospital we had established a bond. They expressed their gratitude with words and hugs.

The critical care staff was also grateful for my help. After the family left numerous physicians and nurses thanked me.

This was a typical example of my responsibility when called to a Cor. Some days the hospital had no Cor's and other days we could experience multiple ones. I recall responding to five Cor's on one shift, each of which ended with the patient's death. On that particular day two patients cored at the same time in adjacent rooms in the Critical Care Unit. Both patients had family members present. It was difficult moving back and forth between those families as they were struggling with the death of their loved one. That stressful event was then followed by three more Cor's later in the shift.

All my life I have had to respond to and function in the midst of life and death crises. Those situations are often chaotic, filled with raw emotion, fear and sorrow. I always approach those events prayerfully, trusting God to empower me with the skill and compassion necessary to help the survivors through the chaos. Those prayers have always been answered. I'm one who never runs from a crisis … just the opposite, I'm usually the first to respond.

A Black Shirt with a White Tab Collar

"I believe my life has a value, and I don't want to waste it thinking about clothing. I don't want to think about what I will wear in the morning. Truly, can you imagine anything more boring than fashion?"

Michael Crichton

When I was enrolled in the Clinical Pastoral Education program at Swedish Hospital the uniform of the day was black trousers and a black clergy shirt with the top button covered by a white tab collar. Among "those who know", it is known as a Roman collar because that is the type of clergy shirt normally worn by Roman Catholic clergy. If I had chosen the collar worn by Anglican clergy, the entire collar would have been a white. I've never cared for that style of clergy shirt because it reminded me of a fancy dog collar.

There were advantages to dressing the way we did. To begin with, it made life simple. I didn't have to begin each day making a lot of choices. I didn't stand at the mirror and say to myself, "…will this blue and white striped tie go with my white shirt that contains green checks?" No. I simply went to the closet, reached into the mass of black shirts and grab the first one my hand reached.

Another advantage had to do with immediate identification. When someone saw me walking down the hall they didn't mistake me for an X-Ray technician or a physical therapist. They knew they were in the presence of clergy. They didn't even need to know my name to address me. They'd say, "Good morning, Father, how are you today?" And, I'd respond, "I'm fine, thanks be to God…", or, something like that.

One other advantage was that my clothing provided me with instant access to restricted areas. No one challenged me when I strolled through the emergency department. Wearing the collar enabled me to enter the nursery at will. And I was considered a welcome presence at Cor-O's because I was expected to provide the suffering family with pastoral care.

Now, I must admit that the black shirt did have its draw backs. There were times, for example, that I'd enter a patient's room and their immediate response was fear. That look on their face would often be accompanied by the statement: "I'm not about to die, am I, Father?" Isn't it revealing that the appearance of a priest evokes the thought of death? No wonder some people avoid church.

Everyone seems to have a stereotypical opinion of clergy. The black shirt brings that opinion to the surface immediately. People who have a positive opinion of liturgical churches tend to feel comforted by the presence of a priest. That is particularly true of Hispanics. It took less than two weeks for most of the Hispanic housekeepers to know my name. They'd encounter me in the halls with a warm: "Hola, Fr. John!" And I could walk into a non-English speaking Hispanic patient's room, bow my head in prayer, and my appearance and conduct would convey the needed pastoral care.

On the other hand, people who came from some protestant backgrounds would respond with suspicion when they encountered a priest. I recall once offering to pray with a woman whose husband had just died. She declined my offer saying: "No thanks, I'm a Christian."

Everyone who encounters a priest seems to feel the need to guard their tongue. They act as if they will be harshly judged if they allow a swear word to slip out. That concern can have its humorous consequences.

One afternoon I was walking through the lobby of Swedish Hospital when I encountered a shabbily dressed man with extreme pain etched on his face. His clothes were dirty and the left arm of his oil stained ski jacket was torn and down feathers were flying out as he walked. His left arm was limp and hanging straight down. His hand and wrist were covered with dried blood.

The first words out of his mouth were: "Where's the emergency room?" I said: "Follow me, it's one floor up and at the opposite end of the hospital." As we headed down the long hall to the elevator he held his arm and moaned. While waiting for the elevator he explained he'd been removing the engine from his car and his home-made engine jack collapsed and the engine fell on his arm. He hadn't removed his coat but he could feel the broken bones in his forearm.

When we entered the elevator, I glanced at the man's face. He was about 30 years old and he hadn't shaved for several days. He was missing some front teeth and he reeked of the odor of alcohol. We made the short trip without a word spoken between us.

When the elevator door opened, I led the way down another very long hall. Each step seemed to send sharp pain down the man's arm. Feeling empathic, I said: "I'll bet your arm feels like the dickens." The man stopped, looked me in the eye and said: "Dickens. Dickens. That's the very word I've been looking for. You're right, Father, my arm hurts like the dickens." That silly exchange broke the tension. I began to laugh and so did he. Then he said: "It's more like Hell, Father." With that, we continued down the hall to the emergency room.

A black shirt with a white tab collar set the tone for pastoral encounters. They are comfortable, convenient, and they identified my task in life. No wonder I ended up with half my closet draped in black.

Birth of our First Grandchild

"Grandchildren are God's way of compensating us for growing old."

Mary H. Waldrip

We had been anticipating the birth of our first grandchild with a great deal of excitement. Our daughter-in-law, Liz, was admitted to Presbyterian/Saint Luke's Hospital because she was experiencing some swelling. After she was examined her doctor determined that the baby she was carrying was breach. Plans were made for Liz to deliver by C-section the next day. Eric told us the plan and asked me to be at the hospital and to pray for them before Liz went into the delivery room.

The day before the birth Carol started a new job. There was no way she could accompany me to the hospital, so I went alone. I must say I was so delighted to be able to be near Eric and Liz when our first grandchild was being born. I say "grandchild" because Eric and Liz had chosen not to know the baby's sex until the birth occurred.

I arrived at PSL at 6:50 AM and went directly to Labor and Delivery room 303. Eric and Liz were pleased to see me but they looked worn and tired. They said they were so excited that they had been awake since about 2:00 AM. Liz hadn't had anything to drink since before midnight and she was thirsty. The air was full of tension, anticipation, and excitement.

Within minutes, Liz's parents, Jay and Sheila, arrived and the room was instantly filled with warm greetings and conversation. Sheila focused on Liz. Jay and I focused on Eric. Finally, Eric asked me to pray for Liz. I got the Holy Oil out of my pocket and invited everyone to gather around Liz's bed. We held hands and I began to pray. Deep within my spirit I could feel the presence of God's Holy Spirit surrounding us. I felt enveloped in peace and filled with joy. It was apparent that we were all about to enter a very sacred moment in our lives. I thanked God for the gift of life He was about to present to us. I asked Him to protect Liz and her baby, and then I anointed her with Holy Oil. When the prayer was over I happened to look at Eric. Tears were running his face. In no time several nurses entered the room and asked us to leave while they prepped Liz and helped Eric dress in hospital garb.

Liz's sister, Ann, joined us as we settled into chairs in the 3rd floor waiting area. We were talking and laughing when suddenly Eric and several nurses appeared, pushing Liz in her bed on their way to the labor and delivery room. We had everyone stop so the procession could be properly recorded on film. I have to say Eric looked great with a bulky blue hair net covering his head. Liz seemed to be at peace.

The next 35 minutes were filled with small talk. As that conversation went on I found myself watching the wall clock. I was anxious for this part of the morning to end. I wanted to meet my grandchild.

A young oriental medical student had requested permission to be present during the delivery. He introduced himself to Eric and Liz shortly after I had anointed Liz, and he was one of the people pushing Liz's bed down the hall. So, it was no surprise when he was the first person out of the delivery room after our baby was born. He asked if we had talked to Eric yet. We said, "No, is the baby here yet??!!!" "Oh yes," he said, "everything is OK." To which Jay said, "Is it a boy or a girl?" With a smile, he said, "Eric will tell you." And then he disappeared.

Several very long minutes later he returned and told us to follow him. We jumped to our feet, gathered our things and hurried after that young man. He took us to a large window that looked into the nursery. Then he went inside, stood facing us and began looking down into a hospital crib which contained a tiny, beautiful baby girl. For the second time that morning, Eric had tears in his eyes. More than that, the tears were running down his cheeks. My heart was filled with joy and love as I looked at my son and granddaughter.

Kylie was absolutely stunning. She had short, curly, dark blond hair, her head was perfectly formed, and she was wiggling all over her crib. The only other time in my life I've felt such deep joy was when I first saw our sons, Doug and Eric, after they were born. That feeling can only be described as Holy.

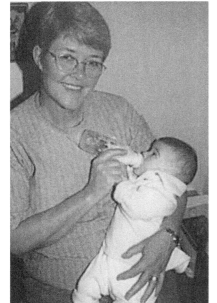
Carol feeling a young Kylie her bottle

I couldn't take my eyes off Kylie. I drank in her beauty like a parched man consumes water. Within me I offered God praise and thanksgiving for the precious new life. Our family must have been a sight to behold. Liz's sister, Mary, had joined us at the window and everyone was "oooing" and "awhing". We made enough noise that people were stepping around the nurse's desk to see what all the commotion was about. They had no idea a baby could receive such adoring attention.

In no time Mary and Ann began spreading the good news via their cell phones. I made my was back to Liz's room to find a phone to call Carol. My first attempt failed. The person who answered Carol's phone said she'd never heard of "a Carol Andrews" and told me I had the wrong number. Phooey. My heart sank. How could I have the "wrong number" at a time like that? I returned to the viewing window and told Jay I couldn't reach Carol. Ann handed me her cell phone and said: "Try again." So I did. Success. And as Carol asked questions I could tell how hard it was for her to not be at her granddaughter's side.

After completing that phone call I was able to go into the nursery. Kylie Jaye greeted me with the most beautiful sounds. Oh, some would say she was crying, but I know better. She was showing Papa that she had great lungs and a powerful voice in spite of her size. I gave Eric a hug and I told Kylie how much Nana and I loved her. That seemed to please her because she stopped yelling and tried to focus on that strange bearded old fella with the soft voice. I knew we would be great friends.

I shall never forget the events of that day, just as I'll never forget Doug and Eric's birth. God richly blessed our family, He gave us a precious life, and he brought Liz through the experience whole and well. Thank you, Lord. Thank you, Lord.

The Birth of John Joseph Andrews II

"What an honor to have someone named after you."

John Andrews, Sr.

When our grandson, John, was born, Carol and I shared the experience together. The birth occurred in Presbyterian/Saint Luke's Hospital. Liz again gave birth by C-section. I failed to take the detailed notes I had taken when Kylie was born. That didn't mean the event was less important. In fact, as the event unfolded I encountered a double surprise.

Carol and I, along with members of Liz's family, were again gathered in the waiting room near the delivery deck. I remember hearing a faint recording of Braham's Lullaby. One of Liz's sisters heard it too and told us that the recording announced the birth of a baby. We all wondered if it was telling us that Liz had given birth. Very soon after that, Eric appeared, told us he was the proud father of a baby boy, and the child's name was John Joseph Andrews, the second! I couldn't believe my ears!

Eric introducing Kylie to her new brother John

Of course, Eric and I were in tears as he led his family to the nursery. There we got to meet the newest member of our family. I was still in shock and it was hard to read John's name which appeared on the tag attached to his crib. I read it and then re-read it. Having my grandson named after me was and is the greatest honor I have ever experienced in my life.

During the first year of his life it was my privilege to baptize John at a Sunday Eucharist service at Epiphany Episcopal Church in Denver. Traditionally, a Christian name is given on the occasion of Christian baptism. After

John's baptism, I wrote John a letter to express by feelings about his name and to provide him with a history of where our name came from. I've included the letter below:

Dear John,

What a privilege it is to share the same name. I can't begin to describe the pride and deep emotions I felt the day you were born and your parents confirmed the fact you and I would share the same name. You are not only my grandson, who, to me, is extremely important; you are also carrying my personal name and our family name. As I reflected on all this I came to the conclusion that you might find the history of our shared name of some interest.

My parents named me after an uncle by marriage and both of my grandfathers. I was named John after my uncle John Johnson. John Johnson was married to my grandmother Hulda Velin's sister, Hanna Hanson. Everyone in our family liked John. He was friendly, fun to be with, and he was a Swede. He had a reputation within the Swedish community for being honest and at times he was referred to as, "Honest John Johnson". I fondly remember Uncle John as a kind man. He was tall and slender and he had a gentle smile. He spoke with a Swedish accent. After Aunt Hanna died, Uncle John married a woman who we called Aunt Ellen. They lived in the suburbs west of Denver and my parents often visited them on holidays. Uncle John always took time to talk with me and he made me feel loved and valued. I've tried to incorporate some of Uncle John's character into my life by being honest and kind.

My middle name, Joseph, came from my grandfather, Joseph Velin. Joseph Velin was born and raised in Sweden. He was oldest child in a family that included seven children. His parents were poor farmers and, when Joseph was old enough to support himself, his parents asked him to move out of the family home because they could no longer feed and support him. He had learned the carpenter trade in school. Using those skills, he built three large tool boxes and filled them with his home-made tools. He then made his way to the coast of Sweden, gained passage on a ship to America, and set sail to a new life. He arrived in Denver, Colorado, in 1902 and made the Mile-High City his home. On February 25, 1911, he married Hulda Velin, another Swedish immigrant. On October 15, 1912, Hulda gave birth to their only child, Helen Josephina Velin, my mother. You'll notice that my mother's middle name, like our middle name, came from her father. So, John, you are the fourth member of our family to bear the name "Joseph".

Joseph Velin was born August 5, 1878, in Friel, Sweden. He was a skilled finish carpenter. He built beautiful homes, fine furniture, tools, and many other useful items. I have possession of an engraved phonograph that he built by hand. It's a piece of furniture that only a skilled craftsman could build. Early in his career he built display cabinets for Daniels and Fishers Department Store in Denver. Daniels and Fishers was an exclusive department store noted for its expensive collection of clothing and accessories.

After Joseph retired, he and Hulda lived in an apartment across the street from our home in Castle Rock. I was a small child at the time and there were several things I remember about Joseph. First, I called him "Papa". Next, he was blind in one eye and was missing the index finger on his right hand. He was blinded when some lime accidentally splashed in his eye while he was mixing it with water. And he accidentally cut off his finger while operating an electric saw. Third, I remember how large his hands were. Each finger and the palm of his hand were massive and I imagine he had a very strong grip. Finally, I remember Papa to be an independent, strong willed and disciplined individual. He lived life on his own terms and took pride in his work and accomplishments. Oh yes, I remember one more thing…no one every touched his tools without permission…I know, I did once and I still remember the consequences. In spite of that, I've tried to incorporate some of Joseph Velin's character into my life. After his example, I've tried to always take pride in the work I've done. "Excellence in all things" could be my motto. Also, I've tried to be independent, a person who sets his own goals in life and then strives to accomplish those goals through disciplined focus.

John, as you know, our initials are J. J. A. My paternal grandfather's name was Jesse Johnson Andrews, making his initials J. J. A. My parents wanted me to carry the same initials as my father's father, therein making me named after both grandparents. That means you carry your grandfather's name and parts of both of your great-great grandfathers. I think that's cool.

Jesse Johnson Andrews was a resourceful and hard-working man who did many things during his life to support his family. He was born on July 15th, 1878, in Olathe, Kansas, and he married Nora Bell Wiswell on November 1, 1900. Prior to marriage, Jesse worked for the Santa Fe Railroad in San Bernardino, California; and later for the Chicago Great Western Railroad in Kansas City, Missouri. He also helped his family farm land near Evant, Texas. After marriage to Nora Bell, Jesse continued to farm in Texas and later took his family to Roswell, New Mexico, by covered wagon where they homesteaded 160 acres of land. He later sold that land and then used the money he obtained to buy and sell other property. Then, for several years he and his family traveled through the West by covered wagon, buying and selling horses. That's right, John, one of your great grandfathers was a "horse trader". After the death of Nora Bell, Jesse moved to Laramie, Wyoming, where he was the proprietor of a rooming house. While there he met and then married his second wife, Nora Ruth. He then moved his family to Brighton, Colorado, where he opened an automobile repair shop. Jesse also worked as a deputy United States Marshall for period of time.

I never knew Grandfather Jesse because he died before I was born. I've heard him described as a strong-willed person who used his ingenuity to provide for his and his family's needs. I was proud of the fact he was a U. S. Marshall and at one time I had possession of his Colt 38 cal. revolver and shoulder holster. Admiration for Jesse's law enforcement background was one of the reasons I developed an interest in being a policeman.

As you can see, there is a lot of family history behind our name. But there is another facet to our name which I think is import and I'd like to share that aspect with you. The names "John" and "Joseph" have a strong Christian connection. There are several New Testament biblical characters with the name John. There is "John the Evangelist". He was one of the Lord's original apostles and he is credited with writing the Gospel of John. He was a preacher, teacher, and healer. Then there is "John the Baptist". He was the Lord's cousin. He announced the Lord's coming, baptized Jesus, and was a powerful preacher who was commended by the Lord, himself. John the Baptist was martyred for his faith. Of these two New Testament heroes, I've always identified most with John the Evangelist. He loved Jesus

289

and he shared that love with others with the hope that Good News would make a difference in their lives. I've tried to do the same.

There are three "Joseph's" in the Bible that have held my interest. The story of "Joseph, son of Jacob" can be found in the Book of Genesis. He incurred the jealousy of his brothers because of a dream he had and shared. His brothers sold him into slavery. He was taken to a foreign country where his character was tested. He proved to be an honest and intelligent man who was selected by Pharaoh to administer the affairs of Egypt. He was very successful and his family ultimately was blessed by his forgiveness, wisdom and generosity.

The first "Joseph" we meet in the New Testament is "Joseph, husband of Mary, step father of Jesus". He was a man who found himself in a very awkward and embarrassing position when his fiancée became pregnant by God's Holy Spirit. He prayed and listened to God. He obeyed God's wishes and proved loyal to Mary. We're told he was a loving and faithful husband and father. All these are wonderful character traits we should seek to apply to our lives.

Finally, we meet a man named Joseph at the end of the Gospels, a man who I really identify with. He was known as "Joseph of Arimathea". This man was someone who admired Jesus. He was present during the Lord's crucifixion. After the Lord died, he went to Pilate and requested permission to remove Jesus from the cross and bury his body in a tomb Joseph owned. With that permission, Joseph performed the sad and difficult task of caring for Jesus' body. He did this at great risk and out of love and respect for the Lord.

I've always identified most with Joseph of Arimathea. I grew up in a funeral home. My father was an embalmer and funeral director. From a very early age I was expected to help my father. By the time I was 14 years old I was removing dead bodies from accident scenes, hospitals and private homes; I helped embalm and assisted my dad at funerals. Like Joseph of Arimathea, I took care of dead bodies. At one point in my life I owned the funeral home in Castle Rock, Colorado, and served as the Douglas County Coroner. My parents instilled within me a deep respect for the dead and my family always considered our work to be Christian ministry. Our goal was to provide loving care and compassion to those in grief. The task was often unpleasant. It's not easy to physically remove, care for and then bury the dead. It's heartbreaking to comfort those in grief. And, our family was often the target of harsh judgment from others. No one in our society feels comfortable with undertakers. But I believed what we as a family and I, personally, did was a blessing that helped and comforted many people. What Joseph of Arimathea did was no less noble. I love the name "Joseph" and for years I've considered Joseph of Arimathea my patron saint.

So, you see, John, names can be very important. I believe we share a very special name. How you identify with your name will have an impact on you throughout your entire life. I hope some of this information helps you grasp the significance of our name and inspires you to identify with the positive characteristics of some of the people who share our name.

With my love,
Your grandfather,
John Joseph Andrews, Sr.

Grandchildren at a Distance

"It's difficult at best!"

John and Carol Andrews

We received a unique announcement of the pending birth of our second grandchild, Rachal. Doug and Sherry were visiting us over the Christmas holiday in 2001. During that visit, Sherry presented us with a wrapped gift. We opened it to find a plastic baby bottle filled with confetti! We looked at it, then at each other and finally at Doug and Sherry. They said, "Yes, we're pregnant!" That was the best gift we received that Christmas.

Doug was attached to the Marine Corp. based at 29 Palms in California; so Rachal's birth was to occur in California in mid-July. My experience of Kylie's birth was so positive; and, the fact Carol had missed being present at Kylie's birth were the basis of our determination to drive to California for the July event. Plans were made and we began our travels west on the 14th of June.

We spent 10 days in Utah, then time in Nevada, including Lake Tahoe. We arrived in California on July 2 and made our way south as we waited for Sherry to go into labor. We were excited about the pending birth and it was hard to wait. Finally, Doug called to tell us Sherry was in labor! We were parked in an RV park in Pismo Beach, about one day's travel from Doug and Sherry.

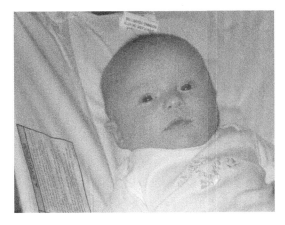

Rachal in hospital at time of birth

Rachal Lauren Andrews was born in the hospital at 29 Palms on July17, 2002. Doug informed us by phone that mother and daughter were well. Our plans were to drive to their home as soon as they were released. Once they arrived home Doug called and told us that Sherry wanted a few days alone with her daughter so that they could "bond". He told us he would let us know when Sherry was ready for us to visit. We moved our RV to Santa Margarita KOA for one night; then we spent two nights at Flying Flags in Buellton; then we moved to Malibu RV park for a week. While in Malibu we received the invitation to come visit Sherry, Doug and Rachal. Planning to spend several nights at a motel in 29 Palms, we packed and drove with our two cats.

When we arrived at the motel the clerk told us he did have a room; however, the motel was full of young, drunk Marines who were competing in a week-long baseball competition. He said they had to call the police numerous times and he knew we would not be comfortable staying there. We decided our visit would last one day.

We drove to Doug and Sherry's, carried our cats into the house and locked them in a closet and then – finally – we got to see our granddaughter for the first time. We visited for several hours. Then we collected our cats and drove back to Malibu.

We didn't see Rachal again until the following November when Doug asked us to fly to California to take care of Rachal while he and Sherry attended the Marine Ball in Laughlin, Nevada. That trip enabled us to spend some quality time with Rachal. We had fun caring for her; and, her response indicated she too enjoyed our visit.

Samantha Dorothy Andrews was born January 22, 2004, in Reno, Nevada. We had been asked to take care of Rachal while Sherry and Sami were in the hospital. We stayed in Doug and Sherry's house during that time. On the day we first got to see Sami, we drove with Rachal to the hospital so she, too, could meet the new family member.

Doug had a deep love and respect for his grandmother, Dorothy Robinson. Sami's middle name was given to honor the relationship Doug had with Dorothy.

A young Sami Andrews

Sherry was raised in the Roman Catholic Church. She once told me that she believed Carol and I were part of another "religion". She obviously did not feel comfortable with our faith. When Rachal was an infant, Sherry's mother made a baptismal gown for her using material from Sherry's wedding dress. That was a gift Sherry really appreciated. Sherry's father was an active member of a Roman Catholic group which met for worship in private homes. When Doug and Sherry visited her parents back East, Rachal was baptized at one of those services. Carol and I were not told so we were not even given the opportunity to attend. We learned about the baptism one day when I asked Doug if the children were baptized. He said Rachal was but Sami wasn't baptized. He did describe Rachal's baptism to us.

Doug and his family have attended very few worship services with us. Since our Christian faith has been the center around which much of our life has revolved, the absence of a shared faith has had its impact on our relationship. We know that God loves Doug and his family, and we pray daily for each one of them.

Quality time with these two granddaughters has been limited due to the great distance that separated us. At different times Doug's family lived in California, North Carolina,

Massachusetts, and New Hampshire. We made visits to each of those locations and the girls accompanied Doug to our 50th wedding anniversary. Knowing our visits would be limited, I began writing each grandchild a personal postcard every week for a number of years. I never got any response from that effort, but I hoped they felt some connection with their "Nana and Papa". We also telephoned regularly. As the girls grew, we always asked to talk with each one. Sherry would hand the telephone to the girls, and if they didn't answer our questions immediately or if they didn't answer the way she felt they should, she would answer for them. It was frustration for both them and us.

When Doug had surgery for colon cancer, we were again asked to take care of the girls. We flew to New Hampshire and spent 10 days caring for both children. In many ways that was the most positive time we spent with them. We saw them off to school and greeted them when they returned. We attended a girl scout event and toured the girl's school. The four of us spent a day at the beach and then ate out. On another occasion, we went on a hike near their home. It was a fun experience in spite of the stress surrounding Doug's surgery.

Grandparenting at a distance has been frustrating. We deeply love Rachal and Sami. They are growing into beautiful young ladies. We wish them the very best as we hold them is our daily thoughts and prayers.

Family Ministry

"The true character of ministry is a servant's heart."

Harold Warner

When I answered God's call to the ordained ministry I gave no thought to the fact I would be called upon to serve my extended family. I could visualize pastoral ministry in a church congregation and I could imagine myself serving as a chaplain in a hospital. But I never gave a thought to being a minister to people I was related to. The situations where my family called upon me to be their pastor often arose as the result of a crisis like death or serious illness. I was always comfortable responding to the need. It felt like the loving thing to do. Then, I began receiving requests to perform baptisms and marriages. I accepted with a deep sense of gratitude that members of my family trusted me with those duties. After all, I know clergy whose families would never call upon them to be the family pastor.

Ministry at the time of death can be very difficult. There is so much involved in planning all the details. Involving family members in the service can be a delicate and sensitive matter. The ministry demands good communication and often involves grief counseling. I was blessed and privileged to officiate at the funerals of my father, Carol's parents, my brother-in-law and my sister-in-law. Three of those services included the celebration of Mass; and I preached at each service. All that was done as I, too, experienced the grief other family members were experiencing.

I've been blessed and privileged to baptize members of my family. My two grandchildren, Kylie and John, were each baptized in Sunday worship services shortly after their birth. What an honor to hold them as I sprinkled water to initiate them into God's family. Each time I was spiritually moved by the experience

My brother and his son-in-law called me to respond to Children's Hospital in Denver to baptize my brother's newly-born grandson. Jarid had been born in Pueblo, Colorado, and then was rushed to Denver due to a dangerous lack of skin covering his head and stomach. His life was in danger. I performed an emergency baptism standing at his bedside as doctors were preparing to treat him. Jarid was hospitalized for a month at Children's Hospital and, unfortunately, his family couldn't be with him because they were needed to care for his twin sister and her brothers and sister in Canon City. During that month, Carol and I sat with Jarid everyday so he would know family love and support.

I baptized Sarah Fawaz, the child of my niece, Jennifer Fawaz. Sarah was raised in the Episcopal Church and she served as my acolyte when I was asked to supply at her family's church in Monument, Colorado. She and her fiancé have asked me to officiate at their wedding later this year. How special.

The first family wedding I participated in was Sarah's parents' marriage. Sarah's mother, Jennifer, is my Godchild. Jennifer asked me to participate in her marriage. It was scheduled just before I was to be ordained. Carol and I flew from Wisconsin to Colorado. I attended the wedding rehearsal, which occurred the day before the ceremony was to take place. I had no idea what my role would be. Jennifer's priest asked me to preach at that service. I had never done that in my life. I spent the rest of that day and the next morning writing and practicing that sermon. Talk about a stressful honor!

Jennifer's sister, Kim, and her fiancé Andy planned their wedding at the same Episcopal Church in Pueblo. Andy's cousin, a Christian minister, was to perform the marriage and I was asked to bless the couple at the end of the service. The wedding rehearsal occurred the night before the service The day of the wedding I arrived at the church about an hour prior to the scheduled beginning. As I walked into the church, Kim and Andy informed me that Andy's cousin had to return home and they asked me to perform the service. After discussing the situation, I gathered the wedding party for another quick rehearsal. The rehearsal the night before was for a non-Anglican wedding and I was going to perform an Episcopal service. By the grace of God, I had brought a wedding sermon with me and I used that sermon during the service. It was a beautiful wedding and Kim and Andy have remained happily married for many years.

I've officiated at other family weddings including my brother's daughter, Megan, and my sister's son, Craig. Years later Megan's son, Devin asked me to bless his marriage just prior to his military deployment. I officiated at both of our son's weddings. Both boys married Roman Catholics and therefore the service included Roman Catholic clergy. Eric and Liz were married at Saint Gabriel's Episcopal Church. Fr. Hoffman from Risen Christ Catholic Church participated in the service. I celebrated Mass but Fr. Hoffman did not concelebrate or receive. Doug and Sherry were married in a Christian chapel on the Hanscom Air Force base in Massachusetts. A Roman Catholic chaplain assisted. There was no Mass. I was the preacher. It was a real privilege to be a part of those two services.

Unction, the sacramental prayers for healing, was a part of the ministry I offered to members of my family. Over the years, I anointed Carol's father, my father, my sister Kendal, my niece Becky's husband, and my nephew Jarid for healing. In each case the recipient was critically ill and I believe the prayers brought an element of healing.

I am writing this on my 74th birthday, a day of reflection and decision. Reflection on my family ministry has been full of all sorts of memories. Some painful and sad. Other memories are full of delight, fun and a sense of humble gratitude knowing my family trusted me with those responsibilities. The decision I've come to has to do with the future. I'm getting old. I'm no longer confident that I can serve with the skill I have in the past. I've decided I am going to announce the end of my family ministry.

The Last Career – Ministry – Then Retirement

"Retirement may be an ending, a closing, but it is also a new beginning."

Catherine Pulsifer

Summarizing 17 years of ministry is complicated. That experience is full of variety. It has to reflect God's action, the commitment of faithful Christians, and an openness to change. I encountered so many wonderful, loving and faithful people; it was exhilarating to encounter all the change that came my way. I feel very blessed to have participated in so many wonderful ministries.

It all began during the last year I was attending seminary. I had begun to wonder if there would be any church in the Diocese of Colorado that needed a new priest. Less than a month before graduation, Bp. Frey contacted me and invited me to be interviewed for the position of vicar in Grand County. I replied in the affirmative without any hesitation; though I have to AM I really didn't know where Grand County was located. I quickly discovered that the position included three small yoked missions: Saint John's, Granby; Trinity, Kremmling; and Saint Columba in Winter Park. A young, dynamic, musically-talented priest had been serving those missions and he was resigning to accept a position in a larger congregation. He had introduced guitar music to the worship services and had attracted a number of young people.

I was older, inexperienced and had absolutely no musical talents. In spite of those negatives, I was hired even before I was ordained! My ordination to the diaconate occurred in my home parish in Castle Rock and one week later I was leading worship in the Grand County Missions.

I served those missions from 1987 until 1991. Every Saturday I would celebrate Eucharist at 5 PM in Winter Park. On Sunday, I would celebrate Eucharist at 8:30 AM in Granby, drive 27 miles to Kremmling where I lead the worship service at 10:30 AM. Every Wednesday at 5 PM I conducted worship services in Grand Lake in the Roman Catholic Church. All that involved a lot of driving and it exposed me to a number of families living in different communities.

A small group of parishioners were interested in weekly classes so I began an Education for Ministry class which was enthusiastically embraced. Carol and I created a Catechumenate program which was designed as a preparation for confirmation.

I joined a group of pastors in Granby to conduct a weekly ecumenical service at the Grand County Jail. That ministry was so successful that I baptized several inmates and one of them went through Catechumenate instruction and was confirmed by Bishop Wolfrum in the jail day-room.

Small communities seldom have churches from all the prominent denominations. As a result, it's not uncommon to become involved with families who come out of other denominations. The first marriage I performed is an example of that. I was asked to marry a woman with a Methodist background to a man who was a Lutheran. They wanted the service in Grand Lake at the Presbyterian Church, but that congregation was searching for a new pastor, so the couple asked me to officiate at their wedding. The result was an Episcopal priest marrying a Methodist and a Lutheran in the Presbyterian Church. That would never happen in an urban area; but it was common in Grand County. I even co-officiated at a wedding at Saint Anne's Roman Catholic Church in Grand Lake. During that service, the Roman Catholic priest and I concelebrated the Mass!

The Roman Catholic congregation had a church in Grand Lake, but none in Granby. So, the Roman Catholic priest held Sunday Mass in the Episcopal Church in Granby and every Wednesday I conducted Episcopal Communion services in the Roman Catholic Church in Grand Lake. The Episcopal Church was too small to accommodate my ordination to the priesthood so my ordination occurred in that Roman Catholic Church!

Several years into that ministry I was elected and served as the dean of the Mountain Deanery. The churches in that Deanery included Saint Paul, Steamboat Springs; Saint Mark, Craig; Christ Church, Aspen; Transfiguration, Vail; Saint John's, Breckenridge; Saint George, Leadville; Grace, Buena Vista; and the three yoked missions in Grand County. I traveled about 3,000 miles a month during the three years I was dean. Some of the duties included negotiating disagreements between clergy and their vestries, officiating and preaching at the installation of new clergy, conducting monthly clergy gatherings, serving on the bishop's Dean's Council, and being a mentor and support to the clergy in the Mountain Deanery.

I loved serving the mountain churches but I felt I had accomplished all I could. Additionally, Carol wanted to move to an urban setting. So I entered the search process and began receiving invitations to be interviewed by vestries seeking a new priest.

In 1991 I was called to serve Saint Gabriel's Episcopal Church, located in Cherry Hills Village, an affluent suburb south of Denver. When I arrived at Saint Gabriel's there were less than 50 active members. Seventy-six percent of those members were over the age of 50. There was one family with 2 children under the age of 13 in attendance. The worship services were conducted using the old traditional Rite I language; and, the music at the 10AM service was selected out of the 1940 Hymnal. There were no adult studies or children's Sunday School. Most of the active members did not live in Cherry Hills Village.

The vestry that called me to serve was very clear about one thing. They wanted a rector who could help the church grow. I remember asking the vestry if they really knew what growth would mean. They said "yes" and asked me if I knew what growth meant. I said, "I do. It's going to mean a lot of change." Everyone agreed.

Well we were right. But neither the vestry nor I, in our wildest dreams, expected the growth and change that came. The last year I was there the congregation had 528 members, 212 of whom were youth. That growth tremendously impacted the finances. The 1991 annual report showed a total pledge of $62,000 from 54 pledging units. The 1997 pledge was triple that number with the pledging units giving $225,000 annually.

While at Saint Gabriel's, the congregation successfully organized a drive to finance a million-dollar building project. That project included a vastly expanded space for new offices, classrooms, and parish hall. We hired an additional priest, a parish administrator and supported an organist and choir director. Adult study, Education for Ministry classes, Lenten programs, a Children's Sunday School, Stephen Ministry, a youth group, Bible studies, and prayer groups were formed, became active and were well supported.

On one hand, ministry at Saint Gabriel's was exciting and rewarding. On the other hand, it was exhausting. I was involved six days a week from morning to night. Additionally, I served on the Diocesan Finance Committee and the Commission on Ministry. During the last year at Saint Gabriel's I conducted 17 funerals. I resigned in April of 1997 with the intention of slowing down. I accepted a position as interim priest at Saint Martin in the Field Episcopal Church in Aurora.

Unlike Saint Gabriel's, Saint Martin's was not traditional. It was a congregation that embraced contemporary worship and music. The church band even included a set of drums! Boy, that was a real stretch for an orthodox and traditional priest like me! The issues facing that congregation were completely different than those I had struggled with at Saint Gabriel's. There were members who embraced fundamentalism, others who had no history with or appreciation for Anglican tradition, and there was little interest in Anglican music. I had to adjust to other styles of worship and music as I tried to share my appreciation for Anglican worship and music. I admit that I did enjoy some of the music, including "My God is an Awesome God", "The Butterfly Song", and "Jesus, Name Above All Names."

Saint Martin's was the one and only time I served as an interim pastor. I moved from that experience to a one-year CPE training program at Swedish Hospital in Englewood. I loved working there and I've included stories of my time there in earlier chapters.

From Swedish Hospital I was able to move to Parker Valley Hope Drug and Alcohol Treatment Center in Parker. This was another positive experience. I functioned as a chaplain, working with people addicted to drugs, alcohol, sex and gambling. I led daily worship services, presented classes addressing the grief one faces when they give up an addiction, and I personally counseled patients as they struggled with the first five steps of the twelve-step program. I came away from that experience with a deep admiration for people who successfully overcome deeply-rooted addictions.

Finally, the last two years of my active ministry were spent as an associate pastor at the Church of the Transfiguration in Evergreen. The rector of that church had been my curate at Saint Gabriel's. I shared preaching responsibilities, taught classes, and assumed full responsibility when the rector was on vacation.

I fully retired after the Easter services in 2003. That marked the end of my involvement in three different careers. I am so glad I have lived at a time I could move from one career to another. I look back on each of them with fondness and I'm so grateful for the rich experiences I've had as a result. It's truly been all about people, dead and alive.

Made in the USA
Coppell, TX
09 February 2025